דברי שמחה

THE BRAUNSTEIN FAMILY EDITION

מה אשיב לה' כל תגמולוהי עלי. כוס ישועות אשא ובשם ה' אקרא: נדרי לה' אשלם נגדה נא לכל עמו.

SUKKOS AND HALLEL

BASED ON

THE MAHARAL

Rabbi Simcha Bunim Berger

ISBN: 979-8-88673-335-8

Book & cover design by:
VIVIDESIGN
SRULY PERL | 845.222.1967
srulyperl.com | info@srulyperl.com

Published and distributed by:

Israel Bookshop Publications
501 Prospect Street
Lakewood, NJ 08701
Tel: (732) 901-3009
Fax: (732) 901-4012
www.israelbookshoppublications.com
info@israelbookshoppublications.com

Printed in USA

Distributed in Israel by:
Tfutza Publications
P.O.B. 50036
Beitar Illit 90500
972-2-650-9400

Distributed in Europe by:
Lehmanns
Unit E Viking Industrial Park
Rolling Mill Road,
Jarrow, Tyne & Wear NE32 3DP
44-191-406-0842

Distributed in Australia by:
Gold's Book and Gift Company
3-13 William Street
Balaclava 3183
613-9527-8775

Distributed in South Africa by:
Kollel Bookshop
Ivy Common
107 William Road, Norwood
Johannesburg 2192
27-11-728-1822

לזכר נשמת

הרבני החסיד המפורסם

לשבח ותהילה, בקרב עם סגולה, מוקיר תורה

ואיש החסד ה"ה

הרב משה ברונשטיין ז"ל

בן הרה"ח מוה"ר ישכר בעריש ז"ל

נפטר בשם טוב

ביום כ"ז תמוז שנת תשנ"ב לפ"ק

ולזכר נשמת האישה החשובה

בעלת חסד בת קדושים

מרת יענטא ע"ה

בתו של רבי ישראל חיים ווייס הי"ד זצוק"ל

בנו הבכור של הגה"ק החקל יצחק מספינקא זי"ע

נכדת מהרש"ם מברזאן זצוק"ל

נפטרה כ"ד אדר ב' שנת תשס"ה

ק"ק ווילעדזש גרין ד'וועסלי הילס
מברכת את המרא דאתרא של קהילתנו
הרב שמחה בונים הכהן ברגר שליט"א

על הוצאת הספר
"דברי שמחה"
על סוכות והלל מפניני המהר"ל

בספר זה הושקעו מאמצים רבים כדי להבהיר ולגלות לרבים את
עומקם של דברי המהר"ל בספר "גבורות ה'".

We take pride in the publication of *Divrei Simchah on Sukkos and Hallel*, written by our מרא דאתרא, Rabbi Simcha Bunim Berger שליט"א.

The Rav's main mission is to help us strive toward and reach greater heights in our closeness to the Ribono Shel Olam.
Our *kehillah* appreciates our Rav's unique ability to articulate the depth and beauty of our Torah. Now others can grow from his Torah as well.

***Mispallelim* of Village Green Shul**

In memory of

Harav **Tzvi Hersh** *ben* Harav **Yoseph Pinchas**
Devorah Sarah *bas* **Reb Meir**

Reb Hershel and Debbi Levinson *zt"l*

Dedicated in appreciation of

Rabbi and Rebbetzin Berger

for all they do for the *kehillah* and for Klal Yisrael, and in honor of our wonderful children.

Izzy and Aliza Zelman

Aliza, Hindy, Yehuda, and Leora

Aviva and Naftali Zelman

Dedicated by

Shmuel and Esther Lapa, New York

in memory of their parents

הר״ר **אברהם** בן הר״ר **אלימלך** לפה ז״ל

מרת **בלומא** בת הר״ר **דוד צבי** צוקרברג ז״ל

and

הר״ר **ישראל יצחק יחזקאל**
בן הר״ר **מרדכי אהרון** הרשקופ ז״ל

In memory of

Bayla Yenta *bas* Reb Yisroel

Sukkos was my mother's favorite Yom Tov. She cherished how the Yom Tov encapsulates the warm embrace Hashem gives us after Yom Kippur, and proudly shared the *chag* with all Jews.

The praises from Hallel that we sang in her *sukkah* still embrace us today.

Rabbi and Mrs. Arye Smith

In honor and in memory of

יצחק אייזיק בן הרב יהודה
ורעיתו רבקה הענטשע בת צבי הירש מאסי

Mr. and Mrs. Joseph Macy

Eliyahu ben Reuven Zarin *zt"l*

By their grandchildren,

Mr. and Mrs. Dovid Gamzeh

In memory of

Larry Rossman *a"h*

אליעזר בן דוד

Dedicated by

Marc and Alissa Rossman

In honor of

Rabbi & Rebbetzin Berger

who welcomed us into their home years ago when we moved to Monsey. Since then, we've been benefiting from their warmth, insight, and inspiration, which are displayed in their genuine love toward Hashem and the Torah.

Rabbi Berger's unique insights and elucidation on Torah subjects, coupled with his enthusiasm and *emunah*, fuel his passion as a *rav* and mentor.

We wish Rabbi Berger continued success in his *meleches hakodesh*. May we merit the ultimate joy with the coming of Mashiach Tzidkeinu.

Michael and Shoshana Raff

In memory of

הרב יצחק מנחם מנדל בן הרב ישראל
Kleiman

הרב ישראל בן ברוך מרדכי
Kleiman

הדסה בת צבי הערש
Kleiman

דוב בן צבי דוד
Himber

שיינדל בת צבי
Himber

בן ציון בן יצחק
Bider

חנה בת זאב וואלף
Bider

לעילוי נשמת אבי מורי

הר"ר **שמואל ברוך** זצ"ל

בן ר' **חיים צבי דוב**

נפטר י"ז אייר תשע"ו

וסבי ר' **חיים צבי דוב**

בן **יהזקאל שרגא** זצ"ל

נפטר כ"ג ניסן תשפ"א

Dedicated by

Mr. and Mrs. Dovid Salamon

This *sefer* is in memory of our beloved uncle

הרב אביעזר שמעון יוסף

בן שמואל זאב הלוי וולפסון זצק"ל

The patriarch of our family
and *rebbi* to thousands.

Uncle Aviezer, this *sefer* would not
have been possible without you.

With fond and eternal memories,

**Simcha Bunim, Batsheva,
and Family**

Approbation received for author's previous work

ישיבת מיר ירושלים

YESHIVAS MIR YERUSHALAYIM

Founded in Mir 1817. In Jerusalem 1944 — 580037638 ע״ר — בס״ד נוסדה במיר בשנת תקע״ז. בירושלים בשנת תש״ד

RABBI E.Y. FINKEL
DEAN

הרב א.י. פינקל
ראש הישיבה

בס״ד — כסלו תשפ״ב

מכתב ברכה

מה נכבד היום בעלות על שולחן מלכים, מאן מלכי רבנן, החיבור הנפלא **דברי שמחה** על סדר הגדה של פסח ועניני ליל הסדר, גלות מצרים חג המצות והמסתעף, ממוהר״ר **שמחה בונים ברגר** שליט״א, אשר יראתו קודמת לחכמתו, וידיו רב לו בעמלה של תורה וחפץ ה׳ הצליח בידו.

המחבר שליט״א מרוב חביבותו את יופי המצוות רחש לבו דבר טוב להעלות עלי גליון את עומק ההתבוננות בדרכי השי״ת ובהנהגתו עם בריותיו, וטרח לברר הדברים על בוריין בדרך רבותינו מצוקי ארץ נ״ע, בשפה ברורה ובהירה בלשון המוכנת לבני חו״ל כדי לזכות את הרבים בדבר מתוקן ושוה לכל נפש. והדברים משמחי לב ומאירי עיניים.

אמינא לפעלא טבא יישר כוחו וחילו לאורייתא, כה יתן וכה יוסיף להרבות חיילים לתורה ולזכות את הרבים בספריו, ויזכה תמיד לשקוד ולהגות בתוה״ק באהלה של תורה ללמוד וללמד לשמור ולעשות מתוך מנוחה ושלוה, וישמחו בו חבריו, ויהא כבוד שמים מתרבה על ידו להגדיל תורה ולהאדירה.

בברכת התורה

אליעזר יהודה פינקל

הרב אליעזר יהודה פינקל
ראש הישיבה

3 Beth Israel St. P.O.B 5022 Jerusalem 9105001 Tel. 02-5410999 Fax. 02-5323446 • 580037638 ע״ר 02-5323446 .רח. בית ישראל 3 ת.ד. 5022 ירושלים 9105001 טל. 02-5410999 פקס

Approbation received for author's previous work

בס"ד

תפארת גדליה

YGW

From the Desk of
RABBI AHRON LOPIANSKY
Rosh HaYeshiva

Kislev 5782

Pesach presents us with the challenge of transmitting the timeless heritage of *yetzias mitzraim*, in all its marvel and depth to the next generation. While many have focused on making the seder as engaging as possible for the younger members of the family, not as much thought has been given to helping convey deeper ideas to the older and more mature participants at the seder.

Yedidi, Harav Simcha Bunim Berger's long career as a master *rebbi*, has made him uniquely suited for giving over many of the deep points expressed by the Maharal in his teachings on yetzias mitzraim. His long association with Rabbeinu Hagaon Harav Moshe Shapiro zt"l, has filled him with a love for the Maharal's unique *derech*, and an ability to transmit those ideas in a more readily accessible format. The *sefer* is sure to deepen and amplify the *seder* experience for those mature enough to appreciate the depths of Torah.

With a *bracha* that you keep enhancing the *ruchnias* of all those people whose lives you've touched, and will touch,

Byedidus chama

Ahron Shraga Lopiansky

YESHIVA OF GREATER WASHINGTON – TIFERES GEDALIAH
1216 ARCOLA AVENUE, SILVER SPRING, MD 20902 ▪ 301-649-7077 ▪ WWW.YESHIVA.EDU

חיים יהודה ליביש הלוי ר"ט
אבדק"ק נצח ישראל פארשעי
מאנסי נ. י.

RABBI CH. L. ROTTENBERG
47 Forshay Road
Monsey, New York 10952
845-362-1979

ב"ה

יום שנכפל בו כי טוב, כ"ג למטמונים לסדר וחי בהם תשפ"ה לפ"ק

הנני באתי בשורותים אלו להעיד על ועידי הנעלה והדגול זה רבות בשנים, ומרביץ תורה לרבים הה"ה מוה"ר ש"ה בעומר שליט"א

זה רבות בשנים שאני מכירו ראיתי הרבה פרי עמלו, בהשפיענו שלום בתוך בתים רעועים, ומתוך לבם של צעירים ונערים, ועל מעשיו בנוים על יסודות התה"ק ובדעת ממליה ומוסקיה, בלי התרחבות צרים, ע"כ אף ידי תיכון עמו ויתכוון מה"ש שתשרה שכינה במעשה ולא יצא מכשול מתחת ידיו ויזכה להמשיך בעומלו צדק במעב ובלשון, ולראות רב נחת דק' מכל יוצ"ח עדי נזכה לביאת ינון בב"א

ועידו הדורשלומו באה"ר

חיים יהודה ליביש הלוי ר"ט

TABLE OF CONTENTS

Acknowledgments

הודו לה' כי טוב כי לעולם חסדו –

*Give thanks to Hashem for He is good,
for His kindness endures forever.*

This statement of gratitude is repeated again and again in Hallel. The fact that we declare this phrase numerous times in our prayers indicates that we really can never do justice to our obligation of thanking Hashem. Yet that does not absolve us from doing our utmost to recognize Hashem's everlasting kindness.

Therefore, first and foremost, I humbly thank Hashem for giving me the *zechus* and the *siyata d'Shmaya* of writing this *sefer* and bringing it to publication. It is my hope and prayer that the *sefer* will inspire all those who read it, giving them and their families an opportunity to have a more meaningful experience while fulfilling the mitzvos associated with Sukkos.

When I went to study in Eretz Yisrael in 1984, it was suggested that I attend a *shiur* given by Rav Moshe Shapiro *zt"l*, who, at the time, was giving a Thursday night *parshah shiur* in Ohr Somayach. I can't thank Hashem enough for giving me the merit of being able to attend those *shiurim* of *mori v'rabi*

Harav Moshe Shapiro *zt"l*. It was then and there that I was first introduced to the writings of the Maharal, and was able to glean somewhat of an understanding of his holy words.

Rav Moshe *zt"l* was more than a *maggid shiur*. He took a personal interest in me, which shaped my life. It is thanks to him that I was able to write this *sefer*.

I would like to give gratitude to Hashem for my family. My father, Reb Hershel Berger *zt"l*, and *tbl"ch* my mother, Frida, are more than just parents. They have always been my biggest fans, giving me the love, confidence, and support that I needed in order to go out into the big world. They understood how to bridge the *Yiddishe* upbringing of the old-world *shtetl* with the modern-day world of America.

I met my wife, Batsheva Ringer, while learning in the Mir. To marry in Eretz Yisrael, without the need to return to America for *shidduchim*, was yet another gift from Hashem. I was never *zoche* to meet my father-in-law, Harav Binyomin Ringer *zt"l*, who was *niftar* six years before my wife and I met, yet my *hakaras hatov* to him knows no bounds. My wife is true royalty. She embodies all the values of *tznius* that *Chazal* have taught in the *pasuk* (*Tehillim* 45:14), *The honor of the noble daughter is her modesty*.

All the blessings in my life emanate from her. Hashem has blessed us with a beautiful family of children and grandchildren, each a brilliant diamond carefully crafted and gently polished by a mother whose mission in life is to raise a family that will advance *kavod Shamayim*. Needless to say, without my *eishes chayil*, this *sefer* could never have been written.

The Wolfson home where my wife grew up was the quintessential *Torah u'gedulah b'makom echad*. The opportunity to be welcomed and become part of the Wolfson family in Israel molded my life in ways I could never imagine. Little did I know, when marrying my wife Batsheva, of the profound influence her uncle, Harav Aviezer Wolfson *zt"l*, would have in my life.

Harav Wolfson was a brilliant *talmid chacham* who knew how to take the deep words of the Maharal and turn them into a language that people of all levels of *Yiddishkeit*, those observant and not observant, intellectual, and not so intellectual, could appreciate. He taught Yidden all across the world: in America, in England, in other countries in Europe, and in Russia/the Soviet Union, even during the years of the KGB in the early 1980s! Yes, even there, in those days, he educated Jews, bringing them back to their heritage.

With the help of my uncle, I was able to develop *shiurim* in Maharal modeled after his method. May he be a *meilitz yosher* for our Aunt Chana *shetichyeh*, his *chashuve rebbetzin*, and for the entire family.

When it came to writing this *sefer*, I was still in need of a *rebbi*. Although Rav Moshe *zt"l* had passed away about seven years beforehand, the loss still felt fresh to me. The reason is simple: As a person continues learning, he has questions and needs someone to turn to, someone who could provide him with answers. Now that my *rebbi* had been *niftar*, I was left with those questions.

Fortunately, over the years, I have been able to create a relationship with Harav Tzvi Cheshin *shlit"a*. He has made himself available to guide me through some of the more esoteric parts of this manuscript.

Many people were involved in the creation of this *sefer*. The editing process went through a number of phases. I have tremendous *hakaras hatov* to Mrs. Chana Nestlebaum, whose knowledge and skills allowed this manuscript to become a book. My heartfelt praise as well to the entire staff at Israel Bookshop, who have been so helpful and easy to work with. Nothing is too difficult for them. Truly, they are masters at providing Klal Yisrael with the *sefarim* necessary for them to grow in Torah.

Finally, I feel overwhelming gratitude toward my amazing and dear friends, partners, and *chavrusos* who donated generously to the publication of this *sefer*, thus allowing it to reach completion. These individuals include Reb Dovid Gamzeh, Reb Naftali Zelman, Marc Rossman, Michael Raff, Reb Shmuel Lapa, Reb Dovid Salamon, Rabbi Arye Smith, Shmuel Dovid Levinson, Hershey Kleinman, and an anonymous friend and *chavrusa*.

Additionally, I want to thank the *kehillah kedoshah* of the Village Green shul, where I have the privilege to serve as *rav* for over ten years. The *ahavah v'achvah* among the members of our shul make us more like a family than a congregation. With your assistance, a dream has come true, and a vision has become a reality. May Hashem repay all of you and your families for the *zechus* of the Torah that emanates from this *sefer*.

Rabbi Simcha Bunim Berger
Monsey, New York

Introduction

The Gemara in *Sukkos* (11b) quotes the *pasuk*, *In order that your generations know that in* sukkos *I placed Bnei Yisrael when I took them out of the land of Egypt* (*Vayikra* 23:43).

What is it that we are commemorating with our *sukkos*?

The Gemara explains that there are two opinions as to what "*sukkos*" in the *pasuk* is referencing. Rabi Eliezer says it is referring to the *Ananei Hakavod*, the Clouds of Glory that surrounded the Jewish people, while Rabi Akiva's opinion is that the *sukkos* which we refer to are actual booths.

Now, Rabi Eliezer certainly agrees with Rabi Akiva that the Jewish people lived in individual booths, and Rabi Akiva cannot argue about the existence of the clouds that surrounded the Jewish people while they were in the desert. Therefore, it is difficult to understand their disagreement, since in reality, both opinions are not mutually exclusive.

How are we to understand their disagreement?

The answer is that, indeed, all agree that the Jewish people lived in booths, *and* that they were surrounded by clouds. One complemented the other: The Jewish people were able to live in booths in the desert because the clouds surrounded them, and the clouds surrounded them because they had the courage to leave Egypt and take up residence in the desert.

In the words of *Chazal*, these two things, the clouds and the booths, represent two different forces: one from Heaven, and the other from earth. They are referred to as an awakening from Above (*is'eirusa d'l'Eila*) and an awakening from below (*is'eirusa d'l'sata*).

Rabi Eliezer and Rabi Akiva's argument is regarding which aspect we are celebrating. Rabi Eliezer is of the opinion that we celebrate Hashem's clouds that protected us, while Rabi Akiva argues that we are celebrating the courage that the Jewish people exhibited when leaving Egypt and taking up residence in the desert in flimsy booths.

According to the opinion of Rabi Akiva, when we leave our homes to sit in our individual *sukkos*, we are replicating exactly what our ancestors did over 3,000 years ago. Indeed, the Yom Tov of Sukkos is a holiday that inspires us to reach greater levels of spirituality.

The inspiration to write this *sefer* on the topics of Sukkos and Hallel came from the Yom Tov itself. Sukkos is a Yom Tov full of mitzvos and themes: the *sukkah*, *arba'ah minim*, *Ananei Hakavod*, *simchas beis hasho'evah*, Hoshana Rabbah, *Ushpizin*, Shemini Atzeres, and Simchas Torah. With a holiday so full of mitzvos and meaning, shouldn't it be appropriate for us to have a deep understanding of each of these mitzvos, as well as how they all fit together with each other?

The Maharal has always been a remarkable source of knowledge, allowing us to have a deeper understanding (according to our capacity) of the ideas that *Chazal* have imparted to us. Although the Maharal had planned to write a *sefer* on the topic of Sukkos (so he wrote in his introduction to his *sefer*, *Gevuros Hashem*), unfortunately we do not have access to it. There is a debate as to whether he wrote the *sefer* and it got lost, or if he never actually authored such a work.

While we don't have a *sefer* from the Maharal that's dedicated solely to the Yom Tov of Sukkos, he does discuss some aspects of Sukkos in many of his other works, such as *Chiddushei Aggados*, *Gevuros Hashem*, and *Nesivos Olam*. This is how we can still glean some of the Maharal's wisdom on these subjects. It is from those *sefarim* that I was able to gather the teachings of the Maharal in order to write this *sefer*.

Along the way, I learned many basic ideas from the Maharal on the concept of Yom Tov in general, as well as on the overall structure of all the *mo'adim*. I incorporated these ideas as well in this *sefer.*

Hallel takes on a whole new meaning when it is recited while holding the *arba'ah minim*. The Maharal in *Gevuros Hashem* explains the deeper understanding of Hallel, which we included in this *sefer*. Also discussed is the fascinating origin of the name "Yom Tov," and how and why it became the standard name for all *mo'adim*.

I realize that my work will not do justice to the great master that was the Maharal, and I ask forgiveness if my words fall short of expressing the meaning that he intended. Still, we will try to comprehend the holy Maharal's work on our level, and we will surely come away inspired.

CHAPTER 1

The Three *Regalim*

The Holidays of *Emunah*

For the Jewish people, a "good day" is a day not merely "good" by the measurement of our physical world; rather it is a day that is better than anything the natural world has to offer. It is a holiday, a "Yom Tov," which is literally, in English, a "good day."[1] Not only does the term Yom Tov describe a day of celebration, but it also denotes a day on which our existence is elevated, on which we do not work at our worldly occupations. Therefore, the term Yom Tov encompasses only Pesach, Shavuos, Sukkos, Rosh Hashanah, and Yom Kippur—holidays when those restrictions are in effect. (The specific name, "Yom Tov," relates to the first six days of creation, each of which is described by Hashem as "*tov*.")

Purim and Chanukah are certainly days of celebration as well. However, since there is no prohibition against work, they are not referred to as Yamim Tovim.

Even within the realm of the Yamim Tovim, there are categories. Pesach, Shavuos, and Sukkos are known as the Three *Regalim*,

1. See Appendix, "Origin of the Name Yom Tov."

while Rosh Hashanah and Yom Kippur are referred to as the Yamim Nora'im. A third name for our holidays is found in the Torah portion of *Parshas Emor*, where the *pasuk* refers to Yamim Tovim as *mo'adim*. This terminology will be discussed in a later chapter.

The Three *Regalim*

In *Parshas Mishpatim* (23:14), we find the commandment, *Three pilgrimage festivals shall you celebrate for Me during the year*. The description the Torah uses for these holidays is *regalim*, which means feet. The Talmud refers to this verse as the commandment of *aliyah l'regel*.[2] To fulfill it, all males were expected to come to the Beis Hamikdash, offer a sacrifice to Hashem, rejoice, and stay at least one night before returning home.

Why does the Torah refer to the holidays as *regalim*? The name *regel* (for a single holiday) can be understood as a reference to the ceremony of trekking up to Yerushalayim. However, it would seem strange to identify a holiday with a family hike to the Holy City. Is there not a more appropriate name for the Yamim Tovim than "the feet"?

Additionally, why do we refer to the Three *Regalim* as a unit? What binds them together as a group? Is the terminology based only on the fact that we go up to Yerushalayim three times annually?

The Three *Regalim*: The Foundations of Belief

The Maharal in *Sefer Gevuros*[3] explains that *Chazal* chose the term *regalim* because feet are the foundation of a person. When we say a person doesn't have "a leg to stand on," we are describing a lack of substance in his argument. On the other hand, when

---

2. The mitzvah of *Aliyah L'regel* will be discussed later in this chapter.

3. Chapter 47.

someone bases his position on a strong, well-rooted foundation, we say that he is someone who has "two feet on the ground."

In referring to the holidays as feet or legs, explains the Maharal, the Torah is teaching us that these holidays are more than just a time of festivity. Rather, they celebrate the foundations of the Jewish religion. These Yamim Tovim celebrate our *emunah* in Hashem, and consequently, our connection to Him. Simply stated, **the Yamim Tovim are the feet we stand on.**

The Three *Regalim*: The Feet of Belief

The Maharal reveals a fascinating insight into the fabric of the Three *Regalim*. These festivals express three forms of belief that connect us, the Jewish people, to Hashem. First, let us identify and explain these beliefs.

In the Torah's account of our exodus from Egypt, it states on three occasions that the Jewish people "believed." Each of these instances arises from a different scenario, and each reflects a different form of belief.

The first time the concept of *emunah* is mentioned is when Moshe, on his mission to take the Jews out of Egypt, first approaches the Jewish people to announce that their time of salvation is imminent.

> ויאמן העם וישמעו כי פקד ה׳ את בני ישראל וכי ראה את ענים ויקדו וישתחוו. [שמות ד׳ ל״א]
>
> *And the people **believed**, and they heard that Hashem had remembered the children of Israel and that He saw their affliction, and they bowed their heads and prostrated themselves.*

The Jewish people ***believed*** that Hashem had seen their pain and shared the weight of their burdens.

The second occasion was at the splitting of the sea, where the Torah states:

ויאמינו בה׳ ובמשה עבדו. [שמות י״ד ל״א]

*And they **believed** in Hashem and in Moshe His servant.*

Six weeks later at Har Sinai, while Hashem was instructing Moshe to give Bnei Yisrael the Torah, Hashem says:

וגם בך יאמינו לעולם. [שמות י״ט ט׳]

*And also in you [Moshe] shall they **believe** forever.*

What is the significance of these three expressions of belief?

The Maharal explains that these represent three distinct dimensions of *emunah*, engendered by the exodus, that forged our relationship with Hashem.

The Three Beliefs of Exodus

A deeper understanding of the exodus from Egypt is that the Jewish people needed to be decontaminated and cleansed from the impurity of Egypt. This purification would allow them to enter the world of Hashem, the world of *emunah*. These *pesukim* reveal to us that in truth, there were three aspects of *emunah* that the nation needed to acquire in order to achieve a full disconnection from impurity. Each belief would bring them a step closer to Hashem. These are the three beliefs:

- Belief in Hashem the Creator.
- Belief that this Creator cares about His world and involves Himself in every aspect of its workings. This is the concept of Hashem as the *Mashgiach*.
- Belief that Hashem gave us the Torah, through which He commanded us to perform His mitzvos.

Conceptually, each belief is independent. By way of example, we can use the structure of a company to explain the first two of these beliefs:

Every company begins with one or more individuals responsible for its creation. These people, who set up the structure of the company, are known as its founders. Once the company is up and running, it hires managers to oversee its day-to-day functions. A diverse company will have many departments, each requiring its own manager to maintain that part of the operation. However, at the core of the company is its product, and the company's legitimacy depends on the integrity of its product.

Boreh and *Mashgiach*

Our example illustrates distinct categories of activity that are completely independent of each other. Likewise, Hashem's role as the Creator does not implicitly include His supervision of the world on a day-to-day basis. Indeed, there are those who believe with complete faith that Hashem created the world, but they maintain that He is uninvolved in the actual running of the world. In their view, such "mundane" activity, necessitating involvement in the nitty-gritty of people's daily lives, is beneath His dignity. It isn't a king's job. Another leg of their argument is that terrible things would not happen in the world if Hashem were running it. Therefore, the belief that Hashem is concerned about the world, and involved in it, is an entirely separate "department," a separate belief from that of His role as Creator. Let us reflect on these distinct categories of belief.

The First Belief: Hashem the *Mashgiach*

The word *mashgiach* can be translated as "supervisor." It is commonly used to refer to a Jew who supervises the kashrus status of a kosher establishment.

When Moshe approached the Jewish people and informed them that Hashem had sent him to extract them from Egypt, the Torah states, *The Jews welcomed Moshe and trusted that Hashem remembered them*. They believed that Hashem had seen their pain and knew of their suffering. In this *pasuk*, the Torah relates the first of three separate beliefs in Hashem. It proclaims that the nation believed in a caring G-d Who saw their perilous plight and would take up their cause.

This *emunah*, explains the Maharal, is the belief in Hashem as the *Mashgiach*.

The Second Belief: Hashem the Creator

Later at the Yam Suf (the splitting of the sea), the Torah states, *The Children of Israel saw the hand of Hashem*. The Maharal reminds us that the miracles in Egypt, the Ten Plagues, were an *etzba* (a finger), a fraction of the revelation of Hashem's power in comparison to the revelation at the sea. There, His miracles are described as a *yad* (a hand). When the Torah declares that *They believed in Hashem and Moshe His servant*, says the Maharal, it is describing their belief in an Omnipotent G-d Who turns water into land and land into water. They experienced glimpses of a Creator Who, in front of their very eyes, changed the rules of nature as He saw fit. The splitting of the sea, together with the Ten Plagues, which also upended nature, formed the foundation for the belief in Hashem as the Creator.[4]

---

4. One might wonder, aren't these two beliefs out of order? Shouldn't the belief of a Creator be the initial and foundational concept, upon which rests the belief that Hashem runs and manages the world? Yet the Torah presents these beliefs in a different order; the Jews believed that Hashem remembered them even before Hashem revealed His power to them. The answer is while conceptually this is backward, practically, the Jews—who were enslaved and tortured in Egypt—were not in a position to internalize the concept of a Creator. Informing or even proving to them that there is a Creator would be futile. They would say, "Of what importance is it to have a Creator when we, the Jews, are all suffering?" Under those circumstances, the first thing the Jews needed to recognize about Hashem was that He cared about their pain and was going to do something about it! After they believed in a G-d Who cared, it was appropriate *and necessary* to educate the Jewish people on the great power that this G-d possessed. This explains why although conceptually their beliefs were reversed, practically, it had to be this way.

The Third Belief: Hashem's Commandments

The third time the Torah mentions *emunah* is and at the revelation at Har Sinai, when the Jews received the Torah. As the *pasuk* (*Shemos* 19:9) relates, Hashem assures Moshe that when the Bnei Yisrael hear Hashem speaking to him, *And also, in you shall they believe forever.*[5]

This is the belief that Hashem has expectations of us. He gave us a Torah with commandments, through which we should live our lives. It is *Toras Moshe*, the commandments that Hashem gave to Moshe Rabbeinu. The Jewish people thereby acquired yet another foundation of belief—that Hashem has expectations of humans, which can only be fulfilled by living according to the Torah, given to Moshe by Hashem.

Having established these three pillars of faith, let us now understand how the Maharal connects them to the Three *Regalim*.

Pesach: The First *Regel*

As we mentioned, a *regel* is not just a time to ascend to Yerushalayim. Rather, it is a foundation of our connection to Hashem. Each of the three Yamim Tovim celebrates one of the three distinct facets of *emunah*.

The holiday of Pesach taught the Jews to believe in Hashem the Creator. The diversity of the Ten Plagues proved that Hashem has dominion over the heavens and the earth and all parts of creation.[6]

---

5. One might ask, why would the belief in Hashem's commandments be linked to the belief in Moshe? The answer can be found in the famous words of the prophet Malachi:

זכרו תורת משה עבדי [מלאכי ג׳ כ״ב]—*Remember the Torah of Moshe My servant.* Since all the Torah's commandments were told to us by Moshe, the Torah is identified with him. The Gemara in *Makkos* calculates that of the 613 commandments of the Torah, 611 were related to us by Moshe. Indeed, the numerical value or *gematria* of the word "Torah" equals 611, justifying the statement, *Toras Moshe.*

6. See Maharal Haggadah for an elaborate connection between each plague and the ten utterances of creation.

This message was eternally imprinted in them when they crossed the Yam Suf, leaving Egypt and Pharaoh behind forever. This culmination of the exodus corresponds to the seventh and final day of Pesach.

Therefore, says the Maharal, *Krias Yam Suf* was a perfect, ripe moment for the Torah to inform us that the Jewish people believed in Hashem. Indeed, the miracles they witnessed at the sea were a re-enactment of creation. At the beginning of the creation, Hashem commanded the water to gather to reveal dry land. *Krias Yam Suf* enabled the people to witness this with their own eyes as the waters gathered with unnatural rapidity to reveal dry land, and later fell back to the sea instantaneously. Seeing this with their own eyes, they could not doubt that Hashem had created the world. Thus, the *regel* of Pesach and its lesson of *emunah* were not complete until the final day of Yom Tov.

On a deeper level, the Jewish people's emergence from the water carried great significance. Not only was the splitting of the sea similar to creation, but it also provided a rectification of creation. With the emergence of the Jews as Hashem's people, a new form of mankind was born: a people created in the image of Hashem, who reflected the original Adam. To understand this idea, let us delve into a few concepts:

- The original man—Adam
- Har Sinai
- The Jewish people—the new Adam

The Original Man—Adam

Adam was created in the image of G-d. He was pure and good. The evil that was in the world at that time existed only outside of man, in the form of the serpent. This was the situation prior to Adam and Chava's sin of eating from the Tree of Knowledge of Good and Evil. After Adam listened to the serpent and sinned, evil became internalized within him; it became part of the form of man. This is referred to as "the contamination/ toxicity of the snake," or in the words of the Gemara (*Shabbos* 145), *zuhamas hanachash*.

Moving forward through the subsequent generations, the power of evil within man began to dominate. By the tenth generation, known as the generation of the flood, man no longer resembled the original Adam. Therefore, Hashem regretted having created man. As the Torah says,[7] *Hashem saw that the wickedness of man was great upon the earth and that every product of the thoughts of his heart was but evil always. And Hashem reconsidered having made man on earth.*

When Hashem brought the flood, He saved only Noach and his family. With them, He started a new world. From that time on, humans were known as Bnei Noach—the children of Noach. The original Adam, with his capacity to connect to Hashem, was lost and destroyed in the waters of the flood.[8] So the situation remained until the exodus.

Har Sinai

The Gemara (*Shabbos* 145b) asks in the name of Rabbi Yosi, *Why are the nations of the world contaminated by the serpent [whereas the Jewish people are not]*? The Gemara answers that they retain this state because they did not stand at Har Sinai. When the Jewish people stood at Har Sinai, their contamination departed.

This was Hashem's plan, and He informed Moshe of

---

7. וירא ה׳ כי רבה רעת האדם בארץ וכל יצר מחשבות לבו רק רע כל היום. וינחם ה׳ כי עשה את האדם בארץ [בראשית ו׳ ה׳-ו׳].

8. Although Noach was righteous enough to survive the destruction of the world, he did not possess the capacity to save the world.

it when He first appeared to Moshe on Har Sinai (*Shemos* 3:12): *And He said, "For I shall be with you and this is your sign that I have sent you, when you take the people out of Egypt and serve G-d on this mountain."*

Hashem informed Moshe that through the process of the exodus, the original sin would be rectified. Har Sinai would re-establish our identification with the original man.

The Gemara states, *You [the Jewish people] are called Adam [man], and the other nations of the world are not called Adam [man].* When did this change happen?

The Jewish People—the New Adam

The process of the exodus is considered a birth, as it is written in *Yechezkel, On the day I gave birth to you.* But what was born? It wasn't just another nation, but rather a new human form. The exodus was much more than the release of the Jewish people from slavery; it was a rectification of creation. From the population that re-inhabited the world after the flood, a new people emerged.

I learned from my *rebbi*, Harav Moshe Shapiro *zt"l*, that the miracle of the splitting of the sea was like a recreation of Day Three of creation, when Hashem said, *Let the waters gather and the land shall be revealed.* There on the dry land, at the bottom of the ocean, the entire world took on a new reality.[9] [10]

This foundation of belief is the celebration of Pesach.

---

9. Every day in our morning blessings of *Birkas Hashachar* we say the blessing רוקע הארץ על המים, acknowledging that Hashem stretches the earth over the water. This recognizes and thanks Hashem not only for the original creation of land, but also the land that He made specifically for us, His people.

10. While this would not be complete until the Yom Tov of Shavuos when they received the Torah, the process began with the exodus.

Shavuos: The Second *Regel*

The next Yom Tov, Shavuos, is the holiday that celebrates the receiving of the Torah. As we count from Pesach to Shavuos, we anticipate a holiday that celebrates our significant role in Hashem's world. Through the Torah Hashem gave us, we have an opportunity to participate actively in the process of bringing creation to its perfection. This is why we celebrate. As we mentioned, our belief in Torah from Sinai is synonymous with the belief that we are here for a purpose. Shavuos especially carries this message because the Yom Tov doesn't exist unless we actively create it by counting the Sefiras Ha'Omer.[11] This is no coincidence: Our belief that Hashem gave us the Torah to teach us how to live our lives and that He expects us to use it to take an active role in His world characterize the Yom Tov that celebrates that experience! *Shavuos is indeed created by us.*

Sukkos: The Third *Regel*

The last of the three *regalim* is the Yom Tov of Sukkos. The Torah states:

> למען ידעו דרתיכם כי בסכות הושבתי את בני ישראל.
> [ויקרא כ״ג מ״ג]
>
> *So that your generations will know that I caused the children of Israel to dwell in booths when I took them out from the land of Egypt.*

We are commanded to sit in a *sukkah* to remind us of the

---

11. *Zohar Parshas Emor.* Counting is so important and individualistic that everyone needs to be involved. The Torah's command to count up to Shavuos applies to every person. One cannot fulfill the obligation by listening to someone else's recitation, as we are permitted to do for Kiddush. Rather, the Torah says וספרתם לכם—*You should count for yourselves.* This is because counting is an exercise in *emunah,* which must be rooted in an internal belief that each person develops within himself. A person cannot acquire a genuine belief in Torah because someone tells him, "It makes sense." He needs to arrive at this understanding on his own. This is one of the messages of "count for yourself."

lifestyle that the Jews lived in the desert for forty years. This is the Yom Tov of the Clouds of Glory, known as the *Ananei Hakavod*.

We lived a pampered existence in the desert, surrounded by glorious clouds as we journeyed through the inhospitable terrain, a place Moshe described[12] as "the great and awesome wilderness of snake, fiery serpent, and scorpion." Nevertheless, the Jews felt safe and secure. Therefore, Sukkos is a celebration of Hashem's compassion for us and involvement in our lives.

The Three *Regalim*

We now can appreciate the Maharal's concept of what the three *regalim* represent. Our holidays are not just historical events, but **celebrations of the foundations of our *emunah*.** This gives us an even deeper insight and a greater opportunity to connect to the happiness we experience on the Yamim Tovim. Since, as we explained, *regel* describes a holiday as a foundation, the *regalim* are times when we connect to that foundation and experience the sense of belonging: the confidence and security of being in Hashem's hands. Each distinct type of *emunah* is one of the three legs that supports the larger, stronger foundation upon which we secure our faith in Hashem.

This opens our minds and hearts to a deeper understanding of the commandment of *Aliyah L'regel*. The obligation to come face to face with Hashem enables us to reconfirm our individual connection to Him.[13]

---

12. *Devarim* 8:15.

13. Belief is personal and individual. As we discussed in the introduction to the Maharal Haggadah, believing because someone else "says so" is not *emunah*; rather, belief has to be personal. Therefore, all males must personally come to the Beis Hamikdash since we must connect individually to Hashem. This commandment takes on a whole new dimension when we understand that each visit corresponds to an entirely different belief. It is quite clear that each of the three annual pilgrimages is independently necessary. One cannot simply excuse

However, *emunah* is something that a person needs to constantly work to develop. How does this happen in the months between the three *regalim*? Fortunately, we do not need to wait for a Yom Tov to tap into the energy of the holidays. Rather, we are given the opportunity to strengthen our three beliefs twice a day, when we recite the Shema.

Shema—Daily Maintenance of the Three *Emunos*

Since our beliefs are the foundation of our relationship with Hashem, any flaw in the *emunah* could erode this foundation and cause an unstable relationship. To maintain a healthy relationship, we recite the three *parshiyos* of the Shema twice a day. These three daily portions of Shema represent the three aspects of *emunah*, as we will now explain.

Shema—the Confirmation of the Almighty

Shema Yisrael Hashem Elokeinu Hashem Echad—"Hashem is the One and only." This is the claim of Hashem's omnipotence. It expresses the belief that Hashem is the Source of all that exists. He is the One, and we put our entire self, with all our possessions, in His service. This corresponds to the holiday of Pesach, when we celebrate Hashem as the Creator of all.

The second portion of Shema deals with reward and punishment:

> *And it will come to pass if you continually hearken to My commandments... then I will provide rain for your land in its proper time. Lest your heart be turned away then I will restrain the heavens so there will be no rain.*

With these words, we declare our belief that Hashem manages and maintains this world. He tells us that He is directly involved in

---

oneself and skip one of the three because "I was just there last Yom Tov." Rather each of the three visits fortifies an entirely different belief that is needed to reinforce, on an annual basis, the complete *emunah* foundation.

our lives and will bring or deny rain in response to man's actions. This belief corresponds to the holiday of Sukkos, which celebrates Hashem's involvement in our daily lives.

The third portion of Shema is the portion of *tzitzis*. Rashi, at the end of this Torah portion,[14] explains that the commandment of *tzitzis* encapsulates all the commandments of Hashem. The Torah states, *This shall be fringes for you and when you see it, you remember all the commandments of Hashem and you will perform them.*

The *gematria* of the Hebrew word *tzitzis* is 600. These fringes are comprised of eight threads that are knotted five times. By adding these eight threads and the five knots to the 600 of *tzitzis* we arrive at a total of 613, equal to the number of commandments in the Torah. The Torah is telling us that one who performs the mitzvah of *tzitzis* properly will be reminded of his service to Hashem and his responsibility to keep all the commandments of the Torah. This corresponds to the holiday of Shavuos, during which we received all 613 commandments.

To summarize, the Shema enables us to maintain, on a daily basis, our three beliefs in Hashem.

A Breach in the Foundation

Until this point, we have discussed the justification of these three beliefs and the basis upon which these foundational *emunos* have been developed. Now we will explore what happens when a person has not fully developed all three *emunos*.

The Maharal, with what seems to be an almost prophetic insight into the Gemara (*Eruvin* 19a), reveals yet another layer of significance in the *emunos* that we established through our experience of *Yetzias Mitzrayim*. The Gemara in *Eruvin*[15] says that

---

14. *Parshas Shelach.*

15. ואמר רבי ירמיה בר אלעזר שלשה פתחים יש לגיהנם אחד במדבר ואחד בים ואחד בירושלים, במדבר דכתיב וירדו הם וכל אשר להם חיים שאולה, בים דכתיב מבטן שאול שועתי

there are three doorways to Gehinnom (hell): one in the desert, another at sea, and the third at the entrance to Yerushalayim. The Maharal explains the sources for these locations and provides insight into the distinct nature of each.

The Desert

The Gemara cites the episode of Korach as the source that identifies an entrance to Gehinnom in the desert. Korach adopted the view that Moshe was a fake. He accused Moshe of concocting the story that Hashem had chosen Moshe's brother, Aharon, for the position of *kohen gadol.* In making this claim, Korach threw into question Moshe's integrity, undermining one of the foundations of belief.

The Talmud teaches us that because of this total fabrication, Korach didn't just die a normal death, nor was he merely swallowed up by the ground. Rather, by negating one of the primary foundations of our faith, Korach lost his right to exist. He therefore disappeared from the face of the earth. His body, soul, and everything that he owned went straight to hell.

The belief that Korach challenged corresponds to the *emunah* tied to the Yom Tov of Shavuos. This is the belief in Moshe: *And also in you [Moshe] shall they believe forever.*

The Sea

The Talmud derives the second doorway from the book of Yonah. Hashem commanded the prophet Yonah to inform the city of Ninveh (the capital of Assyria) that their wicked lifestyle had reached Heaven, and punishment loomed ahead for all the inhabitants of the city.

Instead of heeding Hashem's instructions, Yonah ran away from

---

שמעתי קולי, בירושלים דכתיב (ישעיהו לא, ט) נאם ה׳ אשר אור לו בציון ותנור לו בירושלים ותנא דבי רבי ישמעאל אשר אור לו בציון זו גיהנם ותנור לו בירושלים זו פתחה של גיהנם.

his responsibility. As Yonah fled by sea, Hashem stirred up a great storm that threatened the ship on which the prophet was traveling. The journey became impossible. Yonah was forthright with the crew and took responsibility for the danger to the ship and all its voyagers. The crew had no choice but to throw Yonah overboard, which caused the sea to subside.

Hashem then sent a large fish to swallow Yonah. There, in the bowels of the fish, Yonah says, *From the stomach of hell I cry out to You.* By planning to run away and then executing his plan, Yonah (who was a prophet) was rejecting the foundation of belief in the Almighty G-d. Did he really think he could go to a place where Hashem wouldn't find him?[16]

Yonah's actions, reflecting a lack of faith in an omnipotent G-d, greatly diminished *kavod Shamayim*. For that, Yonah realized, he deserved to end up in a Gehinnom-like environment. Yonah's mistake amounted to a denial of all that Hashem invested in *Yetzias Miztrayim*, and specifically at the Yam Suf.

This is the episode the Talmud cites to identify the sea as another entrance to Gehinnom. The *emunah* Yonah called into question is *And they believed in Hashem and in Moshe His servant*, corresponding to the Yom Tov of Pesach.

Yerushalayim

The third doorway to Gehinnom is in Yerushalayim. The Gemara (*Eruvin* 19a) quotes the *pasuk, Thus says Hashem—Who has a fire in Tzion and a furnace in Yerushalayim.* The prophet Yeshayah guaranteed the Jewish people who inhabited Yerushalayim that they would not be harmed by the troops of Sancheriv. However,

---

16. The Maharal quotes a *Mechilta* explaining that although Yonah knew that Hashem doesn't reveal prophesy outside the land of Israel, his attempt to flee showed disrespect to Hashem, as though it were possible to "run away" from Him.

those who didn't believe in Hashem's protection would be exposed to the fire of the oven in Yerushalayim.

In explaining this Gemara, the Maharal quotes the *pasuk* (*Yeshayah* 62:6), *Upon your walls, Yerushalayim, I have placed guards.* Hashem watches over the city (provided that its inhabitants are doing His will). In general, walls are meant to enclose an area; however, walls around a city are built for protection. The walls of Yerushalayim have no value in the physical world unless they symbolize Hashem's higher protection. This is Hashem's role as *Shomer Yisrael,* He Who cares for and protects His nation.

This concept of *shemirah* connects the holiday of Sukkos to the city of Yerushalayim. Sukkos is the festival of the *Ananei Hakavod,* which protected the Bnei Yisrael throughout their forty years in the desert. As we mentioned, the commandment of Sukkos requires us to leave the safe haven of our homes, expose ourselves to nature, and take shelter in Hashem.

In fact, we mention this connection weekly in our Shabbos evening prayers. In the prayer of *Hashkiveinu*, we conclude: *Blessed are You Hashem Who spreads over us the shelter of peace* (sukkas shalom) *and upon all of His people Yisrael and upon Yerushalayim*.

This trust in Hashem's protection is the *emunah* that the Jews acquired in Egypt: *And the nation believed, and they heard that Hashem had remembered the Bnei Yisrael and that He saw their affliction* (*Shemos* 4:31). A person deficient in this belief lacks the basic understanding that Hashem watches over us.

To summarize, the Maharal explains that the Talmud in *Eruvin*, which identifies three doorways of Gehinnom, symbolically refers to the three fundamental beliefs mentioned above. The Talmud's lesson is that a Jew's deficiency in any of these critical *emunah* foundations creates an opening for him into Gehinnom.

A parallel Gemara, regarding the period during which the Jewish people acquired the promised land, drives home a similar message:

The Gemara[17] relates that the Jewish people entered the land of Israel by crossing the Jordan River in a miraculous way. The water split into twelve passageways for the twelve tribes, quite like the experience the Jews had when crossing the Yam Suf forty years earlier. To commemorate this miracle, they were commanded to take twelve stones that were uncovered by the splitting of the Yarden and place them on the riverbank where the nation first entered the water.

The Gemara explains that this monument was the second of three that the Jewish people of that generation were commanded to establish. Two months earlier, on Rosh Chodesh Shevat, while Moshe Rabbeinu was still alive (he would pass away in the following month, on the seventh of Adar), the Jews gathered to hear Moshe explain the Torah in seventy languages. In the final weeks of his life, Moshe Rabbeinu reviewed all the commandments in seventy languages and had them all engraved on stones. This was the first of three stone monuments to be established.

The third was at Har Gerizim and Har Eval, where the Jews first gathered after entering the holy land. There as well, Yehoshua used stones to engrave all the words of the Torah in all seventy languages. The people then carried all these stones to Gilgal, the location of the Mishkan, where the stones were established as a monument so that the Torah would be accessible to all nations.

What is the meaning of these three stone monuments? And what connection do they have to the Jewish people's entry into the land of Israel? Additionally, it seems that Yehoshua duplicated what Moshe did, albeit in a different location. Why, then, did Hashem not simply command Yehoshua to take the stones that Moshe had already engraved and bring them to Gilgal?

---

17. *Sotah* 35b.

The Foundations of Belief

The Maharsha explains that the stone monuments also represent the three foundations of Jewish belief: in Hashem as the Creator; in Hashem as *Mashgiach* Who rewards good and punishes evil; and in the Torah, by which He gave us the commandments.

This is precisely why Hashem commanded that these monuments be made of stone. **The beliefs of the Jewish people are the foundation on which we stand. Each belief is a cornerstone of our existence**. Therefore, at the most critical moment, when the Jews would be taking possession of the promised land, these stones were placed exactly where those entering Israel could gaze upon them and realize that accountability comes along with this inheritance. The people would be reminded of these three foundations:

- The stones engraved in the desert represent the Torah they received from Moshe in the desert.
- The stones at the river memorialize the omnipotence of the Almighty Who, for a second time, split the waters for them.
- The third set of stones (once again engraved), which were placed at Har Gerizim and Har Eval, the site of the blessing and admonitions, represents the accountability inherent in receiving the Torah. At Har Gerizim and Har Eval, the Jewish people entered into a covenant with the understanding that they would be responsible for all their actions.

These three sets of stones clearly coincide with the concept of the three doorways to Gehinnom mentioned earlier, as well as the three *regalim*. The stones that were engraved by Moshe on the other side of the Yarden (in the desert) correspond to the Yom Tov of Shavuos, the receiving of the Torah.

The stones at the river are testimony to the concept that we celebrate on Pesach: Hashem is the Creator. Just as He demonstrated at the splitting of the sea that He is the supreme and only Power in the entire universe, He did so again by splitting the river for the next generation. He instructed them to place stones on that spot so that the stones could testify to the reality of this belief.

The stones that were engraved at Har Gerizim and Har Eval, and carried to Gilgal, represent Hashem's involvement in our daily lives. This parallels the Yom Tov of Sukkos, as well as the doorway to Gehinnom found in Yerushalayim. However, one question remains: Why was another lesson in the three types of *emunah* necessary? The answer is that the nation led by Yehoshua into Eretz Yisrael had not experienced the foundations of Yom Tov. They were the next generation.

The Next Generation

The Maharal explains this by referring to the sin of the spies, whom Moshe sent to scout out Eretz Yisrael prior to the Jewish people's entry. According to the Maharal, the Jewish people who left Egypt and accepted the Torah played a unique role in the story of the Jewish people. The great events that they experienced comprise the Torah. They were ***the*** Bnei Yisrael who left Egypt, and it was to ***them*** that the mitzvos were given; their life and times are eternal.

Had that generation entered the land of Israel, the Jews never would have had to leave the land. Just as the exodus is part and parcel of our religion, so too is the promised land; it would have been forever ours had ***that*** generation inhabited it. However, since they accepted the testimony of the spies and no longer wanted to enter Eretz Yisrael, they severed the heritage of the Jewish people—the land of our fathers—from the exodus.

Instead, the next generation, the children who were born in the desert, were the ones who entered the land. They, however, didn't experience the Ten Plagues, nor were they at Har Sinai for *Kabbalas*

HaTorah. The experiences that created the foundations of *emunah* for the previous generation were, at that point, part of history.

Entry into the land presented this generation with the opportunity to experience and forge *their own* three foundations of *emunah*. In the last year of Moshe Rabbeinu's life, a mere forty days before he passed away, he explained the entire Torah to the Bnei Yisrael. While they didn't stand at Har Sinai, they still received the Torah from Moshe's own mouth (as celebrated on Shavuos). And while they didn't cross through the sea with the Egyptians in pursuit, they did experience a miraculous splitting of the waters (as celebrated on Pesach). And although they didn't have the *Ananei Hakavod*, they did establish a place for the *Shechinah's* presence when they built the Mishkan in Gilgal (as celebrated on Sukkos, see below).[18] Although the first generation that left Egypt had died, the three episodes of the stones represented this next generation's own personal experience of the fundamental beliefs that define us as the chosen people.

In summary, Hashem instructed those who entered the land of Israel to value and remember the foundations of our inheritance. By engraving and placing these three sets of stones in their appropriate locations, they would engrave these three beliefs into themselves, and into the holy land. This is something that we also experience annually, during Pesach, Shavuos, and Sukkos.

---

18. This is similar to the Yom Tov of Sukkos, just as the prayer we recite on Shabbos night at Ma'ariv expresses the concept of Yerushalayim as the place of *Sukkas Shalom*: הפורש סוכת שלום עלינו ועל כל עמו ישראל ועל ירושלים.

Pesach, Shavuos, and Sukkos: The Three Stages of Physicality

In addition to the name *regalim*, the holidays are known as *mo'adim*. *Mo'ed* means a specific time or event. The Maharal explains that the three festivals not only represent the three different types of beliefs,[19] but also, according to the Torah, Pesach, Shavuos, and Sukkos are unique events that the Torah synchronized with the developmental stages of wheat. Why did the Torah attach these special times of the Jewish year to the agricultural cycle of the land?

The Maharal notes that for those who cultivate fields (as did most of Bnei Yisrael when the land was divided among them), these three festivals align with times of great joy in the physical world. The arrival of spring, the harvest, and the ingathering of produce—marking the end of the year's agricultural cycle—are sources of natural happiness.

The Torah writes:

> את חג המצות תשמר שבעת ימים תאכל מצות אשר צויתך למועד חדש האביב כי בחודש האביב יצאת ממצרים... וחג שבעת תעשה לך בכורי קציר חטים וחג האסיף תקופת השנה. [שמות ל״ד י״ח-כ״ב]
>
> *You shall observe in the festival of matzos; seven days shall you eat matzos... at the appointed time of the month of the springtime, for in it you left Egypt.... And the festival of the harvest of the first fruits of your labor that you sow in the field; and the festival of the ingathering at the close of the year when you gather in your work from the field.*

19. As discussed in the previous chapter.

The Maharal in *Sefer Gevuros*[20] discusses at length the connection between these three holidays and the various stages of the growth and ripening of wheat. As an introduction, let us delve into the Maharal's teachings on the topics of *zman* and *geshem* (time and physicality) to reach an understanding of their essence. By clarifying the essence of each of these seemingly unrelated concepts, we will discover an underlying connection that gives deeper meaning to the three festivals.

Four fundamental ideas are crucial to this understanding:

1. The creation of time
2. The root of physicality
3. The three stages of physicality
4. Times of holiness

The Creation of Time

What does the word "time" really mean? According to the Maharal, it is a profound concept whose essence is contained in the Hebrew word for time, which is *zman*. When we examine broader usages of the word *zman*, we can arrive at a clear understanding of the word's significance. This, in turn, will help us comprehend the Torah's definition of "time" and the concepts it represents.

The word *zman* has many common applications. It is used in the context of preparing for something. For example, the word *l'hazmin* means to place an order; in doing so, we ask someone to prepare something for us. When we order food at a restaurant, we ask the cook to prepare our meal. Similarly, when three men make a *mezuman* for *bentching*, they are preparing to fulfill the Torah's mitzvah of *Birkas Hamazon*. Likewise, when someone sends out a *hazmanah*—an invitation—he is preparing for the upcoming event. "Time" exists because something is "about to happen." In other words, **the concept of *zman* expresses a state of being constantly**

20. Chapter 46.

prepared for change. It reflects the idea that something that is missing is being sought. Therefore, the concept of time relates to change, and indeed, time never stagnates.

Change, Imperfection, Time

Time can only exist because there is a *reality of change*. The duration of change—the span between "before" and "after"—is the time required for this change to occur. Because change is real and necessary in the world, time must exist. If there were no change, there would be no time. Why?

Imagine that you existed in a state of "non-change." You didn't need to seek any information because you already knew everything. You did not need to go anywhere because you had already seen everything. You had nothing to gain through human interaction and therefore you did not speak to anyone. Since your body had no needs, you didn't eat, drink, or sleep. In short, you were anticipating nothing. No path was lying ahead for you to traverse. Does time have any meaning for such a person? In a situation where everything is perfect, time has no meaning, and it doesn't exist.[21]

This leads us to the realization that time is the product of imperfection. It is only because things are imperfect that there is a possibility for change. *This is the rationale for time as a creation*. It can only exist and have meaning when we talk about things that are imperfect: needing, waiting for, and being prepared for a change that will bring them to a form of completion.

The Torah reveals this in its account of creation. Instead of creating the entire physical world in one flashing instant,[22] Hashem created just a part of the world on each day. In this way, time was

---

21. This perfect state of being explains the idea that Hashem is not bound by time.

22. The Mishnah in *Avos* (Chapter 5) discusses why Hashem chose to create the

created.[23] Every day there was change, creating a difference between "before and after." The world was thus imbued with what is commonly known as past, present, and future.[24]

With this deeper appreciation of the concept of time, we understand that the Hebrew word *zman* is not defined solely by the hours on the clock or the days on the calendar. Rather, the word describes the deeper concept of what time is; it is the potential and the *root*[25] of existence. Let us now explore the next point: the root of physicality.

The Root of Physicality

The Hebrew word for physicality is *gashmiyus*.[26] The root of this word is *geshem*, which commonly refers to rain. Why is rain used as the root of the word for all physical objects? What do the two have in common?

Rainclouds are a fascinating phenomenon. To the naked eye, there's no logical way to conceive of the great amounts of water contained in the clouds. It is even difficult to understand how a small amount of water can seemingly be suspended in midair.

---

world in ten utterances over a lengthy period of time instead of just creating it in one utterance.

23. The opening verse of the Torah, *In the beginning*, according to the Vilna Gaon, was the creation of time.

24. The three Yamim Tovim of Pesach, Shavuos, and Sukkos can be explained in terms of past, present, and future, as will be explained later in this section.

25. The point is not only that Hashem created time and imperfection together. Rather, creating an imperfect creation is the root of the existence of time. Because Hashem is perfect, He exists outside of time. Time comes into existence through the imperfection of the beings/world and it is the connecting factor between imperfection and perfection of those creations. In other words, time stands in the stead of perfection, and it will ultimately be replaced by perfection. Time is the creation that comes from a lack of perfection, and through it, we arrive at perfection.

26. The Ramban in *Parshas Bereishis* discusses the idea of *gashmiyus*.

While a cloud has some degree of mass, it's certainly not laden with water, for if it were, the clouds would not be able to remain aloft. Obviously, a process must take place that converts the vapor in the clouds into physical rain. **This transformation from vapor to physical rain captures the essence of physicality according to the Torah.** Therefore, *geshem*/rain is the root of the word the Torah uses for physicality, which is *gashmiyus*.

Herein lies a deeper message. When we observe the physical world, we initially perceive finite objects and a self-contained world. However, *Chazal* teach that our comprehension of the physical world connects us to a higher reality. Our prayers are full of verses that recognize the world and events that are before our eyes, and firmly connect them to the spiritual influence that flows from Hashem (*Tehillim* 33:6,9).[27]

The reason for this is physical as well as spiritual. From the perspective of the Jewish people, everything we perceive in our physical world is rooted in heaven. The source for this is found in the *Zohar*: *There is no blade of grass that exists in this world that doesn't have a higher reality in heaven that is designated to watch and protect and cause it to grow.* ***Gashmiyus*** **not only describes a physical object; it also reveals an item that has gone through a "*geshem*-like" transformation**. Everything we perceive in the physical world has a "rain-like" reality—a potential stored in heaven and released on earth.

This is the secret that explains why physicality in this world is referred to as *gashmiyus*. *Chazal* sought to impart to us the idea that just as rain comes from heaven and goes through a transformation process that renders it a physical reality (for as we perceive it, it would be impossible for it to be physical while in the

---

27. בדבר ה' שמים נעשו וברוח פיו כל צבאם—*By the word of Hashem the heavens were made and through the spirit of His utterance, all legions.* Also, כי הוא אמר ויהי הוא צוה ויעמוד—*For he spoke and it was; He commanded and they were established.*

clouds), so too everything physical begins with the words of Hashem and goes through a process of rain-like reality and is indeed *gashmiyus*.

Based on the understanding that everything in this physical world is connected to and comes from a higher reality, the Maharal reveals that the transformation process of every being, as it goes from its spiritual root to its physical state, is divided into three stages.

Three Stages of Physicality

The Maharal elaborates that every created object has a beginning, middle, and end. All physical entities have their beginning; that is their formation stage. When the creation stage is complete, the "created entity" now exists in its complete form. This is its second stage. Finally, the created entity reaches the objective of its creation—the fulfillment of its spiritual purpose—which brings it back to the root and purpose of its creation. This is its third phase and its completion.

This means that like *zman*, the physical world—*gashmiyus*—is a product of imperfection. Hashem created everything in an incomplete state. Take, for example, a human being: A person's birth and childhood comprise the first stage. This is the stage at which the physical entity makes its appearance in the world and develops its capacities.

Once an object has been created and developed, it enters a second stage as an **independent** item. A person reaches this stage when he or she becomes responsible for keeping the Torah and performing the mitzvos. The capacities that have been developed are now being put to use, being strengthened, refined, and coaxed toward maturity.

The Maharal explains that the third stage is to connect the item back to its Source. Once the creation has returned to where it began, it has come "full circle" and can be considered to have served its purpose. In the life of a Jew, this occurs when he or she is settled with a family and dwelling with Hashem's presence in the home. Yitzchak presents a paradigm of this stage when he brings Rivkah home and the *Shechinah*, which had departed with the death of Sarah, returns. The Jew's purpose in being created—that of bringing Hashem's light into the world—is thus fulfilled.

These three steps can be perceived in the physical world through the growth of produce, and the Torah chose wheat as the example. Without these stages of development serving as our frame of reference, we would have no way to demarcate a beginning, middle, and end in the yearly cycle of nature. There would be no reason to call any particular season the first, since a cycle is by definition a continuous loop. The budding of produce allows us to perceive a starting point.

The second stage in creation arrives when the crops have grown to their full potential. Finally, when they have completed their growth and are being gathered and prepared for consumption, we perceive the final stage in the cycle. Through this cycle, which begins with planting the seeds in the ground, progresses to growth and maturity, and then onto harvest and ingathering, we can observe the complete metamorphosis of a *gashmiyus* creation as it develops from nothingness to reality and finally to conclusion.

Herein lies the connection between *zman* and *geshem*. We mentioned earlier that time can be divided into the past, the present, and the future. Now let us link the three stages of physicality to these three aspects of time: The first stage of creation, the stage of development, is the past. The second stage, the developed creation as an independent entity, is the present. The purpose of the creation—its *tikkun*—is the future. The next step is to understand how this connects to our three holidays: Pesach, Shavuos, and Sukkos.

Three Pillars of the World

The Maharal explains this relationship by quoting the mishnah that states, *The world stands on three things: on Torah,* avodah *(sacrifices), and* gemilus chassadim *(acts of loving-kindness).*[28] Elaborating on these three pillars of creation in reverse order,[29] he explains that they are the "contact points" by which the world is attached to Hashem. The first is the act of loving-kindness. Through this, we connect to Hashem's desire to bestow goodness, which is the *motivator* behind creation and its first pillar.

Another pillar is Hashem's Torah. This was the *means* through which the world was created. As it is written, *He looked into His Torah and created the world.* The third pillar is the *purpose* of creation, which is the opportunity that we have been given to create an eternal bond with the Creator. We accomplish this through the act of service, *avodah*, which allows us to attach ourselves back to the Source. Our three holidays, Pesach, Shavuos, and Sukkos, are the celebration of these three pillars: Torah, *avodah*, and *gemilus chassadim*.

The Maharal elaborates on each holiday.

Pesach: The Inception of Bnei Yisrael

The Torah states (*Shemos* 13:4), *Today you are leaving in the month of the spring.* As we have learned, every item of *gashmiyus* has three stages. The first stage is the inception, which we perceive as the developmental stage. In nature, this is the time of the year when we can clearly perceive Hashem's benevolence, or *chessed*, toward His creation. Springtime is synonymous with renewal, a time when Hashem unfailingly bestows new life upon the world. We naturally perceive this as Hashem sprinkling the world with His goodness.

Since this moment in time is defined as "the beginning," it has a connection to holiness. For example, when a child is born, the

---

28. *Avos, perek* 1 mishnah 2.

29. *Sefer Gevuros*, Chapter 45.

date of his birth takes on significance and is celebrated as the beginning of this child's life. So too, the beginning of the natural cycle is the correct point in time to celebrate the birth of Hashem's nation. This is why the Torah commands that the Yom Tov of Pesach should always be in the spring.[30] As the holiday of our birth as a nation—the inception of our life as a unified entity—it represents the "past" of the Jewish people.

Shavuos: The Yom Tov of Independence

The second stage is when the physical object is fully grown; it is ready to exist as an independent entity. This is the time of harvest. Once again, a defined moment in time is being celebrated. In human development, this is the stage at which the child has become a full-fledged adult. Here too is a moment of holiness, which is identified with the pillar of Torah and the celebration of *Kabbalas HaTorah*—the holiday of Shavuos. The Yom Tov that celebrates *Kabbalas HaTorah* gives the Bnei Yisrael an opportunity to merit its existence. Through keeping Torah and mitzvos, the Jews can lay a claim to the goodness Hashem bestows upon them, giving them an independent and justified life.

Rashi elucidates this point based on the second portion of Shema (*Parshas Eikev*), *And it shall be that if you listen to My commandments that I command you today*. He explains that "today" means that the mitzvos should be as new to us as if we have just heard them that day. The Maharal (*Gur Aryeh*) expands upon this, observing that Moshe commanded the Jewish people regarding the Shema forty years after they had received the Torah. Moshe was thereby teaching them that a Jew's attitude toward the commandments should always be infused with the excitement of receiving something new. This directive would prevent the Torah's commandments from ever becoming a

---

30. This is also the rationale of the Jewish leap year, for we are told to keep a balance between the lunar months and the cycle of the solar year.

matter of routine. It is clear that Shavuos represents the "present" of the Jewish people.

Sukkos: The Ingathering

The third and final stage is when the created object has fulfilled the purpose of its creation and attaches itself back to the Source it emanated from. On Sukkos, we leave our homes and move into a place where we dwell together with Hashem. This is entirely distinct from the previous stages and therefore engenders a holiness of its own. As the Yom Tov in which we leave our material world behind and reconnect to Hashem, Sukkos embodies the ultimate future of the world when everything and everyone returns to Hashem.[31] Therefore, Sukkos is the holiday of "the future."

The World of Reward

In describing the obligation of Torah and mitzvos, the Torah writes: *You shall observe the commandments and the decrees and the ordinances that I command you today to perform them.*

The Gemara (*Eruvin* 22a) infers from the words "today to perform them" that the commandments are meant to be performed today, while we dwell in this world, rather than in the next world. However, we will receive our reward in the next world (*Olam Haba*).

Simply stated, the reward for observance of Torah and mitzvos is not meant for this world (although they are beneficial in their essence in both this world and the next). *Olam Haba* is indeed known as the world of reward.

Based on this understanding, if a person performs Torah and mitzvos for their benefits during his present lifetime, he not only misunderstands the idea of reward, but is completely ignorant of

---

31. As we will discuss in the next section.

the essence of Torah commandments. A life of Torah and mitzvos requires a commitment to a lifestyle whose focus transcends the physical world in which we reside. For example, we have no immediate practical benefit from donning *tefillin*, keeping Shabbos, eating kosher, or observing any other laws, other than the peace of mind we attain by doing the will of Hashem.

To summarize, each of the holidays has its own theme and purpose as an independent Yom Tov. Nevertheless, the three are bound together as one unit under the umbrella of *regalim* and *mo'adim*. Now let us delve into the Yom Tov of Sukkos.

CHAPTER 2

The Yom Tov of Sukkos

The Sukkah: A Portal to the World to Come

The Gemara (*Maseches Avodah Zarah, Daf* 3) gives a fascinating and somewhat prophetic account of the world after the coming of the Mashiach. This era is described in the Talmud as a time when all of humanity will recognize the existence of Hashem, the G-d of the Jewish people, and know that the true purpose of life is to create a relationship with Him. Once humanity realizes this and sees the clear reward for the performance of Torah and mitzvos, everyone will want to be among those who receive this reward.

In describing the events that unfold, the Talmud records a discussion between Hashem and the nations of the world: The nations request a portion of *Olam Haba*. Hashem answers that they can only receive a share of *Olam Haba* by performing the Torah's mitzvos, for through this they can demonstrate their compatibility with the spiritual rewards of *Olam Haba*. Therefore, the nations ask for an opportunity to perform the mitzvos. As the Gemara relates, they will be persistent for the right to such a chance. Hashem will respond that they have already been given a chance and rejected it.

Nonetheless, He gives them a second chance; Hashem commands them to perform the mitzvah of *sukkah*. The Gemara describes their response: Willing and eager to take this opportunity, they will build *sukkos* on their rooftops. At that time, Hashem will fire up the sun, making the *sukkos* unbearably hot and unlivable. The nations will all abandon their *sukkos*, and having failed in their mitzvah performance, each person, as he exits his sukkah, will kick it in disgust.[1]

Many points about this account need clarification: First, why, out of 613 commandments, is the mitzvah of *sukkah* chosen? And how does the performance of *mitzvas sukkah* qualify its participants for a share in *Olam Haba*? Furthermore, why did Hashem "bring the sun out" and make it impossible for them to perform this commandment?

Let us begin by focusing on the mitzvah of *sukkah*. Why this mitzvah? It is because the essence of dwelling in the *sukkah* is to disconnect from this world—to literally leave the comfort of this world and immerse in the environment of the *sukkah*. For the nations to request reward for mitzvos, they would have to be willing to re-evaluate their status in life, and step away from this world. If the nations could accept this mitzvah, this would be the most accurate indicator that they were able to receive the Torah.

---

1. דרש רבי חנינא בר פפא ואיתימא רבי שמלאי לעתיד לבא מביא הקדוש ברוך הוא ספר תורה ומניחו בחיקו, ואומר למי שעסק בה יבא ויטול שכרו, מיד מתקבצין ובאין עובדי כוכבים בערבוביא שנאמר כל הגוים נקבצו יחדו ויאספו לאמים מי בהם יגיד זאת וראשנות ישמיענו יתנו עידיהם ויצדקו וישמעו ויאמרו אמת... אמרו לפניו: ריבונו של עולם! תנה לנו מראש ונעשנה. אמר להן הקב״ה שוטים שבעולם מי שטרח בערב שבת יאכל בשבת, מי שלא טרח בערב שבת מהיכן יאכל בשבת. אלא אף על פי כן מצוה קלה יש לי וסוכה שמה לכו ועשו אותה. ומי מצית אמרת הכי והא אמר רבי יהושע בן לוי מאי דכתיב ושמרת את המצוה ואת החקים ואת המשפטים אשר אנכי מצוך היום לעשותם, היום לעשותם ולא למחר לעשותם, היום לעשותם ולא היום ליטול שכר, אלא שאין הקב״ה בא בטרוניא עם בריותיו.

מיד כל אחד ואחד נוטל והולך ועושה סוכה בראש גגו, והקדוש ברוך הוא מקדיר עליהם חמה בתקופת תמוז, וכל אחד ואחד מבעט בסוכתו ויוצא, שנאמר ננתקה את מוסרותימו ונשליכה ממנו עבותימו.

The Maharal reveals that since the nations are requesting access to *Olam Haba*, Hashem chooses the mitzvah of *sukkah* because it alone can test their ability to partake in that realm. In doing so, Hashem reveals the essence of the mitzvah of *sukkah* and the unique qualities that make it the most appropriate retort to their demand.

Before explaining why specifically the commandment of *sukkah* was chosen, let us understand their request.

Sukkah: Gateway to a Higher Reality

For a person to merit a place in the World to Come, his life must be compatible with the reality of *Olam Haba*. There, life exists beyond the physical; it is a world of pure spirituality.[2] The physical world precludes the compatibility of pure spirituality. However, when a Jew performs Torah and mitzvos, he connects his physical life to a higher state of reality.[3]

It is as though the person is not in this world while doing the mitzvah. In this sense, the performance of every mitzvah is like living in a *sukkah*. This is what makes the *sukkah* unique. It is the prototype of the next world because all the physical actions we perform in the *sukkah* become a part of the mitzvah. We are still in this world, and yet our mitzvos—physical actions—are not associated with this world. Through the *sukkah*, a fusion of *Olam*

---

2. Judaism maintains that in order for a person to experience the afterlife, resurrection must happen. This means our bodies will reconnect to our souls, but the connection will be spiritual in nature, and our bodies will not have any of the physical needs that they currently require in this world.

3. Rav Chaim Volozhiner writes in *Ruach Hachaim* that when a person performs a mitzvah, an *ohr hamakif* (lit. a bubble of light) comes from Gan Eden and envelops the person. Upon completion of the mitzvah, this light is stored in Gan Eden for his future benefit.

Hazeh (this world) and *Olam Hasechar* (the world of reward) is accomplished both physically and spiritually.[4]

The Maharal reveals that if the nations of the world had passed this test and been able to leave their material, natural environment, they would have demonstrated a capacity to develop an entirely different perspective on the world. This would have elevated all their possessions, even their homes, *beyond* the natural, finite world. The test of living in the *sukkah* assessed their attitude toward the material world and their place in it.

Our days of living in the *sukkah* are meant to replace the experience of living in this world. Just as the world was created in seven days, the mitzvah of *sukkah* lasts a full seven days. This period gives us time to completely reidentify our existence here in this world, to perceive it as a much higher reality.

Illustrating this idea, there is a well-known story of a wealthy businessman who came to visit the Chafetz Chaim. He was shocked to find the Chafetz Chaim living in a sparsely furnished house, which was, in his mind, unsuitable for such a great and respected man. The businessman immediately offered the Chafetz Chaim the necessary funds to cover the cost of refurnishing the house in a way that he deemed proper for such a holy sage. However, the Chafetz Chaim politely refused. Instead, he took the opportunity to educate the businessman on the proper view of our life in this world.

---

4. This concept is hinted at in the word *sukkah*. The word *sukkah* in Hebrew has the *gematria* of 91, equal to two names of Hashem—*Havayah* and *Adnus* (26 and 65). The outside letters, *samech* and *hei*, equal 65, which corresponds to the Name *Adonai*—my Master. This is the Name to which human beings can relate in this world. The inside letters, *kaf* and *vav*, equal 26, which is the *gematria* of the *Shem Havayah*, the Name of the Creator of all, Who is far beyond our grasp. These two Names, which connect the physical outer world and the spiritual inner world, are fused together in the *sukkah*.

"How many of your possessions do you bring with you on your travels?" the Chafetz Chaim asked the man.

"Since I'm only away from home for a few days at a time, I don't take much along with me," he answered.

The Chafetz Chaim responded, "So too is the life of a Jew in this world. We are all travelers. Why should I fill my house with large and permanent items if we are just passing through?"

This is the lesson of the *sukkah*! The mitzvah of *sukkah* redefines the perspective of our place in this world. We, as Jews who identify as Hashem's children, must evaluate where such children belong. Our main place of dwelling is in the World to Come, and therefore we must make this world compatible and transient. This is precisely why *sukkah*, out of all the commandments, was chosen by Hashem not only to test the nations but to convey this message.

But there is still one point that needs clarification.

The Gemara continues its narrative: *Hashem turned up the heat of the sun, making it unbearably hot, and thereby causing dwelling in the* sukkos *to become unbearable.* The intolerable heat caused all the people to abandon their *sukkos*. If Hashem was willing to grant the nations' request for an opportunity to perform the mitzvah, why did He make it excruciatingly hot so that the people couldn't stay in their *sukkos*?

The Heat of the Day

When the Talmud relates that the day was unbearably hot, it should be taken literally. However, there is an alternative understanding, based on the Talmud *Yoma* (20a).[5] The Gemara states that there are three powers whose "sounds"—meaning influences—radiate around the whole world. One is the sound of

---

5. ת״ר שלש קולות הולכין מסוף העולם ועד סופו, ואלו הן, קול גלגל חמה, וקול המונה של רומי, וקול נשמה בשעה שיוצאה מן הגוף.

the sun. The second is the sound of Roman culture. The third is the sound of a soul when it leaves the body.

The Maharsha, explaining this Gemara, says that "sun" does not refer only to the luminary in the sky, but also refers to the *concept* of the sun as a power or trend that captures the attention of the entire world.[6] My *rebbi*, Rav Moshe Shapiro *zt"l*, would refer to this "sun" as the power of the culture of today's society. The mitzvah of *sukkah* carries within it the message that if someone really intends to fulfill the commandment of *sukkah*, he must abandon his worldly attitude toward life, and only then is it possible to make his relationship with Hashem his most precious commodity.

***Sukkah* and Living with Hashem**

The idea that the Talmud presents is that when a person is influenced by the "sun" and views his life's priorities through its light, he finds himself inextricably caught up in the world's culture. He is bound to the world's dictates. This concept sheds new light on the concept that *Hashem turned up the heat of the sun, making it unbearably hot*. The weather wasn't the issue; rather, the nations felt trapped. Their hearts were so engaged in the physical world outside the *sukkah* that they simply couldn't stay together with Hashem. Hashem strengthened the sun because the mitzvah of *sukkah* could not truly be fulfilled unless the nations felt the pull of their cultures and *then* stayed in the *sukkah*.

When Hashem gave the nations the mitzvah of *sukkah*, they then realized what it takes to live in the World to Come. To be worthy of this reward, they would need to separate themselves from everything that they had identified as meaningful. They

---

6. The Maharsha notes that the Gemara mentions three sounds that *carry* throughout the world, instead of three sounds that are *heard*. This indicates that the concept is not of voices that are heard, rather they are three powers.

found this test impossible to undertake. Not only did they fail to capitalize on the chance Hashem gave them, but also, by kicking the *sukkah* on the way out, they showed how distant they were from a true relationship with Hashem and a place in *Olam Haba.*

The Yom Tov of Happiness

Each of the three pilgrimage holidays has a characteristic theme. These three themes are mentioned in the specific prayers of each of the Yamim Tovim:

1. Pesach: *Zman Cheiruseinu*—"Time of Our Freedom"
2. Shavuos, *Zman Mattan Toraseinu*—"Time of the Giving of Our Torah"
3. Sukkos, *Zman Simchaseinu*—"Time of Our Joy"

We see that Sukkos is uniquely designated as the Time of Our Joy, but isn't every holiday a time of *simchah*? What makes Sukkos the time that is specifically identified with *simchah*? And if *simchah* is the order of the day, how do we achieve it?

First, let us identify the source in the Torah that commands us to be happier during Sukkos than all other holidays.

The midrash states[7] that the Torah associates three verses of *simchah* with the holiday of Sukkos:

---

7. The original text of the *Yalkut Shimoni* (*Parshas Emor* #654) reads as follows: אתה מוצא שלש שמחות כתיב בחג, ושמחת בחגך, והייתי אך שמח, ושמחתם לפני ה' אלקיכם שבעת ימים. אבל בפסח אין אתה מוצא שכתוב בו אפילו שמחה אחת, למה. אתה מוצא שבפסח התבואה נידונית ואין אדם יודע אם עושה השנה תבואה אם אינו עושה, לפיכך אין כתוב שם שמחה.

דבר אחר בשביל שמתו בו המצריים. וכן אתה מוצא כל שבעת ימי החג אנו קורין בהן את ההלל, אבל בפסח אין אנו קורין את ההלל אלא ביום טוב הראשון ולילו. למה, משום בנפול אויבך אל תשמח ובכשלו אל יגל לבך.

- *You shall rejoice before Hashem your G-d for a seven-day period.*
- *You shall rejoice on your festival.*
- *You will be completely joyous.*

None of the other four Yamim Tovim[8] given to us in the Torah requires *this* amount of happiness. As this midrash points out, Shavuos is the only other holiday that includes a commandment to be happy. For Pesach, there is no mention of *simchah* whatsoever. Why is this so? To properly comprehend the message of the midrash, we need to clarify:

- The nature of holidays as days of judgment.
- Why indeed is *simchah* not mentioned regarding Pesach.
- The definition of *simchah* as a state of security and serenity.

Holidays and Days of Judgment

The Gemara writes[9] that the world is judged four times a year: on Pesach for wheat, on Shavuos for the fruits of the tree, on Rosh Hashanah for all of humanity, and on Sukkos for the rain. Human nature inclines a person to become preoccupied when a judgment is looming over his head. It consumes his mind and prevents him from enjoying life. The midrash explains that since the world is judged on these holidays, people feel an angst or nervousness that precludes the possibility of sincere happiness. This is quite

---

וכן אתה מוצא שאין כתוב בעצרת אלא שמחה אחת, דכתיב ועשית חג שבועות לה׳ אלקיך ושמחת אתה וביתך, ולמה כתב בה שמחה אחת, מפני שהתבואה נכנסת בפנים. ומה טעם אין כתוב שם שתי שמחות לפי שפירות האילן נידונין. אבל בראש השנה אין כתיב שם אפילו שמחה אחת, שהנפשות נידונות ומבקש אדם את נפשו יותר ממנונו, אבל בחג לפי שנטלו הנפשות דימוס ביום הכפורים כמו שנאמר וכי ביום הזה יכפר עליכם, ועוד שהתבואה ופירות האילן בפנים, לפיכך כתב שלש שמחות, ושמחת בחגך. ושמחתם לפני ה׳ אלקיכם, והיית אך שמח.
מהו אך שמח, את מוצא אף על פי שאדם שמח בעולם הזה אין שמחתו שמחת שלמה, היאך, נולדו לו בנים הוא דואג ומיצר עליהן לומר שמא אינן של קיימא. אבל לעתיד לבוא דקב״ה מבלע את המות לנצח, אותה השמחה תהיה שלמה, שנאמר אז ימלא שחוק פינו ולשוננו רנה.

8. Pesach, Shavuos, Rosh Hashanah, Yom Kippur, and Sukkos.

9. *Rosh Hashanah* 16a.

logical: How can we be at peace while we are uncertain about the outcome of our situation? This explains why there is no mention of *simchah* on Pesach.

Since, as the mishnah states, the world is judged on these days, the Torah *cannot* command a person to be happy. It is the first judgment day of the holiday cycle (because Pesach is in the first month). Pesach is a time of judgment on the wheat crop. While the preparation and planting began months earlier, *nothing* has yet been processed at this stage of the agricultural cycle. The farmers have no way of knowing what their efforts will yield, and therefore, there is an underlying feeling of insecurity. Thus, says the midrash, the commandment of *simchah* is not mentioned on Pesach.

On Shavuos, however, which is also known as *Chag Hakatzir* (the Festival of the Harvest), the wheat has been cut. This is a reason for celebration; there is a sense of confidence that allows us to rejoice. Although the future of the fruit crop is being judged at this time, we can enjoy the relief of knowing that the fields have been blessed with wheat. Therefore, the Torah commands, *V'samachta attah*—"You shall rejoice." However, says the midrash, *simchah* is only mentioned once since the ongoing judgment of the fruit engenders a measure of anxiety.

The midrash continues: On Rosh Hashanah, when the life of every single person is being judged, it is unfathomable to require people to be in a state of happiness. Even if the two previous judgments were favorable, what value is there to wheat and fruits without life? Therefore, *simchah* is omitted on Rosh Hashanah, and the same is true for Yom Kippur.[10]

However, after the Yom Tov of Yom Kippur, the Jewish people have been atoned, and the judgment on them has been completed. This deep sense of relief brings about a feeling of security, which

---

10. The Talmud explains that it is due to the judgment that we don't recite the Hallel prayer on Rosh Hashanah and Yom Kippur.

in turn leads to contentment and happiness. The three commandments of *simchah* on Sukkos encompass the positive resolution of all three prior judgments: the wheat (Pesach), the fruits of the tree (Shavuos), and life itself (Rosh Hashanah).

The *Simchah* of Security of Sukkos

This newfound triple-level of security, based on the three judgments, allows us to fully celebrate the holiday of Sukkos. Hence, the Torah calls for *simchah* three times. Nevertheless, there is a glaring question: Even on this holiday of Sukkos, the rainfall for the entire year is being decided. How can a person feel confident and happy if there is still a pending judgment?

Herein lies the true commandment to rejoice on Sukkos. As we mentioned, although a person *could* be concerned about the outcome of the pending judgment, he has seen three previous rulings go favorably, including of course the judgments of Rosh Hashanah and Yom Kippur. That should give him and all of Klal Yisrael confidence that everything will go well in the judgment regarding the rain. Our success with the previous verdicts ushers in a complete sense of security and relief. The fact that we are alive and able to celebrate the holiday is itself a testimony that supports this encouraging conclusion.

On Sukkos we joyfully proclaim, "We made it!"

The Three *Simchos* of Sukkos

We've now learned that the Torah commands us to be happy specifically on Sukkos. We can gain further insight by exploring the three different ways in which this commandment is phrased:

1. *And you shall rejoice before Hashem.*
2. *And you shall rejoice in your holiday.*
3. *And you shall be only happy.*

The first *pasuk* refers to the *lulav*, commanding us to be happy with it before Hashem. The second *pasuk* tells us to be happy on the Yom Tov itself, and the third says to just be completely happy.

What do we derive from these multiple commandments of *simchah*?

Clearly, the Torah isn't just repeating the same thought three times, since each commandment to be happy applies to a different situation. Rather, the Torah imparts to us that there are three different types of *simchah*, each playing a distinct role in a person's life. In truth, these three forms of *simchah* relate to three relationships experienced by each and every person. These, according to the Maharal, are:

1. *Bein adam l'Makom, simchah* between man and Hashem.
2. *Bein adam l'chaveiro, simchah* between man and his fellow man.
3. *Bein adam l'aztmo, simchah* between a man and himself, also known as internal happiness.

But before we examine what happiness means in the context of these three relationships, let us ask a basic question: What does it take for a human being to be happy?

Happiness

One of the prerequisites of happiness is the security that comes from knowing we have what we need. Those who feel insecure do not feel happy. This is not a question of monetary wealth, but rather, it derives from a healthy attitude that enables a person to feel fulfilled. The mishnah in *Pirkei Avos* declares, *Who is wealthy? One who is happy with his lot.* Thus, the Sages tell us that happiness comes from being at peace with our circumstances, whatever they are. The bank account and income level are irrelevant factors; **the grateful acceptance of what we do have is the key to happiness**. With that, we feel complete, and as the Maharal reveals, complete *simchah* can only be achieved when we feel complete in all aspects of our lives.

To achieve *simchah*, we need this sense of wholeness in all three areas of life: with Hashem, with other people, and within ourselves. That is what Hashem is commanding us with the three mitzvos of *simchah*. Through them, He is teaching us how to reach total *simchah*.

The Three *Simchos*

The first form of *simchah*—between us and Hashem—comes from the *pasuk* that commands us to take the four species. In that context, the Torah (*Vayikra* 23:40) declares, *You shall be happy in front of Hashem.*

The second form of joy is happiness among people. In addition to the commandment to feel joy "in front of Hashem" the Torah (*Devarim* 16:14) commands: *And you shall rejoice on your festival, you, your son, your daughter, your slave, your maidservant, the Levite, the convert, the orphan, and the widow who are in your cities.*

The third is happiness with oneself. As the Torah (*Devarim* 16:15) commands, *You shall be only happy.* The Torah does not include anyone else in this joy. It's just *You shall (within yourself) be happy.*

Since the Torah gives us multiple commandments of *simchah*, we understand that it isn't sufficient to be happy in some areas of our lives. Rather, for us to experience true, complete happiness, we have to work on finding joy in every relationship in our lives. We see on a practical level that this is true because sour relationships in one area of life cloud our joy in all the others. For example, a person will find it difficult to experience wholehearted joy in Hashem if his family relationships are filled with conflict. Likewise, it will be difficult for him to truly enjoy his family if he's unhappy with himself. The mitzvos of Sukkos give us the opportunity to actualize all three forms of *simchah*, as we will discuss in the next section.

The Themes of Sukkos: *Sukkah, Arba'ah Minim*, and *Ushpizin*

Sukkos is a multifaceted holiday; no other Yom Tov expresses so great a variety of themes: the *sukkah*, the *arba'ah minim*, the *Ushpizin*, the *korbanos*, Hoshana Rabbah, the *aravos*, *simchas beis hasho'evah*, and after all that, Shemini Atzeres and Simchas Torah, which also includes *Tefillas Geshem*—the Prayer for Rain. Indeed, there isn't a time in the year that's so busy with so much *simchah*. This *simchah* is not limited to the *sukkah* alone, for the mitzvos of *aravos*, *simchas beis hasho'evah*, and *arba'ah minim* were performed in the Beis Hamikdash. For the Jews who inherited the land of Israel, it was also the busy harvest season, when the farmers would gather in the crops from the field and store them for the winter. With the storehouses at their fullest, the people reveled in a sense of security.

Since the Torah commanded us three times to celebrate Sukkos with *simchah*,[11] the Yom Tov gives us three different routes through which we can actualize these forms of rejoicing. These are different kinds of *simchah* and can be understood through the *sukkah*, the *arba'ah minim*, and the *Ushpizin*. How are these forms of *simchah* different from one another?

Lulav: *Simchah* with Hashem

We will first uncover the core of the *simchah* that is specifically aroused by the *arba'ah minim*. The mitzvah, tied to the season in which Sukkos falls, is, *And you shall take for yourselves on the first day, the fruit of the* hadar *tree, date palm fronds, a branch of a braided tree, and willows of the brook,* ***and you shall rejoice before Hashem*** *for a seven-day period* (*Vayikra* 23:40).

---

11. See "The Three *Simchos* of Sukkos."

Key to this commandment is its location—"before Hashem." The *simchah* we experience is that which is felt when we are together with Hashem, feeling His presence vividly. In such a state, we feel whole. This *simchah* occurs in its highest form when we stand in the holiest place in the world—the Beis Hamikdash—which is where the *arba'ah minim* were to be brought. This is *simchah* with Hashem, *bein adam l'Makom.*[12]

To better understand the other two forms of *simchah*, we will first explore the definition of *simchah* from the Torah's perspective.

Simchah: Bursting with Emotions

Simchah is the Hebrew word for happiness, and the root of this word reveals a greater insight into the nature of happiness. My *rebbi*, Rav Moshe Shapiro *zt"l*, explained that there is a parallel between the word *simchah* and the word *tzimchah*, which means "sprouting." Both words describe the essence of a person while he is in a state of happiness. Just as a tree bursts forth with its fruit, so too does a person burst forth with joy.

Let us give an example. When a person hears a funny joke, he bursts into laughter, and immediately wants to find someone who has not yet heard the joke so that he can share the laughter and *simchah* with others. Why? The answer is that he is happy and wants to share his happiness. Both the burst of laughter and the desire to share are functions of *simchah*. This reveals another characteristic of *simchah*—sharing—which is the second form of Sukkos *simchah*, as we will now explain.

Sharing the *Simchah*

We now come to the second *pasuk* of *simchah*: *And you shall*

12. While we now have the custom to take the *lulav* for all the days of Yom Tov, this is only a custom. The original mitzvah took place for seven days in the Beis Hamikdash and one day everywhere else.

rejoice on your festival, you, your son, your daughter, your slave, your maidservant, the Levite, the convert, the orphan, and the widow who are in your cities.

The Rambam writes the following on the laws of Yom Tov:

> When a person eats and drinks [as part of celebrating a holiday], he is obligated to feed "the stranger, the orphan, and the widow" (*Devarim* 16:11). However, someone who locks the doors of his house, eating and drinking with his children and spouse [alone], and doesn't provide food or drink to the poor and depressed, is not participating in the joy of [Hashem's] commandments, but rather, the joy of the gut. About him it says, *Their sacrifices are like bread for the dead; all who eat of them will become impure, for their bread is for themselves* (*Hoshea* 9:4). Joy like this is a disgrace for them, as it says, *I will strew dung upon your faces, the dung of your festival sacrifices* (*Malachi* 2:3).

The Rambam is clear that it isn't sufficient to give the poor people food; that is *tzedakah*, but it is not *simchah. Simchah* must be shared with everyone. This is the second kind of *simchah, bein adam l'chaveiro.*

We find that the theme of sharing is so fundamental to Sukkos that it even extends beyond the relationship within the Jewish people, to all the nations of the world. This is expressed in the commandment to bring sacrifices that correspond to all seventy nations of the world.

Seventy Bulls

The *Zohar* teaches that the seventy bulls of the Sukkos festival correspond to the seventy nations. At the time of the Beis Hamikdash, the sacrifices shielded all the nations from adversity. This was in the merit of the Jewish people. On Sukkos, the Jewish people are meant to share their *simchah* with all the nations of the world so that every person on the planet is uplifted.

Indeed, this is the concept behind wishing each other *chag same'ach*. The greeting arouses in the greeter and its recipient the *simchah* of togetherness. When a person is happy to share, sharing brings happiness.

Internal *Simchah*

The third form of *simchah* is what the Torah calls *ach same'ach*—"just be completely happy." No one is named as the object of this happiness; it applies to each of us ourselves, *bein adam l'atzmo.*

The wholeness of the *simchah* generated by these three mitzvos together brings us to a level of *simchah* that warrants recognition. The person who has acquired all varieties of *simchah* enters what we can refer to as the "spiritual Hall of Fame." He merits the company of some of the greatest Jews who ever lived, known as *Ushpizin*.

Ushpizin

Ushpizin means guests in Aramaic. The *Zohar* reveals that every day of Sukkos, we receive seven special guests: Avraham, Yitzchak, Yaakov, Moshe, Aharon, Yosef, and Dovid. As we will discuss, each day we give special recognition to one guest among these seven.

But where are these guests coming from? They arrive from the Garden of Eden to visit our *sukkos*. This leads us to wonder, what would entice them to leave the Garden of Eden to come visit us? There must be something in each of our *sukkos* that draws them to us. The attraction is not the *sukkah* itself, but rather, it is us. Through our spiritual achievements, our *sukkos* become compatible with those who reside in the Garden of Eden.[13] This is the third form of *simchah*—inner wholesomeness that turns our personal world into a little slice of heaven.

---

13. This will be discussed at length in the section dedicated to the *Ushpizin*.

To summarize, we have arrived, through the mitzvos of Sukkos, at all three forms of *simchah.* We have become wholesome and complete, meriting daily visits by the greatest of Jews. The privilege of hosting the *Ushpizin* indicates that we certainly have reached the level of *ach same'ach,* complete happiness.

Clouds of Glory

The Torah states (*Vayikra* 23:43):

כי בסכות הושבתי את בני ישראל—*For in* sukkos *I encamped the children of Israel.*

There are two opinions as to what we commemorate when we sit in our *sukkah.*[14] One is that the *sukkah* reminds us of the protective clouds with which Hashem surrounded the Jews while they lived in the desert. Indeed, surviving for decades in a hostile environment like the desert is an open miracle. Nevertheless, we might wonder why Hashem chose clouds to be the agents of this miracle.

Clouds and Hashem's Presence

When we examine the role of clouds in the Torah, we see that they are a medium through which Hashem connects to His people. At the beginning of *Parshas Acharei Mos,* Hashem describes how He reveals Himself to Aharon as he enters the Holy of Holies. The *pasuk* states: *For in a cloud I shall be viewed on top of the cover [of the* Aron*].*

In addition, in our prayers, we quote a verse in *Tehillim* (99:7) in

14. מסכת סוכה דף יא: כי בסוכות הושבתי את בני ישראל ענני הכבוד היו דברי רב אליעזר רבי עקיבא אומר סוכות ממש עשו להם.

which Hashem says of Moshe and Aharon: *Through the pillar of a cloud I speak to them*. Why does Hashem choose to communicate with Moshe and Aharon through clouds?

Clouds

The answer lies in both the form and function of a cloud. Clouds are essential to the world because they are the vessels through which we receive rain. Without the clouds and their rain, the earth wouldn't produce life. However, clouds are not merely placed between heaven and earth to bring rain. Rather, they are the conduit of life between heaven and earth. Therefore, clouds are an appropriate symbol to represent Hashem's relationship with the world, as the Giver and Sustainer of life on earth.

In addition, as we discussed earlier, the clouds that contain the water that rains down and gives life to the world have no real substance. Despite the critical role they play, clouds are practically weightless. Clouds represent the "go-between" between the physical and the spiritual in their ability to convert heavenly potential into earthly bounty.

Now it is clear why clouds were chosen as the conduit for Hashem's communication with people in this world. We now also understand why clouds were chosen as the means to guide and protect us while we traveled and dwelled in the desert. We lived in the physical world, yet in a supernatural manner.

Of course, Hashem's relationship and communication obviously do not end at the culmination of Sukkos. How does this relationship continue throughout the entire year? The answer is the rainclouds. Hashem wants to stay in touch with humanity and continue to provide for it, and He does so through rain.

Rain

Rain is often unpredictable; it can rain suddenly and briefly. It can rain for long periods at a time, and sometimes it will not rain for months. The Gemara (*Ta'anis*) explains that the unpredictability of the rain, especially in the land of Israel, is by design. The Torah informs us that Hashem communicates with us through rain. We mention this twice every day in our prayers when we recite the Shema and declare, *And it shall come to pass if you will diligently obey My commandments...I will give you rain for your land at the proper time...* But if the Jewish people turn away from Hashem, *He will close the heavens so that there will be no rain.* Rain allows us to know how we are faring in our relationship with Hashem.

To summarize: We now have a clearer understanding as to why Hashem used clouds as a medium to communicate with Moshe and Aharon. Clouds provide us with a spiritual barometer known as rain. Through the medium of clouds, Hashem spoke to our ancestors. Through clouds, He protected us for forty years in the desert. And through clouds, Hashem continues to stay in constant contact with us.

The *Sukkah*: A Place of Refuge

The Torah commands us to live in the *sukkah* in the seventh month of the year, which is Tishrei. Unlike Pesach and Shavuos, which commemorate events that happened on a specific day, Sukkos recalls a way of life our forefathers experienced for forty years.

As we mentioned, there are two opinions as to what we commemorate when we sit in our *sukkah*. Rabbi Akiva says that the *sukkah* represents the protective clouds—the *Ananei Hakavod* with which Hashem surrounded the Jews when they lived in the desert. However, Rabbi Eliezer maintains that the *sukkah* we construct memorializes the booths in which the Jews dwelled while in the desert. When we reside in the *sukkah*, we relive the lifestyle of our ancestors.

According to both opinions, this was their lifestyle all year for forty years. Therefore, we could, theoretically, celebrate Sukkos *any* time of the year. However, the Torah commanded us to undertake this mitzvah right after Yom Kippur. Why?

***Sukkah*: Safe House from Satan**

Both Rosh Hashanah and Yom Kippur are Days of Judgment. As with any court case, there is a prosecutor and a defendant. Our Sages teach that the prosecutor on the Days of Judgment is the Satan. The Gemara (*Yoma* 20a) explains that to prosecute is *l'hastin*; this is the root of Satan. He is by definition "the prosecutor."

The Gemara states that the Satan plays three distinct roles in the world: First, he embodies the evil inclination, which persuades a person to sin. Second, the Satan ascends to heaven to bring his case against the person who has sinned, and finally, he acts as the Angel of Death, who carries out the verdict. When we are inscribed in the Book of Life, we win, and the Satan loses. But Satan doesn't like to lose and will look for an opportunity to attack. To protect ourselves from his vengeance, we take refuge in the *sukkah*, our safe haven.

A safe house is a shelter from danger or hardship. It's meant to protect a person from those who want to harm him. In addition to the many other themes and messages of the *sukkah*, it is meant to be a safe house that is especially apt at this time of the year. It's a place to which we can run, where we are at a safe distance from the grasp of our enemies. Historically, this is what the *sukkah* meant for our forefathers.

Yaakov's *Sukkos*

The first mention of a *sukkah* in the Torah is in *Bereishis, Parshas Vayishlach,* after Yaakov encounters his brother Eisav. The meeting, which Yaakov had feared all his life, occurred when Yaakov left Charan and headed back to his parents' home. After their reunion, the Torah states, *And Yaakov traveled to Sukkos and built himself a house, and for his cattle he made booths; therefore, he named the place Sukkos* (*Bereishis* 33:17).

Eisav had long declared his intention to kill Yaakov. Now that they had encountered each other and Yaakov and his family were safe, Yaakov sought to protect his family. Therefore, he built them *sukkos*.

From Ramses to Sukkos

When the Jews traveled forth from Egypt after having been enslaved for over 210 years, where was their first destination as a free people? A place called Sukkos!

The Torah states: *They journeyed from Ramses in the first month, on the fifteenth day of the first month; on the day following the Pesach sacrifice, the children of Israel left triumphantly before the eyes of all the Egyptians. The children of Israel journeyed from Ramses and camped in Sukkos* (*Bamidbar* 33:3-5).

Could this be the same location where Yaakov and his family built their *sukkos* 250 years earlier? Yaakov's *sukkos* were in an entirely different location. Charan is east of Eretz Yisrael and Egypt is southwest. The Jews leaving Egypt were hundreds of miles away from Yaakov's *sukkos*. Why, then, did their first encampment receive that name?

The answer is that the Torah gave Sukkos its name when the Jewish people arrived there.[15] The name signified that the Jewish people had successfully exited Egypt and needed to be sheltered in a place that would protect them from returning.

The fact that Sukkos was the shelter for Yaakov *and* for the Jews leaving Egypt indicates a connection; the *sukkah* represents a safe house where Jews could take refuge after freeing themselves from

---

15. This idea is found often in the Torah, where an event is cited as the reason for the naming of a place. For example, Be'er Sheva got its name because of the seven wells that were dug there.

their spiritual enemies. In these instances, the enemies were Lavan and Pharaoh.

In truth, we constantly are battling our evil inclination; the need for shelter from evil doesn't arise just once a year, but rather, it is a daily need. We pray for the *sukkah's* spiritual protection each evening in the prayer of *Hashkiveinu.*

Hashkiveinu

In *Hashkiveinu*, we ask Hashem to *remove the Satan from in front of us and behind us and spread upon us Your* Sukkah *of Peace.* Through our prayer, we recognize that the *sukkah* helps us to free ourselves from the Satan's grasp. How does the *sukkah* protect us?

The safety of the *sukkah* comes from its simplicity. It is where we remove ourselves from our constant pursuit of possessions, for it is this pursuit that provides the Satan with his most fertile ground for sowing misery. *Hashkiveinu* reminds us each evening of a time when Hashem will ensconce us in His protective cover, and we will be permanently free of the pernicious Satan.

Once a year, we physically leave our homes and live in the *sukkah* so that we *actually* live under Hashem's *sukkah* of protection, right here in this world. That time of year rightfully comes right after Yom Kippur when we've separated ourselves from the evil inclination just as Yaakov separated from Lavan and the Jewish people separated from Egypt. The *sukkah* is meant to keep the Satan away.

When observing the entire process of the Yamim Nora'im, we can sum up our efforts as follows:

On Rosh Hashanah, we confuse the Satan with the shofar. On Yom Kippur, we defeat him with our fasting and prayers. And then on Sukkos, we keep the Satan away from us by entering the shelter of the *sukkah*.

CHAPTER 3

The Cup of Blessings

Kiddush

Every Yom Tov formally begins with Kiddush—the sanctification of the holiday. The word Kiddush comes from the word *kedushah*, which the Torah uses to mean holy.[1] The holiday doesn't activate until the declaration of the Yom Tov is made via the Kiddush. This is a unique phenomenon. An announcement isn't needed to transition from Sunday to Monday. Time progresses on its schedule without any need for input from us. Why is the onset of the holidays different? Also, what exactly is Kiddush? Why is wine used rather than any other food or liquid? And why do we need a cup—why not the entire bottle?

Activating the Holiness of the Day

It would seem that since we must make a blessing to activate the holiness of the holidays, a holiday is not a natural part of the

1. The first form of *kedushah* is Shabbos. The Torah says ויברך אלקים את יום השביעי ויקדש אותו—*And Hashem blessed the seventh day and sanctified it.* This is the reason that Shabbos is the introduction to all of the holidays, for the *kedushah* of Yom Tov is sourced in Shabbos.

world. Rather, it would seem that the world is void of *kedushah* until we introduce it. The *kedushah* is a power of holiness that is infused into the world only when someone activates this holiness. Since the cup of wine is the means by which we activate the *kedushah* of the day, it needs a great deal of preparation, as we will see below. This is the premise of a cup of blessings. Let us explore how and why this works.

The Cup of Blessings

To attain a deeper understanding, we will begin with the general concept of the ceremonial blessing recited on a cup of wine, known as *kos shel brachah*. The Gemara (*Brachos* 51a[2]), in its discussion of the requirement to recite *Birkas Hamazon* after a meal, says that ten conditions must be fulfilled to properly make a blessing on a cup of wine. These requirements apply to a cup of wine used for the blessings on all sorts of occasions, for example, Kiddush on Shabbos and Yom Tov, *Birkas Hamazon*, or any ceremonial event, such as a wedding, *bris milah*, or *pidyon haben*.

Below is the list of the ten requirements with a short explanation from the Maharsha for each:

1. **הדחה**—The cup must be washed on the inside.
2. **שטיפה**—It must be cleaned on the outside. The Maharsha explains: This represents the holiness called *kedushah v'taharah*—"sanctified and pure."
3. **חי**—The word *chai* in this context is defined as the pure and undiluted wine that must be poured into the Cup of Blessings. To make it drinkable, it is then diluted with the correct amount of water. While ordinarily this dilution is done before the wine is poured, for Kiddush it is done

---

2. תנא עשרה דברים נאמרו בכוס של ברכה טעון הדחה ושטיפה חי ומלא איטור עיטוף נוטלו בשני ידיו ונותנו בימין מגביה מן הקרקע טפח ונותן עיניו בו ויש אומרים אף משגר במתנה לאנשי ביתו.

inside the Kiddush cup. The Maharsha explains that this pure wine is called *chai*—life—because it represents the specific life force that comes directly from Hashem to us when we recite Kiddush. That is the blessing with which we are required to fill our cup.

4. **מלא**—The cup must be filled to capacity. The Maharsha says that this represents an unflawed cup, complete without a blemish.

5. **עיטור**—The cup must be adorned, which means it has to be crowned or glorified. There are multiple opinions in the Gemara as to what type of adornment is required. Rav Yehuda would crown his Cup of Blessings by surrounding each cup with *talmidim*. Rav Chisda would place many cups of wine around the Kiddush cup.

6. **עיטוף**—The cup must be covered or wrapped.

7. **נוטלו בשני ידיו**—One person raises the cup with both hands and hands it to the person making the blessing. That person accepts it with both hands. The Maharsha says that the two hands represent two characteristics: *rachamim v'din*—"mercy and judgment."

8. **נותנו בימין**—The cup must be held in the right hand of the person making the blessing. The Maharsha explains: Using the right hand represents the side of *rachamim* overpowering the side of *din*.

9. **מגביהו מן הקרקע טפח**—The person making Kiddush raises the cup one *tefach* (handsbreadth). The Maharsha explains: Raising the cup expresses positivity, for although there are cups that are associated with tragedy and loss, a cup raised with pride and honor is a cup of salvation.

10. **נותן עיניו בו**—The person making the blessing should look at the cup of wine. The Maharsha explains that this means he should focus on the cup of wine and all its blessings.

11. Some say there is an additional requirement.

ויש אומרים אף משגר במתנה לאנשי ביתו—The person making the blessing should share the wine with his wife and family. Sharing is a trait indicative of a good person, someone with a "good eye," who is himself a source of blessing. He is a person from whom blessing can spill over. In fact, the Gemara (*Maseches Sotah*) declares that the Cup of Blessings should only be given to a person who is righteous and has a good eye because only such a person will fill the cup with blessings.

The Gemara continues: *Reb Yochanan stated, He who blesses on a cup that is full will receive an inheritance that is not limited by boundaries*—as it says in the blessing of the tribe of Naftali (*Devarim* 33:23): *And of Naftali, he [Moshe] said, "Naftali is satiated with favor and is full of Hashem's blessings. [He shall] inherit the sea and the South."* Indeed, through a Cup of Blessings, we gain the ability to expand the world from its physical limitations to a boundless spiritual reality.

This is the foundation of the power within the Cup of Blessings. The attitude and positivity of he who raises the cup and blesses Hashem is the factor that connects this experience to the Creator, Who created the world with the name Elokim.

The Fusion of the Upper and Lower Worlds

This deeper understanding teaches us that the person who makes a blessing on a cup of wine is combining the upper world and the lower world. By making Kiddush to sanctify a holy day or by blessing Hashem in *Birkas Hamazon* for the bounty with which He sustains us, we are accessing a higher level of sanctity and at the same time, rising to a higher level of spiritual reality.

It seems, therefore, that the cup of wine is the catalyst that activates spirituality. How are we to understand this? Why does it have this power? Let us explore the hints and secrets that hold the answer.

A Cup of Wine

To begin, let us seek a deeper understanding of the following concepts:

- The Name of Hashem the Torah uses when recounting the seven days of creation—Elokim
- The Name of Hashem that is revealed at Mount Sinai —י-ק-ו-ק
- Man's role in creation
- Yosef Hatzaddik
- The word "cup/*kos*"
- Wine

Elokim

The Torah begins with the words, *In the beginning Hashem (Elokim) created the heaven and the earth.* The Name Elokim[3] was precisely chosen because through this Name, Hashem was able to create a world in which humans could exercise free will. Free will, in turn, enables humans to play an active role in the unfolding of Hashem's plan for the world.

From the first act of creation through Hashem's declaration of Shabbos at its completion, the Torah uses only the Name Elokim. Our Sages teach that this Name represents Hashem as the Master of all powers of the world.[4] During the six days of creation,

---

3. When referring to Hashem and His Names, there are a few points to be made so that we understand the concept. (While this subject is beyond the scope of this *sefer*, it is critical that we have at least a basic understanding of the concept of the Names with which Hashem is identified.) Hashem's Names are "titles of roles that Hashem takes on" in His relationship to this world. Our Sages write that the Names of Hashem can be compared to the clothing that we wear. For example, we dress for work in one set of clothing and then change into something else for a wedding. The clothes are not the person; rather they are the external appearance by which others perceive him. So too, when Hashem is associated with a Name, this is the "clothing" that He chooses to wear at that time.

4. The word Elokim means power. Therefore, it is used as a name for the *beis din* (court) for it has the power to enforce law on the people.

Hashem constructed a world that contains these various powers, all of them in sync with each other. Thus, the Name Elokim is the Source of the revealed world. This means that when we perceive that which Hashem created—the sun and the moon, oceans, land, and mountains, as well as all forms of life—we are seeing Hashem as Elokim.

With this explanation of Elokim, we can begin to grasp the concept of nature. Not only is Elokim the Name Hashem used in the creation of the world, but it is also the Name through which He maintains and oversees the world. This is the phenomenon we call nature, or in the language of our Sages, *teva*.

Nature—*Teva*

Nature is the organized order of the world as we perceive it. We can see that clouds produce rain and seeds produce vegetation, that the sun rises in the morning and sets in the evening. These are reliable, observable elements of our world. Judaism teaches that Hashem constantly maintains this order and that He is aware of everything that happens in the world—from the great upheavals to the most minor occurrences. (It is important to clarify that the Torah's definition of nature is very different from that of the secular world. The popular concept that "Mother Nature" is a cause-and-effect natural force that is not controlled or directed in any way is entirely rejected by Judaism.)

By adding the letter[5] *hei* to the word *teva*, we turn it into *hateva*, which means a specifically *designated* nature. This form of the word tells us that nature is not a force of its own, as it appears to be. Rather, it has been precisely programmed. It is Elokim, expressing His will in our world. Reinforcing this idea, *hateva* has

---

5. When used at the beginning of a word, this letter turns the meaning of something general into something specific, unique, and well known. For example, מקום means "a place" and המקום means "a well-known and specific place," אדם means "a person" while האדם means "that person."

the numerical value of 86, which is the same numerical value as Elokim.

This *gematria* conveys two thoughts: First, the Name Elokim is the Source of nature. Second, on somewhat a deeper level, *hateva*—nature—is the physical manifestation of the Name Elokim. Through creation, we can connect to Hashem.

Unlike the Name *Yud-hei-vav-hei*, which is so far beyond our comprehension that we are not even permitted to pronounce it, Elokim is a Name we relate to on several levels.

We connect to Hashem not only through His creation, but also through the events of our daily life. The Torah uses the Name Elokim when describing law and order. For example, in *Parshas Mishpatim*, the word for judges is *elohim*. The Torah is not referring to Hashem in this instance, but rather, to court. Nevertheless, the word *elohim* is used, for the courts are responsible for maintaining an organized society. This usage shows us that Elokim is not only the Name of creation but also the Force that maintains creation according to Hashem's purpose and plan.

Let us delve a little deeper into this Name.

The Vacuum of Darkness

Before Hashem created the world, His presence pervaded everything. Since nothing can exist outside of Hashem, He had to "make space" for creation. Otherwise, there would be no possibility of independent existence on any level whatsoever. It is only because Hashem restrained and concealed Himself that creation could come into existence. This is the basis of one of the fundamental concepts of Kabbalah called *tzimtzum*—contraction or self-constriction. *Tzimtzum* enabled creation to take place and exist as an independent entity, but because of it, creation cannot be totally infused with Divine light. *Tzimtzum* causes a vacuum of the perceivable presence of Hashem, which allows for the existence of darkness.

Elohim Acherim

This darkness is so great that it allows people to manipulate creation to the extent that they can believe in other deities. The name that the Torah gave to these powers is *elohim acherim*—other powers.[6] The vacuum of light is so dangerous that the Torah warns a person to be on guard, *lest you raise your eyes to the heavens and you see the sun and the moon and the stars–the entire legion of heavens; and you will be drawn astray and bow down to them and worship them.*[7]

This darkness, consistently associated with tribulation and evil, comes from the absence of Hashem's light, which is caused by His own self-constriction. Many Torah sources identify the *sitra acher*—"the other side"—with this vacuum of Divine light.

Darkness to Light

However, the same vacuum allows human beings the opportunity for personal growth. The Torah commands us to "choose life" (*Devarim* 30:19), a choice that is available to us *because* there is darkness. Otherwise, there are no choices to make, and without our ability to make choices, Hashem's purpose for creating the world and humanity cannot be achieved. The good in the world can only take place within the vacuum that itself is darkness. How do we grasp the opportunity provided by this void?

Tov and *Tov Me'od*

Regarding every day of creation except the second day, the Torah relates that Hashem *saw what He had created, and "it was*

---

6. In the second chapter of Shema, the Torah warns, *Beware for yourself lest your heart be seduced and you will turn astray and you will serve other gods* (elohim acherim) *and prostrate yourself to them.*

7. *Devarim* 4:19.

good—ki tov." But at the culmination of creation on the sixth day, it adds a modifier: *And Hashem saw all that He created and behold it was **very** good*–tov me'od–*and it was evening, and it was morning the sixth day*. Here at the conclusion of creation, the Torah adds that the world is not merely "good" but "very good." But if the Torah's definition of good is absolute good, what does "very" add to the description?

From Good to Very Good

The answer is that "good" refers to something we expect to be good, and it fulfills our expectations. However, there are also negative elements in the world. We cannot imagine anything positive coming from them, but when they do indeed yield good, this is *tov me'od*—very good. For example, getting a lucrative new job is "good," but benefiting from being fired from a job is "very good." The "very good" of the sixth day of creation refers to the places of darkness inherent in creation—an element from which no positive could be expected. The *me'od*—the very good—emerges because man can bring light to the places where light doesn't shine. And how is this achieved? This is the secret found in the word for man—*adam*.

Tov Me'od/Tov Adam

In Hebrew, the word *me'od*—very—is comprised of the same letters as the word *adam*—man. The *tov me'od* with which the Torah describes the end of creation is more than a description. It is the ultimate purpose of creation. This *tov me'od* is achieved through *tov adam*—the good that man creates. This means that the world, which is good (as is written regarding six days of creation), can get better only through the choices man makes while in a state of darkness. Man's choices allow light to emanate from darkness, and that is why Hashem endowed man with the power to choose. But how can a physical being know how to choose the option that reveals Divine light in the world? To accomplish this mission, Hashem created the human being in His image, with a *Tzelem Elokim*.

This brings us back to the Name Elokim as it relates to creation. Not only did Hashem create the world through the Name Elokim, and not only does He supervise nature through this Name, but Hashem also empowered man to bring completion to the creation with the same Name! As written in *Bereishis* (1:27), *And Hashem formed the man in His image; in the image of Elokim He created him.* We were created with the power—and the mission—to bring light into the dark places. Man's choice to act in accordance with his *Tzelem Elokim* fulfills the words, *Ta'ir eretz mikvodecha*—"May the Earth shine from Your honor," which we recite in the Shabbos *zemer* of *Yedid Nefesh.* Humanity thus reveals the Source of creation, and in doing so, becomes a partner in creation.

To better understand this concept, we will study the example provided for us in the Torah through the story of Yosef Hatzaddik. His rise to power and his position in Egypt illustrates perfectly what it means to bring light into darkness.

Yosef in Egypt

Egypt was a morally degenerate place. Going back to the times of Avraham, the Torah introduces Egypt as a decadent society where the inhabitants might be expected to snatch a woman away from her husband. Avraham and Sarah protected themselves by claiming they were siblings.

Egypt was clearly a very dark place for any person to dwell in, but this was especially so for a righteous man like Yosef. Nevertheless, it was the will of Hashem that he was thrust into both physical and spiritual danger. Furthermore, the series of events that brought him to Egypt was possibly an even greater example of darkness.

First, his own brothers, the ten sons of Yaakov, plotted to kill him. Then they decided to spare his life and sell him as a slave.

The fact that they could conceive of such plans illustrates conclusively that Hashem's presence was hidden from the scene. Additionally, the specific conditions of Yosef's enslavement, working in the home of Potifar, whose wife relentlessly tried to seduce him, made the situation even more challenging. Everything about his life in Egypt went against his own moral fiber; it was total darkness.

Then, after successfully staving off Potifar's wife, he was accused of succumbing to the very temptation that he had successfully withstood. As a result, he found himself imprisoned in the dark dungeons of Egypt. However, through this entire saga, from the moment he was sold through his imprisonment, he remained deeply connected to Hashem. Eventually, Yosef was lifted from the dark dungeon and clothed and groomed properly for an audience with Pharaoh.

If we contemplate for a moment the drastic change and the stark comparison between Yosef's "before" and "after," we gain an insight into the transformation of dark to light. Yosef instantly went from being among the lowest and most unwanted people in Egypt to having an audience with the single most powerful person in the country, Pharaoh, who wanted to hear what Yosef had to say about his dreams. When asked by Pharaoh for an interpretation, Yosef took no credit for his insight. Rather, he said, "Elokim will provide the peaceful answer."[8] **This is the essence of Kiddush! It reveals the power of Hashem in creation and thereby elevates the world to recognize the true power and the holiness that was infused in the world by its Creator.**

From that time onward, Yosef serves as the conduit of Elokim in delivering life-saving measures that ensure nourishment for Egypt and the entire world. The gains that Yosef achieved were clearly

---

8. Yosef was able to steer Pharaoh and the entire country away from their idols, to believe in one Power, the true and only G-d, Elokim.

only possible because of the darkness that enveloped him. He achieved the ultimate success of bringing light and life into the darkest place in the world. The benefit of this transformation of darkness into light was not just for Yosef personally, but rather, it was a *tikkun* for the entire Jewish nation that would be born in Egypt. Yosef's achievements were not just his own, but rather, they were universal. To gain an even deeper understanding of the extent of Yosef's success in bringing light into darkness, let us examine Dovid Hamelech's rendering of this event.

Yosef and Yehosef

This transformation from *galus* to *geulah*—darkness to light—is noted in *Tehillim* (81:6): *As a testimony for Yehosef (b'Yehosef), He ordained it when He went forth over the land of Egypt. I understood a language that I had not known*. The Gemara (*Sotah* 36) relates that the night before Yosef stood before Pharaoh, the angel Gavriel appeared to Yosef and taught him seventy languages so that Yosef could prove that he was worthy of the power with which he was about to be invested. However, Yosef was unable to learn the languages. Gavriel then added a *hei* from Hashem's Name to Yosef's name, and Yosef became capable of the task.

Yeho-sef

The Gemara (*Sotah* 36) says that the added letter *hei* served as a testimony to Yosef's righteousness. By connecting Yosef's name to His own, Hashem publicized Yosef's devotion and loyalty to Him, even in the privacy of his master's home.[9] This loyalty

---

9. This testimony is also recorded with regard to the Jewish nation when the Jewish people were counted according to their families. The *pasuk* states, שבטי י-ה עדות לישראל–*The tribes of Hashem, this is a testimony to the Jewish people.* The Name of Hashem that is used to testify is י-ה. These are the letters found in the words for man and wife: איש אשה. The two letters י and ה represent a man and woman when their unity is based on their connection not just to each other, but to each other with Hashem as their source of unity. This testimony to the families of the

provided Yosef with the opportunity to continue bringing public honor to Hashem's Name. With the addition of the letter *hei*, Yosef possessed most of the letters of Hashem's Name. (The letters *hei*, *yud*, and *vav* are three of the four letters of the Name.)

After correctly interpreting Pharaoh's dreams, Yosef rose to power in Egypt and merited to become the source of all sustenance not just for Egypt but for the entire world.[10] The story of Yosef in Egypt is a prime example of bringing light into darkness, and the benefits of his deeds lasted long after the famine ended.

Tehillim (105:17) states, *A man was sent before them. Yosef was sold as a slave.* The midrash explains that Hashem sent Yosef to Egypt ahead of his entire family, where he successfully lived a moral life. In doing so, he created a cocoon of morality and holiness that permeated the Jewish people. With this core of holiness, every man was able to remain loyal to his heritage and to Hashem. (In a sense, Yosef "made Kiddush" over the land of Egypt, allowing all the Jews who entered the country to live a life of holiness. In fact, the entire Jewish nation was created in the land of Egypt because of the *kedushah* that Yosef brought to the land.)

This is the ultimate accomplishment of bringing light into darkness—the achievement that the Torah describes as *tov me'od*. Let us take this a step further by exploring the role played by a cup of wine as it connects to Yosef's accomplishment of turning good into very good.

Jewish nation is rooted in the actions of Yosef as he successfully refrained from the advances of the wife of his master.

10. The Ari Hakadosh writes that our Sages teach us that there are 310 worlds; Yosef in Egypt brought light—*ohr*—to 207 of those 310, leaving 103, which is the value of *egel* (the Golden Calf).

Elokim = *Kos*

The Hebrew word for cup is *kos*, which has the *gematria* of 86. That is the same as the numerical value of Hashem's Name Elokim, the Name the Torah uses in describing the creation of the world. Since words with the same *gematria* are perceived as having an underlying connection to each other—through which we can gain a deeper grasp of both—let us examine the *kos*-Elokim connection. We will see how the cup serves as the catalyst that moves us beyond the world of nature, enabling us to perceive the higher reality of Hashem.

The Dream of the Cupbearer

When the time came for Yosef to leave jail, he received a heavenly message. He had understood that the dreams of the royal cupbearer and royal baker were meant for him. But how did he know that? In fact, there is a special hint in the dream that the cupbearer shared with him: the image of a cup of wine. What did this have to do with Yosef?

Kos Yayin = Yosef

The numerical value of *kos* is 86. Wine—*yayin*—is 70. 86 + 70 = 156, which is the numerical value of Yosef. When Yosef interpreted the dream of the cupbearer and foresaw that this imprisoned servant would once again place a cup of wine in Pharaoh's hands, Yosef understood that Hashem was sending him a prophetic message. Yosef would be delivered into the hands of Pharaoh. He understood that *he was that cup of wine*!

Amazingly, the dream that Yosef interpreted came to fruition exactly the way Yosef understood it. Although Yosef was not released immediately upon interpreting the dream, eventually, it was the cupbearer who suggested his release to Pharaoh. This resulted in "the cup of wine" being placed before Pharaoh. This cup of wine was the catalyst for Yosef's transition from darkness to light.

Kiddush

The role of the cup of wine in Yosef's story gives us insight into the significance of Kiddush and the process of sanctifying a holy day. If we did not make Kiddush and bring the holy light of Shabbos into the world, the day would not be holy and indeed Friday would not turn into Shabbos. Just as a cup of wine signaled to Yosef his upcoming transition from darkness to light, it also serves to move the world from mundanity to holiness. When we make Kiddush on Friday night or any holiday, we are opening the connection between this dark physical world and Hashem's holiness and spirituality.

This is how Hashem's light permeates the natural world. Both Elokim (86) and *hateva*/nature (86) have the same numerical value as *kos*/cup (86); the revelation that emerges from this numerical correlation is that the "cup of creation," which signifies the world's capacity to receive Hashem's bounty and humanity's opportunity to "make a difference," is revealed through the Name Elokim. It is through the sanctification of a cup of wine that the world shines with the glory of the Creator.

The holiness of Shabbos is a new and higher revelation of Hashem, which connects us back to the Torah at Har Sinai. Let us understand this by analyzing one aspect of that revelation.

The *Kedushah* of Shabbos

When we make Kiddush and sanctify Shabbos, we reveal not only the *kedushah* of Shabbos and the Name of Hashem as the Creator, but we also gain access to a Name of Hashem that is beyond the scope of creation. This Name was revealed to the Jewish people at Har Sinai when Hashem revealed His identity with the words, *I am Hashem, your G-d, Who took you out of the land of Egypt.* In this pronouncement, Hashem identifies Himself with the name *Yud-hei-vav-hei.* The Name that is revealed with the giving of the Torah is not Elokim, the Master of the process of creation, but rather, it is the Name that is the root and cause of creation.[11]

The Revelation at Har Sinai: Hashem Is Elokim[12]

When Hashem introduced Himself on Har Sinai with the words, *Anochi Hashem (Yud-hei-vav-hei) Elokecha*, He revealed that all the powers of creation that are perceived to be Elokim are in reality a manifestation of Hashem, Who is the Source of Elokim. As we say in our prayers, *Hashem, Hu HaElokim.*

The Maharal (*Derech Hachaim* on *Pirkei Avos*[13]) quotes a midrash that relates the following scene: When Hashem created the world, all the letters of the *aleph-beis* came before Him to request that they be the letter upon which creation begins. Starting with the last letter, *taf*, each letter was allowed to make its case. Hashem found a reason to disqualify every letter until He reached the letter *beis*, which He chose as the appropriate starting point of creation. Therefore, the Torah begins with the word *Bereishis*—"In the beginning."

The midrash continues, noting that the letter *aleph* stood silently despite the fact that it had not been given an opportunity to make a case for itself. Noting the humility of the *aleph*, Hashem comforted it with the promise that in the future, when He gives the Jewish people the Torah, it would begin with *aleph*.

---

11. It is fascinating to note the order of the first of the Ten Commandments. The first and second are connected: The first is *I am Hashem* and the second, *You may have no other G-d*, which is the exclusivity of Hashem's revelation. Then the third mitzvah is *Do not desecrate My Name*. This too is logically connected. The fourth mitzvah is *Remember the day of Shabbos to sanctify it*. How is this connected to the first three? The day of Shabbos reveals that Hashem is not merely Elokim in creation, but rather, Elokim is the Name of Hashem that is responsible for creation.

12. This statement, *Hashem, Hu HaElokim*, is made when Eliyahu Hanavi challenged the prophets of the *Baal* at Har Carmel.

13. *Perek* 6 Mishnah 1.

The Maharal interprets the midrash as testimony to the virtue of humility, and its critical importance as a trait of those who study Torah. Furthermore, as the first letter of the *aleph-beis*, the *aleph* testifies to the primacy of Torah, even over creation. It is appropriate that the first letter of the first of the Ten Commandments, which announces to the Jewish people and the world *I am Hashem your G-d*, be the *aleph*.

In summary, the first letter, *aleph*, reveals Hashem with the Name *Yud-hei-vav-hei*,[14] for it is with that Name that Hashem gives us Torah and mitzvos. On the other hand, the Torah's account of creation begins with the second letter, *beis*. This flows from the concept that "two" represents something that has expanded. Since creation represents Hashem's expansion of the universe to include mankind and our contribution to His plan, it rightfully begins with *beis*. But the Name *Yud-hei-vav-hei* is the Name through which Hashem gave us the tool—the Torah—that empowers us to achieve His purpose in creation. Until the exodus, however, we perceived Hashem only in His Elokim state.

Hashem, Hu HaElokim

When Hashem revealed Himself as *I am Hashem, your G-d*, and gave us the mitzvos, He revealed the true purpose of creation. We declare this understanding when we say, "*Hashem, Hu HaElokim*," meaning that all of creation—the world of Elokim—is nothing other than an expression of the Name *Yud-hei-vav-hei* and His plan for creation. This is the ultimate goal of *tov me'od*—very good.[15] Additionally, this connection to the higher level of

---

14. The connection between the letter *aleph* and the name *Yud-hei-vav-hei* can be seen in the structure of the letter *aleph*. *Aleph* is comprised of three letters: two *yuds* and one *vav*. The numerical value is 26, the same as the name *Yud-hei-vav-hei*. It is therefore appropriate that the letter *aleph* begins as the power that reveals the Name *Yud-hei-vav-hei*.

15. At the culmination of creation on the sixth day, the Torah says, *And Hashem*

Hashem—His ultimate purpose—enables us to better understand the power of the letter *hei* that was added to Yosef's name. As we mentioned, Yosef incorporated Hashem into every part of his life, but this became most noteworthy when he was tested by Potifar's wife. He found the strength to suppress his natural instincts in favor of doing Hashem's will. No other creature would be capable of doing anything other than that which came naturally, and yet Yosef was able to choose to rise above his nature.

Kiddush Hashem

The Gemara in *Sotah* referred to this as "Sanctifying the Name of Hashem." The subtle message in the Gemara's words is that when man honors the Name of Hashem, he reveals a connection to Hashem that is eternal, extending far beyond the scope of the physical, observable world. This was Yosef's accomplishment. Since Yosef's connection went beyond the natural human capacity, he earned the addition of the *hei* to his name. He became *Yehosef*, which signified the extent to which he was at one with Hashem's purpose.

This is the capacity that exists in mankind. We are able to reach beyond the natural world and connect ourselves, our reality, and all that exists to Hashem, the Source of creation. This is the meaning that underlies the term *kiddush Hashem*. In this sense, every mitzvah is a *kiddush Hashem* because a person who performs a commandment is heeding the will of Hashem as *Anochi*—the G-d who appeared to us at Har Sinai—and thereby connecting to Hashem at a level that is beyond the scope of nature.

The Shelah reveals that this connection is contained in the word

---

saw all that He created and behold it was very good. And it was evening, and it was morning, the sixth day. Rashi quotes the Gemara that "the sixth day" represents the sixth of Sivan, the day the Jewish people received the Torah. This means that in addition to the basic understanding of the *pasuk*, the verse implies that everything was *tov me'od* because of the sixth day.

"mitzvah." He uses the *gematria* known as *at-bash*, where the first letter (*aleph*) is replaced with the last letter (*taf*), the second (*beis*) with the second to last (*shin*), and so on. Applying this method to the first two letters in the word "mitzvah," the letter *mem* is interchangeable with the letter *yud*, and the letter *tzadi* is interchangeable with the letter *hei*. This spells *Yud-hei-vav-hei*.[16] According to the Shelah, this *gematria* indicates that when a person performs a mitzvah, he connects to the Name of Hashem revealed at Har Sinai and thereby fulfills his mission of bringing holiness into the world.

We now have a clearer understanding of the Kiddush of Shabbos and the other holy days that Hashem commanded us to observe. By fulfilling Hashem's commandment, we reveal the *tov me'od* that only we, through our free choice, can reveal. This brings us to *Yom Hashishi*—the sixth day, when Hashem completed the heavens and the earth. The world on Shabbos reveals the higher reality of creation. It is a time when all is One,[17] as we declare in the

---

16. My *rebbi*, Rav Moshe Shapiro *zt"l*, explained this as follows: The word "mitzvah" contains three components: the Commander, the one who is commanded, and the command. We can understand this through other similar concepts. For example, the word describing a loan in Hebrew is known as a מלוה—*milvah*. It also has three components: the lender (מלוה), the borrower (לוה), and the loan, which once established by the borrower and the lender is known as a מלוה. The same is true with the word used for judgment: *mishpat*—משפט. But the component of the judgment itself is the result of two other components—the judge (שופט) and the one who is being judged (נשפט). All three together comprise *mishpat*. When one performs a mitzvah, he is not merely following the commandment, he is connecting to the Commander—since the Commander is incorporated in the mitzvah.

17. This is known as *Hashem Echad*. The revelation at Har Sinai is just the prototype of what will exist in the world with the coming of the Mashiach. Eventually, the world will achieve its completion, together with the revelation of Hashem as the Source of creation, as the *pasuk* says, *On that day the world will know that Hashem is* Echad *and His Name is* Echad.

Shemoneh Esrei of Minchah on Shabbos: *You are One and Your Name is One, and who is like Your nation Israel, the one nation on earth.*

Now let us return to Kiddush to explore the purpose of wine and specifically, the rationale for making Kiddush on wine.

Wine: The Catalyst for Happiness and Holy Days[18]

Wine is the physical manifestation of the spiritual and kabbalistic nature of creation. As we mentioned earlier, the Name Elokim, with which Hashem created the world, encompasses both the good we see around us and that which appears bad as well. So too, wine is the catalyst for all good and all bad. Indeed, the Talmud praises a person who uses wine in a positive way, comparing him to none other than Hashem his Creator and also to the entire Sanhedrin.

The Gemara (*Eruvin* 65a)[19] states that anyone who can be appeased (and overlook an injustice afflicted upon him) by drinking wine, possesses one of the attributes of his Creator, Who was appeased by the pleasant aroma of Noach's sacrifices and therefore promised never to bring another flood to the world. The message of this statement is that Hashem was willing to go beyond His attribute of strict judgment and grant the world a permanent existence. Likewise, a person who uses wine to open his heart to mercy and forgiveness has an attribute similar to that of Hashem.

The Gemara adds that anyone who is in a settled state with a clear mind after drinking wine possesses the attributes of the seventy judges of the Sanhedrin. Wine has a Hebrew numerical

---

18. I heard this explanation from Harav Tzvi Chechin *shlita*.

19. אמר ר׳ חייא כל המתיישב ביינו יש בו דעת ע׳ זקנים. יין ניתן בע׳ אותיות וסוד ניתן בע׳ אותיות נכנס יין יצא סוד. א״ר חנין לא נברא יין אלא לנחם אבלים ולשלם שכר לרשעים שנאמר תנו שכר לאובד ויין למרי נפש.

value of 70, which equals the numerical value of the word *sod*—secret. What is this secret?

The source is found in *Shoftim* (9:13): *But the grapevine said to them, "Shall I give up my vintage that gladdens G-d and men?"*

Dovid Hamelech writes (*Tehillim* 104:16): *And wine will gladden the heart of man,* meaning that when wine is used as Hashem intended, it can bring happiness. In fact, the purpose of its creation according to the Gemara (*Eruvin* 65a) is to console mourners.

Having seen that wine has the capacity of expansiveness which leads to happiness, we now have a clearer understanding of the mechanism of making Kiddush on a cup of wine. The cup that we fill with wine represents the cup of creation as it expands to a higher reality. Since wine (when used properly) elevates a person, the cup of wine with which we make Kiddush carries within it the power to elevate the physical world and make it holy. Now this elevation through a cup of wine is not limited to Yamim Tovim; we can access these blessings even during our regular days of the year, through *Birkas Hamazon* and a *kos shel brachah.*

Birkas Hamazon and a *Kos Shel Brachah*

The Maharal (*Sefer Nesivos, Nesiv Ha'avodah,* Chapter 18) discusses the *kos shel brachah* on which *Birkas Hamazon* is recited. The halachah states that the person who leads a group that is reciting this *tefillah* must raise a cup of wine while reciting the entire *Birkas Hamazon* so that all the prayers and blessings within this *tefillah* are recited accompanied by a full cup of wine. This combination, says the Maharal, bestows an abundance of blessings on those who participate. What is the source of these blessings and why are they linked to reciting *Birkas Hamazon*, specifically with a cup of wine?

To properly understand this connection, let us lay the groundwork with the following points:

- The distinctiveness of *Birkas Hamazon*
- The concept of *parnassah*
- Man in the Garden of Eden
- Streaming blessings—*V'yitein lecha*

Birkas Hamazon

The Maharal observes that of all the blessings a Jew recites, *Birkas Hamazon* is the only one that is commanded in the Torah; all the rest are of rabbinical origin. The mitzvah of *Birkas Hamazon*, which is found in *Devarim* (8:10), instructs us, *You shall eat and be satiated*[20] *and bless Hashem on the good land that He has given you.* Why is this blessing the only one the Torah specifically commands us to recite?

Food Directly from Hashem

We are required to recite *Birkas Hamazon* after satisfying our appetite on a meal that includes bread. Its words uniquely capture the intimate devotion of a Father sustaining His children. They speak of lovingkindness and affection: *Blessed are You, Eternal, our G-d, King of the Universe, Who nourishes the whole world in His goodness with grace, kindness, and mercy.*

According to the Gemara (*Brachos* 48b), this praise was composed by Moshe when the *mann* fell from heaven. (It is most likely the oldest prayer in our possession.) The backdrop to this commandment appears in *Parshas Eikev*, when Moshe tells the Bnei Yisrael: *He afflicted you and let you hunger, then He fed you the* mann *that you did not know nor did your forefathers know, in order to make you know that not by bread alone does man live; rather by*

---

20. The requirement of *bentching* depends on a person eating a satisfying amount; this will be discussed later in this chapter.

everything that emanates from the mouth of G-d does man live (*Devarim* 8:3).

The *mann* was meant to ingrain in the hearts and minds of the Jewish people that the sustenance we receive comes *directly* from Hashem. This is a stirring realization: The *brachah* that we recite today on our bread, which we procure after a long, roundabout route from the wheat fields to the flour mills to the bakery to our table, is the *exact same* blessing that Moshe instituted for the Jewish people while they were living on *mann* that fell straight from heaven. It is the same blessing because our bread comes from the same Source as the *mann*. *Birkas Hamazon* commands us, for all generations, to know in our hearts that our sustenance comes directly from Hashem. Bread became the focus of this lesson because it is the staple of human consumption.

Bread that Sustains the Soul

This gives a clearer understanding of Dovid Hamelech's words in *Tehillim* (104:15): *And bread, which sustains the heart of man*. The Maharal explains that the heart sustains the entire body. Therefore, when Dovid says that the bread "sustains the heart," he conveys that bread is not merely the basis of a person's survival, but rather, it is an opportunity to acquire a direct connection to Hashem.[21]

Indeed, the phrasing of our *bentching* reflects a direct connection to Hashem, indicated by the words: *Who, in His goodness, provides sustenance for the entire world with grace, with kindness, and with mercy. He gives food to all flesh, for His kindness is everlasting. Through His great goodness to us we continuously do not lack [food], and may*

---

21. The Torah says, *You shall eat, be satiated, and then bless Hashem*. *Birkas Hamazon* does not follow eating if there is no satiation. No other "after blessing" has the requirement of being satiated. The reason *bentching* is different is that the meal is based on bread, and as Dovid says in *Tehillim*, *And bread, which sustains the heart of man*. Hashem's blessings should leave a person feeling complete and lacking nothing; therefore there is a requirement to be "full."

we never lack food, for the sake of His Great Name. For He, benevolent G-d, provides nourishment and sustenance for all.

His Great Name

These words tell us that when we eat bread and are sustained, we have received sustenance from the One above. The reference to "His great Name" connects to a similar blessing in *Hallel Hagadol*. There, we praise Hashem for all the good He has bestowed upon the Jewish people throughout our existence, culminating in the final praise to the One Who *gives nourishment to all flesh, for His kindness endures forever*. This constant sustenance, tailor-made for each of us, is what we call *parnassah* (livelihood).

But why is *parnassah*—the very epitome of mundane concerns—elevated to the pinnacle of all praises in this *tefillah*? The reason is that *parnassah* is much more than money in the bank and food on the table. The Maharal teaches that *parnassah* constitutes Hashem's highest and most profound connection to this world.

Parnassah: The Stability of Existence

Parnassah is the entity that sustains and stabilizes an otherwise deficient world. Hashem created a needy world that survives only because of the support it receives.

The Maharal explains that every created object is inherently deficient. That is because anything that has been created lacks self-sufficiency; it needed someone or something to create it. Because it is dependent, it needs to be sustained. Only Hashem, Who has always existed and therefore did not need to be created, is completely independent and self-sufficient. Everything else is a creation, and therefore, it is lacking.

This dependent world is sustained through the *parnassah* Hashem provides. Therefore, *parnassah* illustrates both how vulnerable the world is—for it would not last a minute without His sustenance—and also, how stable it is, for He never fails to provide. Hashem is committed not only to creating the world but to continuing to provide the life-source and support that the world needs.

This is the greatness embodied in *Hallel Hagadol*. The Talmud expresses it in a description of Hashem as, *He Who sits high above the world and yet gives food and sustenance to all creations*. These praises recognize Hashem's power across the entire spectrum of existence.

He exclusively, without any intermediary, provides sustenance to all forms of life. When all the world's creatures eat, they are testifying that Hashem feeds all of creation. In other words, all meals are "home-cooked" (directly by Hashem). There is no "take-out food" or "I'll make it myself." *Even the consumption of the food* is an act of connecting to Hashem.

This is reflected in the final two praises of *Hallel Hagadol*: *He gives food to all creatures, for His kindness endures forever. Give thanks to the G-d of heavens, for His kindness endures forever.* We recognize that all life is connected back to G-d of the heavens, the Source of all that exists—Hashem's great Name.

Birkas Hamazon is our opportunity to offer this extraordinary praise every time we eat a meal with bread. We emulate the precise praise of *Hallel Hagadol*, recognizing Hashem's "goodness, grace, lovingkindness, and mercy" as He provides food to all living things. We thank Hashem for the bounty we eat, and in the process, we connect to His great Name.

We can now grasp the unparalleled beneficence we access through eating bread and then thanking Hashem for what He has given us—a dual stream of connection that is as earthbound as the bread on our plate and as lofty as the Source of it all. Now, with one further step, we have the opportunity to *capture this connection* to Hashem and instill it into every part of our lives.

How do we achieve this? Through the *kos shel brachah*!

As we discussed in the section on "*Hashem, Hu HaElokim*," Hashem is the power behind all the powers we perceive in the natural world. The *kos shel brachah* of *Birkas Hamazon* gives us access to blessings far beyond the meal that was eaten. We add a *kos* to our *bentching* to capture the blessings of sustenance and channel them into our entire lives.

How does a *kos shel brachah* activate this energy?

V'yitein Lecha and *Kos Shel Brachah*

The Maharal explains that there is an exact correspondence between the ten rules in the Gemara regarding a *kos shel brachah* (as listed earlier) and the ten blessings that Yitzchak gave to Yaakov in the chapters of *Bereishis* (27:28-29) known as *v'yitein lecha*—"May [Hashem] give you..." The Maharal (*Sefer Nesivos, Nesiv Ha'avodah*, Chapter 18) explains that the Gemara enumerates the ten rules of the *kos shel brachah* because the number ten represents a complete conduit of blessings. These rules are a means by which to access the blessings, which have been the source of security and prosperity for all Jewish people throughout our existence. Although Yaakov received the blessings over 3,500 years ago, they are an ever-expanding resource that we can tap into through *Birkas Hamazon* when it is recited with a *kos*. Let us begin exploring the Maharal's ideas by explaining the blessings of *v'yitein lecha*.

One of the main points of contention—arguably the biggest—between Yaakov and his brother Eisav was the blessings given by their father Yitzchak. In *Parshas Toldos*, the Torah relates that Yitzchak had told Eisav to prepare food for him, intending to bless him upon receiving it. Meanwhile, Yaakov, with the urging of his mother, impersonated his brother Eisav and acquired the blessings meant for Eisav. Yaakov risked his relationship with his father in order to acquire these blessings. When Eisav found out that Yaakov had "stolen" his blessings, he was unforgiving and plotted to kill his brother. What was so important about these blessings?

The Blessings of the Garden of Eden

Both Yaakov and Eisav wanted these blessings because they were unanimously perceived as the key to prosperity and security in this world. They were the conduit for connecting heaven and earth.[22] (See footnote for the full blessing.)

When Yitzchak blessed his son Yaakov with *v'yitein lecha*, he bequeathed to his son all the bounty of heaven and earth. What are these ten blessings and how do they connect to the blessing Yitzchak gave Yaakov?

Adam Harishon

Looking deeper into the words of our Sages, we find that the blessings Yitzchak imparted to Yaakov were meant to imbue him not only with the goodness of heaven and earth, but with the majesty of Adam Harishon, the original man.[23]

When Hashem created Adam and placed him in the Garden of Eden, He surrounded Adam with vast natural bounty to satisfy all his physical needs. The world and all that it had to offer were created for him. He did not need to exert any effort to sustain himself. In that state, before his sin, Adam enjoyed a complete relationship with Hashem that allowed him to focus on spirituality instead of physicality.

Once Adam sinned, he was banished from the garden. Because

---

22. ויתן לך האלקים מטל השמים ומשמני הארץ ורב דגן ותירוש. יעבדוך עמים וישתחוו לך לאמים הוה גביר לאחיך וישתחוו לך בני אמך אורריך ארור ומברכיך ברוך—*And may the Almighty give you from the dew of the skies and from the fatness of the earth, an abundance of grain and wine. Nations will serve you, kingdoms will bow down to you. You will be a master over your brothers and your mother's son will bow down to you. Those who curse you will be cursed and those who bless you will be blessed.*

23. ויברך אתם אלקים ויאמר להם אלקים פרו ורבו ומלאו את הארץ וכבשה ורדו בדגת הים ובעוף השמים ובכל חיה הרומשת על הארץ—*And Hashem blessed them. Hashem said to them, "Be fruitful and multiply and fill the earth and take control of it. Rule over the fish of the sea, the birds of the sky, and over all the wild animals that move upon the earth."*

Adam was not loyal to Hashem, Hashem cursed him and the ground from which he was taken: *With the sweat of your brow shall you eat bread.* This situation persisted throughout the world until our patriarchs arrived on the scene.

The Patriarchs

Our forefathers, through their unwavering devotion to Hashem, were able to re-establish a Divine connection, transforming the world into a place that was once again compatible with Hashem's presence.[24] Although they didn't live in the Garden of Eden, they merited a taste of the blessings of the "future good" that Hashem has promised to all those who follow His commandments.[25]

The Blessing of the Garden

Yitzchak's blessings were meant to give the world a connection to Hashem that mirrored that which existed in the Garden of Eden. Rashi (*Parshas Toldos* 27) provides the source for this idea based on the *pasuk*: *And he [Yitzchak] smelled the fragrance of his [Yaakov's] garments, and he blessed him and he said, "Look, the fragrance of my son is like the fragrance of a field that Hashem has blessed."* Rashi expounds that this "fragrance of a field" was none other than the smell of the Garden of Eden.

But how did Yaakov acquire this fragrance when the only man to have ever lived there was Adam?

---

24. The Beis Hamikdash was Hashem's residence in this world. Its existence was due to the loyalty and devotion of the *Avos*. Each of the *Avos* had a vision and perception of the Beis Hamikdash. It was their connection to Hashem that made it possible for Him to once again establish residence in this world. The Gemara, at the end of *Maseches Sotah*, lists the blessings and good fortune that existed when the Beis Hamikdash stood, and what was lost with its destruction. This reality will manifest across the entire world when the third Beis Hamikdash is built and Mashiach brings forth world unity.

25. The Gemara (*Bava Basra* 16b) states that Avraham, Yitzchak, and Yaakov all had a taste of the good of the next world while still living in this world.

Yaakov and Adam

The Gemara (*Bava Metzia* 84) says that the beauty and countenance of our forefather Yaakov resembled that of Adam. The Sages, citing the Ari Hakadosh, teach that this refers to the original Adam, before he sinned. With this fragrance lingering in the air, Yitzchak begins his blessing of[26] *v'yitein lecha*, indicating that the blessings of the Garden of Eden are enfolded in the blessings given by Yitzchak.

This clarifies why Yitzchak's blessings are said to convey the majesty of man. However, we have yet to explain the content of the ten blessings, and how they connect to the *kos shel brachah.*

Birkas Hamazon with a *Kos Shel Brachah*

Yitzchak's blessings start with the words, *V'yitein lecha haElokim*—"And may Hashem give you"—using the Divine Name that identifies Hashem as the Creator and corresponds to His power over nature. It was in His role as Creator that Hashem endorsed each day's accomplishments with the words *ki tov*—it is good. In total, there are ten utterances of creation, corresponding to the ten blessings of *v'yitein lecha*; indeed, Yitzchak was blessing Yaakov with all the *tov*, all the good Hashem had placed in the world.

Most of the blessings parallel the rules of *kos shel brachah* and are self-explanatory. They correspond as follows:

1. "From the dew of the skies" corresponds to שטיפה—the *kos* must be cleaned on the outside.
2. "And from the fatness of the earth" corresponds to הדחה —the cup must be washed on the inside.

---

26. ***V'yitein lecha***—"**and** He shall give." The blessings begin with the letter *vav*, which means "and," indicating a connection to the previous statement. However, in this instance, since Yitzchak was just beginning his blessing, it would seem that the word "and" is inappropriate. The explanation is that since Yitzchak had smelled the sweet, pure aroma of the Garden of Eden, his intention was to channel that energy onto his son as a form of blessing that would endure forever.

3. "Abundance of grain," meaning full storehouses, corresponds to מלא—the cup must be filled to capacity.
4. "Wine" corresponds to חי—the pure and undiluted wine.
5. "Nations will serve you" means they will glorify you, corresponding to עיטור—the cup must be adorned.
6. "Kingdoms will bow down to you" corresponds to עיטוף—the cup must be crowned.
7. "You will be a master over your brothers" corresponds to נוטלו בשני ידיו ונותנו לימין—one must raise the cup with both hands. The hands represent a person's power; furthermore, the cup is transferred into the right hand, exhibiting the might of the right hand.
8. "And your mother's son will bow down to you" corresponds to מגביה מן הקרקע טפח—we raise the cup, which means we will be uplifted and exalted.
9. "Those who curse you will be cursed" corresponds to ונותן עיניו בו—the person making the blessing should look at the cup of wine.[27]
10. "And those who bless you will be blessed" corresponds to אף משגר במתנה לאנשי ביתו—the person making the blessing should share the wine with his wife and family. Sharing is a trait indicative of a good person, someone with a "good eye," who is himself a source of blessing.

In summary, to grasp the complete opportunity that *Birkas Hamazon* has to offer, we are required to prepare the cup so that it can activate all the blessings of *v'yitein lecha.* Using wine for this purpose provides us with a higher state of reality. With this insight, we can comprehend the power of a blessing on a *kos shel brachah*, and why this is a cup well worth adorning!

27. The Gemara (*Nedarim* 7b) relates that in any instance where a rabbinical scholar would look [disparagingly], there would either be death or poverty.

CHAPTER 4

The Four Species: *Arba'ah Minim*

The *Arba'ah Minim* and Mashiach

There is a link between the *arba'ah minim* and Mashiach, which is found in the Gemara (*Pesachim* 5). It quotes Rabbi Yishmael, who says that through three specific mitzvos, we will merit three aspects of redemption. These mitzvos are the *arba'ah minim*, *sukkah*, and the eradication of *chametz*. These mitzvos correspond, in relative order, to the eradication of the children of Eisav, the building of the Beis Hamikdash, and the name of Mashiach. The Talmud then goes on to explain the connection between these three mitzvos and the three events.

Each of these mitzvos shares the common feature of being a *rishon*, or a beginning. *Arba'ah minim* and *sukkah* are commandments for the first day of Sukkos, and the mitzvah of ridding ourselves of *chametz* on Pesach, as it is stated in the Torah, pertains to the first day of Pesach.[1]

The Gemara[2] explains that as a reward for performing these

---

1. אך ביום הראשון תשביתו.

2. דתנא דבי ר׳ ישמעאל בשכר שלשה ראשון זכו לשלשה ראשון, להכרית זרעו של עשו, לבנין בית המקדש, ולשמו של משיח.

three "*rishons*," we will merit three other *rishons*. The first of these is to eradicate the children of Eisav, who is a *rishon* because the Torah (*Bereishis* 25:25) refers to him as "the first one" of the twins who were born to Rivkah. The second is to merit the building of the Beis Hamikdash, about which it is written, *Like the throne of glory exalted from at first, is the place of our sanctuary*. The last is the name of Mashiach, which is known as *rishon* because it is written, *The first of Zion, behold they are here*.

Although the Gemara conveys these overall connections, it does not reveal the specific link between each "*rishon*" and its counterpart. The Maharal[3] fills in the gaps, connecting the mitzvos and their counterparts as follows: The mitzvah of burning the *chametz* corresponds to ridding the world of Eisav. The mitzvah of *sukkah* corresponds to the building of the Beis Hamikdash, and the mitzvah of the *arba'ah minim* is the catalyst for the Mashiach.

He elaborates, explaining that the common denominator of all these "first events" is that they will all happen at the time of redemption. When the Mashiach arrives, we will once again have a Beis Hamikdash and we will be rid of those who oppose us. At that time, the world will reach spiritual completion.

The Maharal then asks the obvious question: What connection is there between these three mitzvos other than the fact that the Torah tells us that they must be performed on *yom rishon*—the first day of the Yom Tov? What makes this *the* significant feature? Also, how does the mitzvah of *arba'ah minim* serve as the catalyst for the "name of Mashiach"?

Yom Rishon: The First Opportunity

Yom rishon means the first day. However, this designation of *rishon* doesn't relate solely to the Yamim Tovim that the Torah refers to. To understand the full impact of fulfilling a mitzvah on

---

3. *Sefer Netzach Yisrael* Chapter 62 and *Drashos* דרשות לשבת הגדול p. 63.

yom rishon, says the Maharal, we must look at the Torah's first mention of a "first." That is *Bereishis*—in the beginning. This is the original *rishon*. It is the state of existence in which Hashem acts as the Source and Creator. Therefore, when we execute a mitzvah on *yom rishon*, we gain access to Hashem in this role. His power of creation is, in a sense, contained in these *rishon* mitzvos.

Additionally, the beginning of creation was the time when the world was in its closest connection to Hashem, in its purest and holiest state. Its existence was one of unadulterated *kedushah*. Once the world was established as a physical creation, however, it could be perceived as a separate entity. In truth, this is only a perception because the world cannot exist if Hashem doesn't constantly infuse it with life. The created, physical world provides space for this perception of independence from Hashem in order to allow the possibility of free will. This, in turn, allows for human choices that bring the world into a state of unholiness. From a human perspective, it can seem that the world is disconnected from Hashem, operating outside His control.[4] How do we reconnect the world to the pure state in which it was created?

Back to "The Beginning"

Hashem created a world that regenerates; this empowers it to reach back to its Source and repurify. Every new yearly cycle brings us back to "in the beginning." According to our Sages, this cycle begins with the month of Nissan, when the world was created. To enable us to maximize the opportunity to attach ourselves to the time, and subsequently, the Source of creation, Hashem gave us the three *rishon* mitzvos. These commandments are scheduled for the times of the year that, in themselves, constitute a beginning. For example, we rid ourselves of *chametz* in the spring, the beginning of the growing cycle. By performing

---

4. This idea was developed in the previous chapter regarding the name Elokim.

rishon mitzvos at *rishon* times of year, we can access the regenerative powers that are rooted in the beginning of creation.

Rishon Mitzvos

The Maharal explains that the Torah's commandment, *But on the first day you shall clear all leaven from your houses* (*Shemos* 12:15), comes at the time of year when wheat that was planted in the winter is growing taller, and we separate the weeds and waste from the good crops. In line with this "clean-up" of the fields, we clean out the *chametz* from our homes. The Gemara teaches that a person who fulfills this mitzvah merits ridding the world of the toxic spiritual waste that emanates from Eisav.

Each of these three *rishon* mitzvos, says the Maharal, are "firsts" both at the beginning of creation and at the end of creation, each in its own way. But how can there be more than one "first day"? The answer, explains the Maharal, is that just as the fifteenth of Nissan is the beginning of the year in terms of the rebirth of the world, the fifteenth of Tishrei is similarly a beginning. It is the commencement of the completion of the world—a concept we will now examine more closely.

Cycle of Seven

In *Sefer Bereishis*, the Torah presents the creation of the world as a seven-day process. Rashi questions why we need to have this step-by-step account. There are many answers; one is that this teaches us that everywhere the number seven appears, it signifies a **completed creation**. For example, the Torah describes Shabbos as the culmination of creation: *Thus the heavens and the earth were finished on the seventh day. By the seventh day, Hashem had completed His work.* The number seven is the foundation of wholeness and completion, which we refer to as *shleimus*.[5]

---

5. The Maharal explains that the word seven—שבע—has the same root as שובע,

We see this concept emerge again with the giving of the Torah, which is the event that completed the world in a spiritual sense.[6] It occurred after seven cycles of seven—the seven weeks between *yetzias Mitzrayim* and the Jewish nation's arrival at Har Sinai. Indeed, many mitzvos are characterized by a cycle of seven, such as the seven days of the marriage celebration, which completes a new Jewish home, and the seven days of *shivah*, which completes the separation of the body from the soul of the person who has passed away. Each unit of seven is its own, miniature, completed creation.

The Seventh Month

The seventh month, Tishrei, is the holiest month of the year. It is the month of the Yamim Nora'im, Sukkos, Shemini Atzeres, and Simchas Torah. It is also the season when the world has reached the completion of the natural agricultural cycle. The produce has been harvested, gathered, and stored. The world has reached the state of "seven," a stage of wholeness not only in its physical development, but also in its spirituality; Rosh Hashanah and Yom Kippur have wiped humanity clean of sins. The Maharal calls this the "first" because it brings us to a closeness with Hashem that resembles the beginning of creation. It is the most complete capacity of our existence (this will be explained below).

Additionally, the Maharal says that the wholeness and completion of the seventh month exists on dual levels, for it applies to both the lower world and upper world. That is why Sukkos includes two *rishon* mitzvos—dwelling in the *sukkah* and taking the *arba'ah minim*.

Since the natural world develops each year during a seven-month period, from its beginning in Nissan (the first month) until

---

which means full and complete. Hence the number seven is a concept of wholeness.

6. See Rashi on the *pasuk* ויהי ערב ויהי בוקר יום השישי.

its completion in Tishrei (the seventh month), **the Yom Tov of Sukkos and the mitzvah of *arba'ah minim* express the *shleimus* of the seventh month of the year.** Once this world has achieved its natural wholeness, it connects to a higher level of wholeness and *shleimus* through the mitzvah of rejoicing with the *arba'ah minim* "in the presence of Hashem." It is because of this duality of *shleimus* that the fifteenth of Tishrei is identified as *rishon* twice; these two different attainments, the mitzvah of the *arba'ah minim* and the mitzvah of *sukkah*, bring us to the level at which we merit the Mashiach *and* the Beis Hamikdash.

Shleimus

Shleimus is the key to our connection to Hashem.[7] While we can never achieve the perfection of the Almighty—for He is completely flawless—we can connect to Hashem through our own relative *shleimus*. The Ramchal writes that the path to *Olam Haba*, which is an eternal connection to Hashem, is through the constant human struggle to perfect ourselves to the best of our ability.

In the annual cycle of time, the most complete and wholesome time of the year both physically and spiritually is in the month of Tishrei, the seventh month. On the fifteenth day when the moon is full and has reached its *shleimus*, the Jewish people can rise above the physical world and take up residence in the *sukkah*. There, under the shade of the mitzvah, their entire body and world are enveloped in the presence of Hashem. Additionally, they can take the produce of the earth, the *arba'ah minim*, enter the Beis Hamikdash, and stand before the Creator. This is the dual *shleimus* of the fifteenth of the month.

In summary, the *rishon* mitzvos have the power to enable the world—with all the toxicity and negativity created by humanity's

---

7. A more complete discussion of the concept of *shleimus* is found in Chapter 5.

bad choices—to still find favor in the eyes of the Creator, and to come to a place of completion. These mitzvos enable us to reclaim the state of purity and holiness the world possessed at its inception. This indeed brings home the idea that the fifteenth of Nissan is the first beginning, and the fifteenth day of the seventh month is also a beginning. We can appreciate Sukkos as an "ingathering" that reflects the beginning.

Sukkah and *Arba'ah Minim*

The Maharal's insight into the Gemara provides us with yet another connection between the mitzvos of *sukkah* and *arba'ah minim*, which further explains why the exalted state of dual completion will bring us success in meriting the Mashiach. Mashiach's mission, explains the Maharal, is to elevate the world to a higher state of reality, bringing about the realization that everything in the world comes from Hashem. It is obvious that the prerequisite for this attainment is the fulfillment of these two "firsts"—*sukkah* and *arba'ah minim*—each doing its part to complete the world.

Now that we've gained a deeper insight into the mitzvah of *arba'ah minim*, let us take a closer look at the role played by each of these four species.

The *Lulav*

When we take the four species in hand to fulfill the commandment of the *arba'ah minim*, we make the *brachah* "*al netilas lulav*." The Gemara (*Sukkah*) asks why we single out the *lulav* as the subject of the *brachah* when all four species are essential to the mitzvah. It answers that the *lulav* is chosen to signify the entire mitzvah because it is the most prominent, noticeable component of the *arba'ah minim*. However, this answer isn't fully satisfying; would the wording of the *brachah* be based on appearances alone? We sense inherently that there must be a deeper answer.

Leaves of Loyalty

To find that answer, let us first seek to understand what the *lulav* symbolizes. The Gemara (*Brachos*) reveals that if a person sees a *lulav* in his dream, it is a positive message from heaven, assuring him that his heart is properly devoted to Hashem.[8] This is reflected in the structure of the *lulav*, with all its leaves closely attached to its spine. Rashi (*Sukkah*) explains that this tight bond signifies loyalty. But the precious message of the *lulav* lies in both its physical appearance and in its name.

The Gemara states that a *lulav* whose leaves are separated is not usable. One explanation it offers is that the leaves separate from the spine when the palm frond stays on the tree for too long, which causes the leaves to harden. In this condition, the leaves are not flexible enough to be bound together with the spine, as is required for the mitzvah of *netilas lulav.*[9] Rashi describes this condition with the following words: *The hardened leaves will not be able to gather together with their father (the spine) to whom they are attached.*

The message is a powerful one. The *lulav* is only kosher for a *brachah* when its leaves lay on the spine, "from where they emerge

---

8. The word לולב can be divided into two words, לו לב, meaning "to Him is my heart," indicating one's devotion to Hashem.

9. The *lulav* needs to be cut from the tree while it's still young and bendable. If the *lulav* is on the tree too long, the leaves harden and are no longer bendable. This would disqualify the *lulav* since it is lacking the requirement of being tied as one. Rashi explains it this way: שאם היה פרוד יכפתנו והרי זה פרוד ואין אתה יכול לכופתו שיהו ענפיו הפרודים כאן וכאן נכפתים ומתמעכים אצל אביהם שהן מחוברין בו לפי שקשין הן—*The requirement to have the* lulav *tied* לולב צריך אגד *requires that the* lulav *can be bound together so that all the leaves are closely attached to the place from where they grow.*

[their source/their father].” This symbolizes the loyalty of the Jewish people to their Father in Heaven. As we mentioned earlier (in footnote 7), the word *lulav* can be read as *lo lev*—“to Him is my heart.” This is a powerful reason to focus on the *lulav* when making the *brachah*.

The *Esrog*

Regarding the *esrog*, the Torah instructs, *And you shall take a fruit of a tree that is beautiful.* It does not specify the fruit in any other way. How, then, do we know which fruit to use to fulfill the mitzvah? The Talmud states that the tradition of using an *esrog* is based in the Oral Law. However, we would expect that law to be derived from some hint in the relevant Torah *pasuk*. Why is the Torah so vague? Further, why is the *esrog* uniquely designated “beautiful” when every fruit is beautiful in its own way? Lastly, what trait of the *esrog* confers this chosen status on it?

The Tree of Knowledge

Rashi provides us with the answer from the Gemara (*Sukkah* 35a) that tells us that, unlike any other fruit, the *esrog* tastes like the tree on which it grows. The Maharal explains that there is a hint of this distinction in the *pasuk*. Normally, the fruit of a tree is called *pri ha'etz*. However, in the *pasuk* that refers to the *esrog*, the Torah uses the term *pri eitz*. This indicates that there is something unique about this tree and its fruit.

The Disobedient Earth

The Torah (*Bereishis*) relates that Hashem commanded the earth to produce trees whose fruits tasted like the trees that bore them. However, the earth disobeyed and produced fruits that tasted better than the trees on which they grew.[10] There was, however, one exception to this disobedience: the *esrog* tree, whose fruit and bark have the same taste. Because the *esrog* tree was the only tree that faithfully reflected the will of heaven, it earned the designation of "a tree that is beautiful." As a unique symbol of the harmony and unity of heaven and earth, the *esrog* was the only species chosen to be brought before Hashem on Sukkos. Furthermore, since the *esrog*, like the *lulav*, symbolizes loyalty to Hashem, it is appropriate that the two species be taken together.

Another explanation of the *esrog's* identity as the Torah's "beautiful fruit" is based on an alternative definition to the word *hadar* (beautiful). It can also mean "one that dwells."[11] This reflects the fact that *esrogim* dwell on the tree longer than any other fruits. Uniquely, these fruits never "just fall off," which implies that these fruits were not meant to be taken. This supports the opinion that the *esrog* tree is none other than the original Tree of Knowledge of Good and Evil. This means that by including the *esrog* in the *arba'ah minim*, we are enacting a grand correction of Adam and Chava's sin, for the fruit that was the object of the sin now becomes the object of a mitzvah.

Furthermore, the Sages teach that the fruit of the *Eitz Hada'as*

---

10. The obvious question is, does the earth have free will? Can it disobey Hashem's commandment? The Maharal in *Gur Aryeh* (*Bereishis*) explains this, providing a deep insight into the nature of heaven versus earth. Heaven is Hashem's "place," where His presence is perceived more strongly than it is on earth. The source for this can be found in *Tehillim* (115:16): *The heavens are the heavens of Hashem and the earth He gave to the sons of man.* Although our belief is that Hashem is everywhere, we perceive earth as a place in which Hashem allows mankind the freedom to make their own choices and create their own destiny. Therefore, when the earth was created, it could not uniformly obey every command of Hashem, for in doing so, it would not have been earth at all, but rather, it would have become like heaven, where free choice doesn't exist.

11. The word "to dwell" in Hebrew is לדור. A place to live is called a דירה. Hence, *hadar* is "one who dwells."

was only forbidden on that one Friday of man's creation. Hashem wanted Adam and Chava to wait for His permission to eat from the tree, which He would have granted on Shabbos, the next day. They took the fruit without Hashem's permission, but every Sukkos, through the mitzvah of the *esrog*, we take that fruit *with* Hashem's permission. This means that our taking of the *esrog* for the *brachah* on the *lulav* is a *tikkun* for the fruits of the *esrog* tree, and in a sense for all trees.[12]

To summarize, both the *lulav* and the *esrog* represent a form of loyalty to Hashem. Therefore, the mitzvah of "taking the *lulav* and *esrog*" is a *tikkun* for us as individuals, and for the earth.

The *Hadassim*

In addition to expressing the concept of loyalty, the *arba'ah minim* give us access to the powers of *kedushah* that would normally lie beyond human grasp. The Gemara writes that we fulfill the mitzvah of the *arba'ah minim* with a total of seven items: one *lulav*, one *esrog*, three *hadassim*, and two *aravos*. These seven correspond to the seven *middos*[13] and the seven guests who visit us in our *sukkah*. Specifically, the three branches of *hadassim* parallel the three patriarchs: Avraham, Yitzchak, and Yaakov.[14] The energy of our Patriarchs, who forged a significant connection to

---

12. Before eating from the *Eitz Hada'as*, the entire world was a place that naturally accommodated the life of Adam and Chava. However, after the sin, the world was cursed, so that there was no blessing. By rectifying the source of sin, the world once again becomes a place of blessing.

13. We will discuss the seven *middos* in the introduction to the section on *Ushpizin*.

14. The two *aravos* correspond to Moshe and Aharon; the *lulav* to the *middah* of

Hashem, brings blessings to this world.[15] One way to access this energy is through the mitzvah of the four species. But what is it about these four species that allow us to access such holiness and prosperity?

The Form of Man

The *Midrash Rabbah* (*Parshas Emor*) states that the *arba'ah minim* represent man. The *lulav* is like the spine; the *aravos* are shaped like lips; the *hadassim* are shaped like the eyes; and finally, the *esrog* resembles the heart. We can understand why the heart and spine are represented. They are two vital organs that have central functions that are unique to man, who was created in Hashem's image.[16] But the eye and the mouth are no less important, for Hashem used the powers of speech and vision to create the world. Day after day in *Bereishis*, the Torah relates that Hashem created the world with His speech: *And Hashem **said**...* after which, *He **saw** that it was good.* Therefore, the *hadassim* and *aravos* parallel

---

yesod, which corresponds to Yosef; and the *esrog*, which is separate from the other six, corresponds to the *middah* of kingship represented by Dovid Hamelech.

15. The Gemara (*Bava Basra* 16b) writes that there were three people (Avraham, Yitzchak, and Yaakov) who in this world already enjoyed a taste of the goodness of the future world. Although the world was cursed due to Adam's sin, Avraham, Yitzchak, and Yaakov succeeded in reconnecting themselves to Hashem and bringing blessings back to this world. (These are the two attributes we mentioned earlier regarding the *lulav* and the *esrog*.).

16. The *Tzelem Elokim*—the image of Hashem—manifests itself in human beings in that humans are endowed with spiritual capacities that animals do not have, and also, these attributes have a physical expression that makes the human body different than that of animals. Therefore, although humans and animals have many things in common, like eyes, a nose, ears, hands, and legs, man is the only creature created with a spine that enables him to stand upright rather than walk on four feet. This indicates the human capacity for free will that allows a person to stand tall to make his own decisions. Further, although animals also have physical hearts, a human has a spiritual capacity of *lev meivin*, an understanding heart.

the powers of creation and connect those powers to the *lulav* and *esrog*—the heart and spine.

The four *arba'ah minim* symbolize a human being who bears the image of Hashem and is totally connected to Him. Such a person has the capacity to bring blessings into the world.[17]

The *Aravos*

The midrash identifies the four species with four types of Jewish people. The variables that define these groups are Torah and good deeds. Some people possess both qualities, some have just one or the other, and some have neither. Parallel to this, each component of the *arba'ah minim* is characterized by two variables—taste and fragrance.

The *esrog* has both taste and a pleasant aroma; it represents the righteous people of Klal Yisrael who are filled with Torah and mitzvos. The *lulav*, which is a branch from a date palm, has taste but no aroma. It represents those who have Torah knowledge but are not steeped in good deeds. The *hadassim* have a pleasant smell but no taste. They represent those Jews who are full of good and caring deeds but lack Torah knowledge. Finally, there are the *aravos*. Lacking both taste and aroma, they represent the wicked Jews who have neither Torah nor good deeds.

Nevertheless, the Torah requires that all four species be *tied together* to fulfill the mitzvah. This means that without the full, united participation of the Jewish people (regardless of their observance level), the mitzvah is deficient.

---

17. This will be discussed at length in the section *Na'anuim*.

Unity

By requiring us to not only "take" the *arba'ah minim* but also to bind them and hold them together, the Torah teaches us a lesson in unity and love for one another. To fulfill the mitzvah of the *arba'ah minim*, all types of Jews need to be connected and attached. This requires more than just tolerance. When people are distant from one another, they find it far easier to be patient and accepting. However, when they are together, interacting with each other, preserving the harmony requires true *ahavas Yisrael.* We define this as the mitzvah of "Love your neighbor as [you love] yourself," which in this context means to appreciate the struggles of others rather than judging them harshly.

This is the special message conveyed by the inclusion of the *aravos* in the four species. It has no taste or smell, which means it lacks any spiritual qualities, and yet it is a necessary part of the mitzvah. What value is there in this seemingly useless branch?

The Essence of *Zera Kodesh*

Rav Tzadok Hakohen writes that **in the *aravos*, we find the foundation of our relationship with Hashem**. We are His children whether we observe commandments and learn Torah, or we do nothing at all. This concept is found in the Gemara (*Kiddushin*): *Rabbi Meir says you are children of Hashem even when you do not do His will. This is the essence of the fatherhood of Yaakov.*[18]

---

18. Rav Hutner writes that each of the three *Avos* were founding fathers in their own way. Each merited to be called a "father" for each created a "first" in the formation of the Jewish nation. Avraham was the first Jew. He created the nation by choosing service of Hashem as his way of life. Yitzchak was the first person to be born as a Jew, and Yaakov solidified the nation, creating a status of "born a Jew, always a Jew" regardless of observance. The importance of Yaakov's contribution is that although Avraham and Yitzchak made the choice to commit themselves completely to Hashem, Yishmael and Eisav did not continue in their path and none of their descendants are Jewish. Yaakov, on the other hand, was so connected to Hashem that his offspring are Jewish regardless of whether they

It is not a coincidence that the numerical value of *aravah* (277) equals that of *zera*, children. The holiness of the *aravos* is the basic, essential holiness that is found inside every single Jew, simply because we are Jewish children.

Lulav: The Symbol of Victory

The midrash addresses a famous question that we discussed earlier: Since the Jewish people dwelled in *sukkos* throughout their entire forty years in the desert, Sukkos could have been celebrated during any week throughout the entire year. Why is it celebrated directly after Rosh Hashanah and Yom Kippur?

The midrash explains with a *mashal*: Two people bring a dispute to court. When the two parties emerge from the courtroom door, the onlookers have no way of knowing which one is the victor. They discern the answer when one of the parties raises his hands in a symbol of victory (similar to when one pumps his fist into the air in a gesture of triumph). Likewise, on Rosh Hashanah, the Jewish people are engaged in their judgment. The contest is between good and evil, between the Jewish people and those who would like to see them annihilated. For this reason, directly after Rosh Hashanah and Yom Kippur, we are confident that we've emerged victorious, and we celebrate Sukkos by raising our *lulav* in the air.

The *lulav*, with the other three species, is indeed a symbol of

---

identify as Jews. Yaakov created a foundation for the Jewish people that cannot be severed. This is the message of the *aravos*; although they do not represent any Torah or mitzvos, they do represent the basis of Judaism. Hashem loves us unconditionally.

Jewish victory. And the ultimate victory is our unity, which we testify to when we hold the *arba'ah minim* together.

The *Arba'ah Minim* and the *Sukkah*

Now that we have explained some of the symbolic ideas of the *arba'ah minim*, we are ready to understand how this mitzvah connects to the mitzvah of *sukkah*. While some are accustomed to saying the blessing of the *lulav* in the *sukkah*, this is certainly no more than a custom. On the contrary, the *sukkah* is meant as a place of residence, while the *lulav* is meant to be used during prayer in shul. How are we then to understand the connection between these two commandments? We can find the answer in the custom of *na'anuim*.

Na'anuim

The word *na'anuim* means multiple acts of shaking or waving. *Na'anua*, the singular form, means to shake. The Gemara (*Sukkah* 37b) teaches that it is a mitzvah to hold the *lulav* and the other three species and to wave them at certain intervals while reciting Hallel. Since we wave the *lulav* multiple times in multiple directions, we use the plural word *na'anuim*.

There is a debate as to when in Hallel we make the *na'anuim*. There are also differences of opinion as to the sequence of the direction of these wavings. However, all agree that the species are waved in six directions, toward the four corners of the earth, up toward heaven, and down toward the earth.

The source for holding the *lulav* during Hallel is found in a midrash that quotes the verse, *Then all of the trees of the forest will praise Hashem*. When we recite Hallel while holding the various species that grow from the ground, we fulfill that verse. But what is the concept underlying the *na'anuim*?

Staving Off Evil Powers

The Gemara cited above explains that *na'anuim* are not exclusive to the *lulav* and the Yom Tov of Sukkos. The same type of waving is used also for the sacrifice of the two sheep and two breads on Shavuos. The Gemara cites Rabbi Yochanan, who says that we wave the two sheep and loaves of bread forward, backward, and in all directions to indicate that the entire world belongs to Hashem. Rav Yossi bar Rav Chanina says the procedure is meant to ward off evil spirits and negative energy.

The Maharsha (*ad loc.*) explains that the two loaves of bread represent the two *luchos* on which the Ten Commandments were written, indicating that through the Torah, Hashem continues to invest in the world. This protects the world from all negative forces. Likewise, with the *lulav*, the *na'anuim* are meant to surround a person with a "force field" of protection.

The Gemara then quotes Rav Acha bar Yaakov, who would say that when he shook the *lulav*, he would use the opportunity to poke the Satan in the eye. (The Gemara goes on to warn that a person should be careful not to antagonize the Satan.) Herein lies the answer to the connection between the *arba'ah minim* and the *sukkah*; both have the power to keep evil away.

A *Sukkah*-Type Protection

To summarize, the *arba'ah minim* correspond to a righteous person who is loyal to Hashem, and such a person can use the *arba'ah minim* to surround himself with protection against evil. This is precisely the concept we discussed regarding the *sukkah*. It too is a place of refuge. As we discussed earlier, it is the place where Yaakov put his belongings after departing from Eisav. It is where the Jewish people found refuge after leaving Egypt. The *sukkah* is meant to keep the Satan away.

Once a year, we physically leave our homes and live in the *sukkah* so that we actually live under Hashem's shelter, right here in this world. That time of year rightfully comes immediately after Yom Kippur, when we've separated ourselves from the evil inclination just as Yaakov separated from Lavan, and the Jewish people separated from Egypt. It is precisely during this holiday that we take the *arba'ah minim* and wave them in all six directions to create a personal "force field" of holiness. Through this mitzvah, wherever a person finds himself, he can feel the same sense of security that he feels when sitting within the walls of the *sukkah*.

CHAPTER 5

The *Ushpizin*

The *Sukkah* and Its *Ushpizin*

Ushpizin means guests in Aramaic. The *Zohar*[1] states that on each day of Sukkos, we receive seven special guests: Avraham, Yitzchak, Yaakov, Moshe, Aharon, Yosef, and Dovid. They come from the Garden of Eden to visit us in our *sukkos*. While all seven guests are there for all seven days, on each day a different guest comes to the forefront and is recognized individually, while all the others take a secondary role. Avraham is honored on day one, Yitzchak on day two, and so on until Dovid Hamelech presides on day seven.

This completely mystical experience raises many questions:

- Why seven guests?
- Why *these* guests?
- Why do they visit us in the *sukkah*, and not in our house?
- What is the purpose of their visit?
- Why do they all come together instead of a different one coming each day?

---

1. *Parshas Emor* p. 103b: תא חזי בשעתא דבר נש יתיב במדורא דא צלא דמימנותא שכינא פרסא גדפהא עליהא מלעילא ואברהם וחמישא צדיקייא אחרין שויין מדוריהון עמיה. אמר רבי אבא ואברהם וחמישא צדיקייא ודוד מלכא שויין מדוריהון עמיה—*Come and see, when a person resides in this dwelling [the* sukkah*] known as "The Shadow of Belief," the* Shechinah *spreads its wings upon him from above and Avraham and five righteous ones dwell with him. Rabbi Abba says Avraham and five righteous ones and Dovid Hamelech.*

- Is there any precedent for this type of visitation?
- Without question, these guests are among the greatest, if not *the* greatest, Jews who ever lived. How is it possible that all of us have the merit to host them in our *sukkos*?

The key to answering all these questions lies in the connection between us and these guests at ***this*** particular time of the year, specifically as we sit in our *sukkos*. The *Ushpizin* do not visit us in shul or come along on our Chol Hamoed outings, but rather, they are only drawn to us in this one location. That is where we are worthy of greeting them. What is there about the *sukkah* that elevates us to a level worthy of these guests?

The answer is *shleimus*. And it is with the mitzvah of *sukkah* that we celebrate our *shleimus*.

Shleimus

Shleimus, as we discussed earlier, is a state of wholeness and perfection.

The root of the word is *shaleim*, which means "complete." Before we relate this concept to Sukkos, let us gain a better understanding of the concept of *shleimus*.

Rav Moshe Chaim Luzzato (the Ramchal) explains in his *Sefer Daas Tevunos* that something that has *shleimus* is whole; it lacks nothing. Furthermore, it has never lacked anything and will never become deficient in any way. This means it never needed to be created and needs nothing to complete it. As we discussed previously, this state of perfection is inherent in *shleimus* because anything that needs to be created is in essence a "creation." It is dependent on a creator for its existence, and that dependency is a deficiency.

Only Hashem, the Creator, is and can be truly complete, for Hashem wasn't created. His eternal existence precludes being created. If, theoretically, Hashem needed to be created or needed anything to be created, that would indicate a lack of wholeness (*shleimus*). Simply put, there is nothing outside of Hashem, and therefore there is nothing that He is lacking.

But what about the rest of creation? Is there a way for people to achieve *shleimus*? The answer is that for any created being to achieve any level of *shleimus*, it needs to connect to Hashem.

How is this accomplished?

Shleimus within Creation

The Ramchal explains that the greatest level of *shleimus* a person can achieve is through a connection to the Source of all *shleimus* and that of course is Hashem. **The less separation there is between a creation and its Creator, the more complete that creation is**. The goal of humanity and, ultimately, each person's destiny is to attach to Hashem. The more we attach ourselves, the more *shaleim* we become. Conversely, the greater the separation, the further we drift from wholesomeness. This is the basic rationale for the Torah and mitzvos; they provide the opportunity for us to connect ourselves to Hashem. As we learn more Torah and we perform more mitzvos, our connection strengthens, and we reach greater levels of *shleimus*.

While we are living in this world, we struggle to connect to Hashem. Our body, its sensations, and its consciousness do not always appreciate this association. There will always be some pushback, whether internally or from the world in which we live, that challenges us and our loyalty to Hashem. Entering the *sukkah* is one remedy to this dilemma. It provides us with the opportunity to unite our body and soul in a unique way, for eating, drinking, sleeping, and even just having a conversation with a friend becomes a mitzvah when done in the *sukkah* on Sukkos.

The commandment of *sukkah* is *the mitzvah* that a person accomplishes with the entirety of his being. There's no battle between our physical and spiritual selves. In the *sukkah*, we are sitting together with Hashem in the Shade of His presence.[2] As we will see, the *sukkah* and spiritual completeness are linked together.

Sukkas Shelomecha

In our daily evening prayer of *Hashkiveinu*, we ask Hashem to "spread upon us the *sukkah* of Your completeness (*sukkas shelomecha*)." One way to understand the association of *shleimus* with the *sukkah* is to fully understand the challenge the mitzvah of *sukkah* presents to us. As we mentioned, this mitzvah requires us to "step away" from the comforts of this world. In general, our possessions give us a sense of identity and security. Normally, a person feels safest in his own home, surrounded by his belongings. If someone were to take all that away from him, he would undoubtedly feel uncomfortable. This could even lead a person to wonder, "What am I? Who am I without my possessions?"

Indeed, this is the mindset the mitzvah of *sukkah* is meant to evoke. The sense of emptiness gives us space to fill with something else.

Living with Hashem

The message of the *sukkah* is to replace everything you possess with Hashem. As the Torah instructs, *You shall make a* sukkah *and you shall live there, seven days for Hashem.* Leaving our permanent dwelling to reside in a shaky, temporary dwelling for an entire week is an act that requires faith and trust. In many ways, the *sukkah* is like exile, which removes a person from his safe, familiar surroundings. But the similarity stops there because exile

---

2. In the previous sections on the subject, "The *Sukkah*: A Portal to the World to Come" and "The *Sukkah*: A Place of Refuge," we addressed a number of points that are relevant to our discussion here. Please see there for more on how the *sukkah* represents separation from this world and ultimately, attachment to Hashem.

is a punishment. *Sukkah* is an opportunity. Sitting in our *sukkos* outside our homes shows loyalty and devotion. The trust in Hashem that allows us to "step away" thus proves itself to be more than lip service. We demonstrate with our actions that our relationship with Hashem is more precious than all our worldly possessions.

This is the *shleimus* that the *sukkah* provides. It is what the *Zohar* describes as *Tzila D'm'heimnusa*, "the shade of belief and trust." That is why the *Ushpizin* come to visit us in our *sukkos* and not in our homes.

Dwelling in *Tzila D'm'heimnusa*

Let us now address the question of why we celebrate Sukkos at this specific time of year, directly after the Yamim Nora'im. This is because the Yamim Nora'im prime us to perform this mitzvah and appreciate it at its highest level. We enter the *sukkah* elevated by the new beginning that Rosh Hashanah ushers in, and the purity that we've attained through our repentance on Yom Kippur. This state of wholeness that the Jewish people experience annually is precisely the preparation needed.

We are then ready to achieve the state of *shleimus* that the *sukkah* is meant to provide. This is simply because we have the confidence that comes from faith in Hashem and His judgment. Our Sages teach that one reason we blow the shofar at the conclusion of Yom Kippur is to sound an uplifting blast of *simchah* and joy.

Further, *Koheles* (9:7) urges us, *Go with joy. Eat your bread and drink your wine with a glad heart, for Hashem has already approved your deeds.* This is the confidence we carry with us from the concluding moments of Yom Kippur into the celebration of Sukkos.

Through the happiness and wholeness that we've achieved, we merit the visitation of our illustrious guests. While we are light-years behind their level of *shleimus*, we nonetheless are engaged on *our* level in this mitzvah of *sukkah*, which embodies *shleimus*. Whenever we are in the *sukkah*, at whatever level of connection we have, we are with Hashem. It is for this reason that the *Ushpizin* come to us in our *sukkah*.

Now that we've answered the question of why the *Ushpizin* see fit to visit us, let us explore another question: Why are there seven of them, and what message does that impart to us?

These last two questions[3] can be explained by studying the Ramban's writings on the beginning of *Parshas Vayeira*, where he expounds on Hashem's visit with Avraham following Avraham's performance of *bris milah* on himself. Hashem came to check on Avraham's well-being after he had undertaken this mitzvah, which was so significant that it separated Avraham from all of mankind. He was the only person in the world worthy of entering into the covenant.

Victory Visits

The Ramban explains that this visit was unique because Hashem did not appear to Avraham in order to command him. Rather, it was a friendly visit meant to "celebrate [the *bris*] rather than dictate." The Ramban offers a few examples of this type of revelation (some performed by angels and others by Hashem Himself):

After leaving Egypt and being miraculously saved through the splitting of the sea, the Jewish people experienced a revelation of

---

3. What is the purpose of their visit? And is there any precedent for this type of visitation?

Hashem far beyond what would have been appropriate for their level of righteousness. They declared, "This is my G-d and I will glorify Him!" as they were shown a vision of Hashem in His glory. *What a maidservant saw on the sea, the prophet Yechezkel did not see [in his Divine visions]* (*Mechilta*).

The Ramban cites a similar revelation after the Jewish people completed the Mishkan. The Torah states, *They [Moshe and Aharon] went out and blessed the nation and the presence of Hashem appeared to the entire nation.* Because they had undertaken and labored to build the Mishkan and brought the commandment to successful fulfillment, they merited Hashem's appearance. The Ramban explains that this revelation was a reward. Hashem wanted them to know that He was pleased by their accomplishments.

On a different occasion, Hashem's angels were the ones to convey His recognition of a successful effort to fulfill His will. When Yaakov returned from Lavan's house after twenty years, Yaakov encountered angels of Hashem.[4] They did not come to command Yaakov in any way; rather, this was a victory celebration. Hashem sent an escort of angels to welcome Yaakov upon his return to his father Yitzchak.[5] This type of appearance is similar in spirit to Hashem's appearance to Avraham after he performed a *bris milah.*

Each of these revelations of Hashem came after a significant spiritual achievement. Avraham and Yaakov, in their own personal growth as servants of Hashem, as well as the entire Jewish nation at the splitting of the sea, had all reached spiritual milestones in their lives.

These achievements, in the words of our Sages, are characterized

---

4. ויעקב הלך לדרכו ויפגעו בו מלאכי אלקים—*And Yaakov went along his way and he encountered angels of Hashem.*

5. It is comparable to parents who come to the airport to greet their child after having been abroad for an extended time. It is simply an act of honor and love.

as *shleimus.* A state of wholeness was achieved, and Hashem's appearance was meant to celebrate the triumph. Let us investigate the events leading to each of these three revelations.

Yaakov and Lavan

Yaakov had spent two decades away from his parents and homeland. The purpose of his departure was to marry and establish a family, which, as the Torah tells us, Yaakov fulfilled perfectly. Nevertheless, living in the house of Lavan was a daily challenge. As the Torah informs us, Yaakov met privately with Rachel and Leah. He spoke to them about Lavan's disfavor toward him and the need to leave immediately. Only someone of the stature and saintliness of Yaakov could have survived that long.

Not only did he survive, but he returned with four wives, eleven children, and tremendous wealth, all of which he acquired without any compromise of his spiritual values.[6] Upon his return, he encountered angels of Hashem. Rashi explains that these were angels from the land of Israel who came out to greet him. Hashem gave Yaakov the revelation of these welcoming messengers as a salute to his accomplishments.

Krias Yam Suf

The same theme applies to the Jews at the splitting of the sea. After over two hundred years in exile, the Jews had strayed far from the principles of Avraham and their ancestors. Their loyalty to Hashem had been lost during the exile.[7] At the Yam Suf, the Heavenly Court claimed that the Jews didn't deserve to have the sea split for them, for the Jews were as guilty of idolatry as the Egyptians were.

---

6. As Rashi quotes the famous statement of *Chazal*, עם לבן גרתי ותרי״ג מצות שמרתי—*With Lavan I lived yet I still kept all 613 commandments.*

7. See Rambam, *Hilchos Avodah Zarah.*

However, as the Jews faced the sea, they showed remarkable faith, forging ahead into the water before it split. Contrary to the common belief that they were neck-deep in the water when Hashem intervened, they were in fact totally submerged, unable to breathe. That is the point at which Hashem performed the miracle. Because this independent nation showed their courage and faith in Hashem by putting their lives at risk to follow Him, they merited a miracle: The sea split for them so that they could cross it on dry land. Once again, Hashem showed His approval by revealing His presence and allowing the Jewish people to bask in His glory.[8]

Avraham and *Bris Milah*

This is the same revelation that Avraham experienced after entering the covenant through the mitzvah of circumcision. The midrash informs us that with his circumcision, Avraham was able to take the position of Adam, the first man. This is because although Adam was created circumcised, he ruined his stature and form when he sinned. As a result, says the midrash, the form of the human man changed to include the presence of a foreskin. Avraham, as a faithful and devoted servant of Hashem, achieved a status like that of Adam before his sin. To celebrate and recognize Avraham's achievement, Hashem appeared to him and created a closer bond. Avraham had become a person with a *Tzelem Elokim*, the form of man that reflects the image of Hashem.

When the *Ushpizin* visit us in our *sukkos*, we experience this same type of revelation. Our achievement is in leaving our worldly possessions behind so that we can dwell with Hashem, immersed in His presence as we go about our lives—both the holy (reciting Kiddush, taking the *arba'ah minim*, learning Torah) and the mundane (eating, sleeping, conversing). The seven holy guests

---

8. ראתה שפחה על הים מה שלא ראה יחזקאל בן בוזי.

come to celebrate the fact that in our own way, we are following in the ways of Avraham after his circumcision, Yaakov leaving Lavan, and the Jewish nation crossing the sea.

The *Ushpizin's* visits are both a result of our *simchah* and a reason for our *simchah*. In our state of *shleimus*, we enjoy a level of happiness that is uniquely a product of the *sukkah*.

The Maharal (*Nesivos, Nesiv HaShalom*) explains the connection between *simchah* and *shleimus* by quoting a *pasuk* in *Mishlei*: *And for those who seek peace, they will find happiness.*[9]

The Seven *Ushpizin*

As we sit in the *sukkah*, we have an opportunity to further elevate our meals with *divrei Torah*. Naturally, many people like to share a *dvar Torah* on the subject at hand—the *sukkah* itself. Further, in recognition of the *Ushpizin* who are among us, we have a unique opportunity to honor them with *divrei Torah* that give them the proper recognition.

This section is devoted to the *Ushpizin* and serves two separate purposes: First, it provides insight into the direct, individual connection each of the seven *Ushpizin* has to the *sukkah*. Second, it explains how the nature of the *sukkah* differs on each day of the Yom Tov because of the differing influences of these seven guests. This gives us a deeper and more penetrating insight into the holiness of the *sukkah*.

These insights and explanations are organized for the reader's easy access so those who would like to enhance their mitzvah of dwelling in the *sukkah* will be able to focus on the relevant *divrei Torah* for each day and each night. The nighttime *divrei Torah*

---

9. ...וליועצי שלום שמחה.

concentrate on each of the individual *Ushpizin*, and the daytime insights focus on the *Ushpizin's* connection to the *sukkah*.

As we have noted, each day we have the privilege of hosting all seven guests, but every day, a different one of them takes center stage.[10]

Seven Guests and the Seven Days of Creation

Let's start by exploring three questions:

---

10. Author's note: I would like to share a personal story of *siyata d'Shmaya* connected to this section of *Ushpizin*. Being a *rav* and *maggid shiur*, I often write during flights to visit my mother in Los Angeles. This section of the *sefer* was written as I returned from such a visit. While pondering how to explain the awe-inspiring concept of *Ushpizin*, I overheard a conversation on an airport shuttle.

Two people who had just met on this shuttle had traveled to Los Angeles from different cities to attend the same event. While at the event, one related that he noticed a photographer taking pictures of a cornered-off area behind him. When he asked why the area was separated, the photographer whispered that a certain celebrity had secretly entered after the lights dimmed and was sitting just feet away. The fellow shuttle passenger responded enthusiastically, "You sat near [the celebrity]? Wow! Amazing!"

I truly wondered why I needed to hear all of this. I had purposely gone to the back of the bus to get away from all the passengers; however, these two people sat down near me. Later, while preparing my *Daf Yomi* lecture on *Gittin* 19 on the plane, I realized why Hashem caused me to overhear this conversation.

The Gemara discusses whether a *get* is valid in languages besides Hebrew, and if secular court documents can be kosher if properly written. It relates how Rav Pappa validated a *get* by gathering information from two gentiles indirectly—using testimony they provided unknowingly. This is known as *meisi'ach l'fi tumo*. This mirrored my earlier experience! I overheard two people excitedly discussing being near a celebrity.

This coincidence illuminated the concept of *Ushpizin*—our spiritual *sukkah* guests. While incomparably greater than celebrities (*l'havdil elef alfei alafim*), if we truly sensed these holy visitors' presence, we'd be overwhelmed with joy. The shuttle passenger merely sat near a celebrity, but our *Ushpizin* come specifically to visit us! Though they are invisible to us, our *emunah* should help us appreciate being in the presence of these seven greatest Jews, elevating our *sukkah* experience. This timely conversation helped me better understand and explain the significance of the *Ushpizin*.

- Why were these *tzaddikim* chosen over others?
- Why seven?
- Why do all seven come to visit together every day?

In addition to what we learned earlier about the number seven as it relates to *shleimus*, this number has other connotations as well. One of the most common is the seven days of the week. In *Bereishis*, the Torah describes each day of creation as a distinct entity, different from the day before it and the day after it. On Day One, Hashem created light. On Day Two, He divided the waters, creating a separation that would eventually become heaven and earth. On Day Three, Hashem finished what He began on Day Two and revealed the earth as well as the grass and produce. On Day Four, Hashem created the sun, moon, and stars...and so on until the seventh day, when the Torah states that Hashem completed all creation. The seventh day synthesized the creations of all the previous days so that from that day forward, the universe would be perceived as one unified creation.

Seven Days, Seven *Middos*

On a deeper level, as we will see, each day's creation was a manifestation of a different one of the seven *middos*.[11] This correlation can be gleaned by analyzing the specific *perek* of *Tehillim* we recite for each day of the week.[12] The Gemara (*Rosh Hashanah* 31a) explains why each of these chapters of *Tehillim* was chosen for the particular day on which it is recited. This offers us greater insight into the *middah* that Hashem projected into His creation on that day.

The *perek* for the first day of creation is *Tehillim* 24, which begins with the words, *To Hashem is the earth and its entirety.* The Gemara

---

11. See Reb Tzadok Hakohen רסיסי לילה.

12. These were the hymns recited by the *levi'im* at the wine libation as it was poured onto the *Mizbei'ach*, accompanying the daily morning *Tamid* sacrifice. There was a different hymn for every day of the week.

explains that on the first day of creation, Hashem acquired the universe and bequeathed it to mankind. Therefore, in the words of our Sages, *The world is built on* chessed. The act of giving springs from the *middah* of *chessed* (kindness), which is the *middah* that Avraham represents.

On Day Two, we say *perek* 48, *Great is Hashem and exceedingly praised.* This is the day on which Hashem restrained the waters and separated them. The Gemara states that Hashem divided and separated the products of His actions and reigned over them. In doing so, He invested the world with the trait of *yirah* (awe), which springs from *gevurah* (strength)—the *middah* of Yitzchak.

On Day Three, we recite *perek* 82, *Hashem stands in the Divine assembly*. On this day in creation, Hashem revealed the dry land so that it could produce vegetation and host all the forms of life that live on dry land. Thus, He crowned the natural world with His glory, projecting *tiferes* (beauty)—the *middah* of Yaakov.

The correlation of the next three days of creation to the *middos* and the *tzaddikim* is a bit more complex. The first step in understanding these connections is to know that according to the midrash (*Bereishis Rabbah* 12:5), the first three *middos—chessed, gevurah*, and *tiferes*—are each parallel to the second three, which are *netzach, hod*, and *yesod*. This second set of days completes and perfects the first set. We see an exact mirror of this relationship in the connection between the first three days of creation and the second three. The midrash expounds: On the first day, Hashem created light; on the fourth day (the first of the second set of three days), He created the luminaries, the completion of light. On the second day, Hashem created the oceans by dividing the waters, and on the fifth day, He created fish, the completion of water. On the third day, Hashem created dry land; on the sixth day, He created man, who perfected dry land by bringing out its potential.

Returning to the *middos* of the *tzaddikim*, we can understand how they compare and contrast with each other as follows: The first three attributes describe a person's inner trait, while the second three describe how that trait expresses itself in interaction with others. In other words, *chessed* is an internal desire to give. *Gevurah* is inner restraint. *Tiferes* is an internal sense of balance between the first two traits. When we take these three inner traits and apply them to an interaction with someone in the outside world, we see the second three traits expressed. *Chessed* manifests itself as *netzach*; *gevurah* as *hod*; and *tiferes* as *yesod*. Let's spell out these connections.

Netzach: When someone bestows pure *chessed* upon another person, the recipient cannot resist it. The goodness is precisely what the recipient needs and therefore, any resistance he might have had is overpowered. *Netzach*, victory, is the condition engendered by *chessed*.

Hod: When someone receives *chessed*, his natural response is to pour out words of praise glorifying the giver. But the giver will not receive that praise unless he exercises *gevurah* by restraining himself from overwhelming the receiver with his acts of kindness, which would render the receiver unable to give praise. By exercising this restraint, the giver is glorified.[13]

Yesod: Like the inner balance characterized by *tiferes*, *yesod* is the balanced connection between the giver and the receiver, in which each feels that he is the true beneficiary of the interaction.

Let us now return to the song of each day:

On Day Four, we recite *perek* 94, which begins, *The G-d of vengeance is Hashem.* This is the day on which Hashem created the

---

13. As an analogy, we sometimes find ourselves in the presence of a person who does so much, he leaves us without the opportunity to thank him for all he does. We can feel overwhelmed by the giver (*netzach*). Therefore, the giver must exercise restraint and stop giving to allow us to recognize and thank him. That restraint that emanates from the *middah* of *gevurah* is the submissiveness found in the attribute of *hod*.

sun and the moon, and He will one day bring retribution to the nations that serve them. That ultimate victory over false gods expresses the *middah* of *netzach* (victory), which is associated with Moshe. This is because in giving the Torah to the Jewish people, his prophecy was so clear that it overpowered the resistance of all those who received it. They recognized Moshe's teachings as the ultimate *chessed* upon which their lives depended, and thus had no choice but to embrace it.

On Day Five, we recited *perek* 81, which begins, *Sing joyously to the G-d of our might.* The Gemara explains that this *perek* refers to the birds and fish that Hashem created on this day so that they would give praise to Him. Since this is a day of praise, it corresponds to the *middah* of *hod* (splendor) and is associated with Aharon. This is because the Torah commands Aharon, the *kohen gadol*, to dress in magnificent garments woven with gold thread and set with jewels to reflect the honor of his service in the Mishkan.

On Day Six, we say *perek* 93, beginning with *Hashem has reigned. He has clothed Himself in grandeur*. This expresses the *middah* of *yesod* (foundation), which connects to Yosef, who, as the viceroy to the king of Egypt, provided sustenance to the entire country, the region, and his family during the time of famine. He was thus the foundation upon which millions of lives depended.

Finally, on Shabbos, the day we welcome the Shabbos Queen, we recite *perek* 92, starting *A song, a hymn for Shabbos.* This day, corresponding to Dovid Hamelech, embodies the *middah* of *malchus* (royalty). Indeed, it is the day of the week on which Dovid was born.

Olam, Nefesh, Shanah

On an even deeper level, these seven days and their *middos*, which parallel the seven *middos* of the *Ushpizin*, can be understood through a concept known as *Olam, Nefesh, Shanah*. My *rebbi*, Rav

Moshe Shapiro *zt"l*, explained that every physical entity has a parallel in time (*shanah*), in a place (*olam*), and in the soul (*nefesh*). This means that everything we find in a human—for example, mouth, ears, nose, and eyes—is found in the context of time. There are months and days that represent eyes, ears, nose, and mouth. Each entity also exists conceptually as a place.

For example, he observed that just as a human being has a physical mouth, there exists a parallel, spiritual mouth in place and in time. We encounter the "place" manifestation of the mouth in *Sefer Bamidbar* when the earth opens its mouth to swallow Korach. In addition, the mouth exists in the framework of time. As we know, on Pesach—which our Sages say can be expressed as *peh sach* (the mouth that speaks)—we have a mitzvah to tell the story of the exodus and fully elaborate on the details. We open our mouths to relate the praises of Hashem at the Seder. This is the "mouth" of time. The parallels in *nefesh*, *olam*, and *shanah* also apply to the seven *middos* (*chessed, gevurah, tiferes, netzach, hod, yesod, and malchus*). In *shanah*, they are the seven days of the week as we designate them on the calendar—Sunday through Shabbos. In *nefesh* they are the seven *Ushpizin*, and in *olam* they are the world, as each day, at the time of creation, expressed a different *middah* (as discussed above). However, after the sin of the *Eitz Hada'as*, and Hashem's declaration that the earth was "cursed," the world was no longer naturally compatible with Hashem's presence. The *olam* of these *middos*—their "natural habitat"—became the *sukkah*.

Now we have an entirely new appreciation for our Sukkos guests. These invitees are not just paying a visit to our *sukkah*. Rather, they are providing us with a valuable service. The mitzvah of *sukkah* requires seven days (like the seven days of creation), yet these days are not identified as the days of the week—Sunday through Shabbos. Sukkos isn't bound by those seven days. Rather, the days of Sukkos are identified by the seven guests who visit the *sukkah*. Each of these *tzaddikim* served Hashem in a distinctive way,[14] with a *middah* so perfect that he was able to forge a unique connection of heaven to earth, and in doing so, to bring forth the *middah* of one of the days of creation. By embodying these *middos*, the *Ushpizin* connect us to the world before Adam's sin—a world like the Garden of Eden.

Together, the *Ushpizin* give new meaning to the seven-day cycle of life in this world. This is why there are seven *Ushpizin* and they are grouped together. Of course, there have been many other *tzaddikim*, but these seven comprise a group that is responsible for producing a unit of Divine influence that connects heaven and earth, the seven-day period known as Sukkos! These *Ushpizin* are much more than just guests; they give each day of Sukkos its own individual identity and spiritual power, linking back to the week of creation.

We can now have a greater appreciation of the *Ushpizin* as one entity. The mitzvah of *sukkah* is, as the Torah declares, *seven days to Hashem*, with each day distinct from the others.[15] Only together, however, do the days comprise an entire spectrum of holiness. Therefore, all the *Ushpizin* visit together.

Seven Kinds of *Sukkah*

With this understanding, we can perceive that each of the seven days of Sukkos has a different theme, determined by the attributes of that day's guest. In essence, we have seven different types of *sukkos*.[16] For example, on the first day, Avraham, whose *middah* is *chessed*, turns the *sukkah* into a place to perform *chessed*. On

---

14. Each of the *Ushpizin* fashioned and represented one of the seven *middos* of Hashem. This will be discussed as we progress to delve into the contribution of each guest.

15. Unlike Pesach, which is a seven-day Yom Tov, on which a full Hallel is not recited, on Sukkos the *korbanos* of each day are different, and the full Hallel is completed every day.

16. This concept parallels the seven weeks between Pesach and Shavuos, during which each week is defined not by the Sunday through Shabbos week, but rather

Yitzchak's day, the *sukkah* is a place of *gevurah*, where those who don't belong are kept outside the protective walls.[17] Yaakov's *sukkah* is a place of holiness, reflecting his connection to Hashem and Yerushalayim, the holy city. Likewise, each of the other *Ushpizin* imbue the *sukkah* with his special *middah* on his special day.

The United Form of Man

In addition to the seven *Ushpizin* providing a framework of time for the mitzvah of *sukkah*, they unite to create a force that unifies the *tzuras ha'adam*—the form of man, bringing it to a state of *shleimus*. This is a prerequisite for their connection to the mitzvah of *sukkah* because in order to be a guest in a place known as *Sukkas Shelomecha* (the *sukkah* of wholesomeness) one must be wholesome. Each of these *Ushpizin* possessed this virtue, and together, they unite to complete the spiritual form of man.

To understand why they all come together, we must delve into the origins of Hashem's relationship to our finite world. On a very basic level, since Hashem is infinite, He needed to create a channel through which He would interact with a finite world. This medium is known as the ten *sefiros*. These *sefiros* are divided into a group of three and a group of seven. The *Ushpizin* correspond to the group of seven.

The *sefiros* are Hashem's most basic mode of creative power, and since Hashem created man in His image, the human being encompasses these attributes.

However, Adam's sin distorted the *tzuras ha'adam*, which necessitated repair. The seven *Ushpizin*, each through his own *middah*, accomplished this repair. Each added his own step in the process until together (as they are when they visit the *sukkah*),

---

by the *middah* of the week: For example, there is a week of *chessed*, a week of *gevurah*, and so forth.

17. This will be discussed on Day Two, when Yitzchak is the preeminent guest.

they re-established the complete *tzuras ha'adam*. Rav Tzadok Hakohen writes that these seven *tzaddikim* caused these seven attributes to become a reality within Klal Yisrael, and thus fashioned our nation.

Let us now explore each of the guest's specific attributes as he makes his presence known in our *sukkah* during our festive meals.

Day One: Welcoming Avraham (Nighttime)

Avraham connects to the *sukkah* on several levels. According to the midrash, the Clouds of Glory that we celebrate on Sukkos were provided to us in his merit. At the beginning of *Parshas Vayeira*, Avraham is visited by three angels who take on the form of traveling Arabs. Avraham offers them food, drink, and shelter under a tree. The midrash states that in return for Avraham's hospitality, Hashem provided the Jewish people with the *mann* to eat, the well of Miriam for water, and the Clouds of Glory for shelter. Avraham's three acts of kindness were "paid forward" to his children hundreds of years later. In a sense, Avraham was the first to create a place of shade to protect his guests when they came to visit him. Therefore, he is a most appropriate guest in the *sukkah*. His deed catalyzed the miracle of the Clouds, which is one of the main reasons we are sitting in the shade of our *s'chach*.

Day One: Avraham's Kindness and His *Sukkah* (Daytime)

On a slightly deeper level, Avraham's connection to the mitzvah of *sukkah* is based on his spiritual accomplishment of kindness. He reached a level of *shleimus* by providing for others in a way that gave him renown as the pillar of *chessed* in the world. As we say in our daily prayers: *Give truth to Yaakov and* chessed *to Avraham.* As we see from the story of his hospitality to the angels, he reached so lofty a level in his *chessed* that he was even providing for those who had come down from heaven. Although as spiritual creatures they did not need food, once they took on human characteristics, they had human needs, and only Avraham had the *shleimus* required to be worthy of serving those needs.

The source for this idea can be found in Hashem's commandment to Avraham to perform *bris milah*: *Go before Me and be complete.* Hashem was telling Avraham that the *bris* would provide him with *shleimus*, which would enable him to be a *mashpia*—a source of giving—like Hashem. Thus, Avraham becomes a source for not only those in the world below, but even for those from the world above. In this mode, he provides shade for the angels; he created a *sukkah* with his *middah* of *chessed.*

His ability to do this came from the level of completeness he achieved through *bris milah.* Once he had performed that mitzvah, Hashem gave him a new name, changing Avram to Avraham. The *gematria* of Avraham—248—is the number of all the positive commandments, as well as the number of bones in the body. Avraham's new name embodies his new identity as a complete person.

Furthermore, his name means the "father of nations," signifying the vast expansion of his role in the world. He was no longer the founder of a local tribe but rather, he became the father of the nations of the world, the "giver"—the *mashpia*—to all. Our connection to the *sukkah* through Avraham is based on this role. It reflects Avraham's *shleimus*, and he therefore dwells with us in the *sukkas shelomecha.*

This idea of *shleimus* is particularly relevant for every one of us at this time of year. As we discussed earlier, the proximity of Sukkos to Rosh Hashanah and Yom Kippur brings us into the *sukkah* in our most wholesome state. Although we are far from the saintliness of our patriarchs, feeling cleansed and free of sin as we do after the Yamim Nora'im enables us to relate to them, at least on our level. To the extent that *we* are on the three levels of security/sharing/wholesomeness inherent in this season (see earlier in this section, "Living with Hashem"), *we* merit the presence of Avraham, the founder of *shleimus*, as well as all the *Ushpizin* who accompany him.

Day Two: Welcoming Yitzchak (Nighttime)

On the second night of Sukkos, we welcome our forefather Yitzchak, who possesses a multifaceted connection to the *sukkah*. The first of these correlations relates to Yitzchak's name, which means laughter. The Torah relates that when Avraham heard from Hashem that he would be having a son with Sarah, *Avraham fell on his face and laughed* (yitzchak) (*Bereishis* 17:17). Based on this reaction, Hashem told Avraham, *You shall call him Yitzchak*.

Sarah had a similar reaction when she overheard the *malach* giving Avraham the news. *And Sarah laughed within herself.* On the surface, this would seem to be a natural reaction from someone who has been childless for decades, for whom nothing short of a miracle could bring about the birth of a child. Yet there seems to be much more than simple joy in Sarah's gleeful expressiveness because the Torah makes a "big deal" about her reaction.

The *pasuk* explains her laughter by relating her thoughts: *After I have withered shall I again have delicate skin? And my husband is old!* Hashem disapproved of this reaction:

> *Then Hashem said to Avraham, "Why did Sarah laugh, saying 'Shall I in truth bear a child though I have aged?'" Is anything beyond Hashem? Sarah denied it, saying "I did not laugh," for she was frightened. But he [Avraham] said, "No, indeed you laughed."*

This whole episode is puzzling. Why does Hashem focus on Sarah's laughter? We see right away that it is an issue because when Avraham accuses Sarah of inappropriate laughter, she denies it. This too is problematic, for it certainly isn't appropriate for Sarah to lie. The episode concludes with Avraham telling Sarah, "No, indeed you laughed," to which Sarah offers no response. We learn from the Talmud that "Silence is like an admission." Therefore,

Sarah's lack of response seems to affirm Avraham's claim. What was wrong with Sarah's response and what is the Torah teaching us through this episode?

We can arrive at an answer by focusing on several interrelated points:

- The essence of laughter
- Yitzchak's name
- Avraham and Sarah's respective responses to the prophetic knowledge that they were going to have a child
- Yitzchak's connection to laughter

Good and Bad Laughter

Laughter is a powerful expression of emotion, both the positive and the negative. On the positive side, laughter can be very therapeutic, relieving a person of stress and defusing tense situations. At times, laughter expresses amusement. It reveals that a person feels happy, satisfied, and in "a good place." However, laughter can also be a sign of doubtfulness and disbelief. Worse yet, it can be evil, for it can be used as a form of mockery or even an expression of haughty superiority. We find all these types of laughter in the Torah.

The negative laughter appears in *Bereishis* when the cities of Sodom and Amorah are about to be destroyed and Hashem sends angels to extract Lot and his family. The angels allow Lot to gather his family before the disaster strikes. Lot approaches his sons-in-law, requesting that they leave the city with him, "before it is too late." Their response, says the Torah, was, *And he [Lot] seemed like a jester in the eyes of his sons-in-law.* They mocked him and discredited his efforts by laughing at him. This is one example of negative laughter.

On the other hand, we find a beautiful expression of

positive laughter in *Shir Hama'alos*, which captures the elation that will be ours in the times of Mashiach, when we will finally be able to laugh with a full heart: *When Hashem will return the captivity of Tzion, we will be like dreamers. Then our mouths will be filled with laughter and our tongues with glad song.*

We see that laughter is the perfect response to remarkable and potentially uplifting news. Such news gives the listener the opportunity to either believe and be elevated or be doubtful and remain lowly and unaffected. Furthermore, if the source of the information is Hashem, a person's response is a test of his faith.

This is indeed what happened the first time Hashem informed Avraham that he would merit having children. As the Torah relates (*Bereishis* 15:3): *And Avram said, "You have not given me children." Hashem took him outside and told him, "Gaze toward the Heavens and count the stars, if you can count them. So shall your offspring be!" And Avram trusted Hashem, and Hashem considered it as righteousness.* Avraham's response demonstrates the positive attitude that uplifts the listener who accepts and believes in Hashem's promise of the future.

Now let us return to Avraham's and Sarah's respective reactions to the news that they would become parents.

Laughter and Belief

When Hashem first told Avraham that he and Sarah would have a son, Avraham had already fathered Yishmael. This fulfilled Hashem's promise that Avraham's own offspring, not that of his servant Eliezer, would inherit all his blessings. Nevertheless, at the time of Avraham's *bris milah*, Hashem promised him another son, this time with Sarah. With complete faith in Hashem's words, Avraham became elated and laughed with joy. Immediately thereafter, Hashem told Avraham to name the child Yitzchak, which means laughter. The name was a salute to the complete faith Avraham's laughter represented, which was the level of faith Hashem expected from him; it was essential if Avraham was to merit the promised miracle. Having spurred this response from Avraham, Hashem then turned to Sarah, the other half of the equation.

Sarah had received the news by overhearing the words of the angels Hashem sent to Avraham at the beginning of the *parshah*. The Ramban explains that Sarah had no idea that these guests were heaven-sent.[18] She was inside the tent and hadn't seen them. When she overheard one of them saying that she would have a child in a year, she laughed at the news in disbelief.

In her defense, she obviously didn't know that this was a message from Hashem, for had she known, she would have received the information differently. However, Hashem still expected a better response from Sarah.[19] She should have considered that maybe this was indeed a message from above, for *Is the hand of Hashem limited?* Hashem informed Avraham of Sarah's response because He wanted Avraham to know that Sarah needed to move up to his level of *emunah* regarding the promise of a son. Avraham therefore sought to inform Sarah that her type of laughter was inappropriate. But why indeed was this an issue?

---

18. See Ramban *ad loc.*

19. הקדוש ברוך הוא מדקדק אם הצדיקים כחוט השערה—*The Almighty expects much more from the righteous than He expects from ordinary people.*

Yitzchak and Sukkos

Many people are blessed with children as soon as they are ready to start the next generation. For some, however, the process is not simple. At times, it can require years of prayers and medical intervention, and even then, there can be a long road ahead until they merit to conceive and have a child. So it was with Avraham and Sarah; neither could have children. Regarding Sarah, the Torah states, *And Sarai was barren; she had no child.*

The Gemara (*Yevamos* 64) expounds on this *pasuk*, asking why it must state both that she was barren and that she had no children. Surely, a barren woman has no children. The Gemara explains that "barren" refers to her physical inability to have children, for she was born without a womb. In short, in their natural state, Avraham and Sarah had no possibility of having children.

The Miracle of Yitzchak

According to the midrash, when Hashem told Avraham to step "outside" and count the stars, he was not referring solely to the outdoors. Rather, Hashem asked Avraham to step outside the realm of reason and nature, thereby informing him that his children would transcend the physical world. This was a *sukkah* type of experience. The birth of Yitzchak required Avraham and Sarah to reach a level of belief that surpassed all boundaries of this world. They had to find it within themselves to feel joy in Hashem's promise before they had seen any sign of fulfillment, feeling with certainty that a child was on the way although they had not yet conceived him. They needed to achieve this despite decades of proof to the contrary. That was the state of belief Hashem required and they ultimately reached.

Yitzchak's name expresses that faith. Because Avraham accepted the good news with laughter (which in the *pasuk* is written *yitzchak*), and Hashem then told Avraham to call his son Yitzchak, we understand that it was through Avraham's *emunah* in Hashem's ability to do the impossible that he would merit such a child.

And that is the basis of Yitzchak's unique connection to Sukkos. When we leave our homes and enter the *sukkah*, we are leaving the organized and scheduled world to dwell in a flimsy, insecure hut. This is much more than a physical mitzvah; it is an attitude of detaching from the world's limitations. Like Avraham when he went "outside" to see the stars that represented his progeny, we too go "out of this world" when we enter the *sukkah*.

It is appropriate that Yitzchak visits us in the *sukkah*, for the *sukkah* experience matches his personal beginning. With this understanding, we gain greater appreciation for the *Zohar's* name for the *sukkah* as "the shade of belief." Through Avraham's deep belief in Hashem, the Jewish nation was born. This is the association of Yitzchak and the *sukkah* that is based on his name.[20]

There is yet another level of connection between Yitzchak and the *sukkah*, and that is based on the walls

---

20. The happiness of Sukkos, which is identified as *z'man simchaseinu*, has many meanings. According to this perspective (the long-awaited birth of Yitzchak), it is similar to the future happiness of the redemption for which we yearn when saying the *Shir Hama'alos* before *Birkas Hamazon*: אז ימלא שחוק פינו—*laughter will fill our mouth*.

of the *sukkah*. Just as halachah specifies that a *sukkah* must have a roof, it dictates that there be walls around the *sukkah*. A *chuppah*-like structure with the *s'chach* supported by four poles does not qualify as a *sukkah*. How many walls are required, according to the Gemara (*Sukkah* p. 6), is derived from the number of times the Torah says the word *sukkah* in the *pesukim* commanding the mitzvah. Thus, a *sukkah* is defined both by its unique roof—the *s'chach*—and its walls.

These two components of the *sukkah* reflect the distinct paths through which our *Avos* served Hashem. As we have explained, the *s'chach* is in the merit of Avraham's *chessed*, which is exemplified by his exertion to offer shade and refreshment to the *malachim* posing as desert travelers. The walls are in the merit of Yitzchak, reflecting the *middah* of *gevurah* with which he served Hashem. More insight into the role of *gevurah* and walls can be gleaned by examining the Jewish people's experience at Har Sinai.

Day Two: *Choshech, Anan V'arafel*[21] (Daytime)

The standard and most basic definition of the word *sukkah* is something constructed "to cover and create shade" as it is defined in the verse,[22] *And the* sukkah *shall be for a shade of the day.* However, it is clear that the word *sukkah* also means to "separate between two places." The use of the word *sukkah* to mean walls is certainly supported by the fact that the Jewish people had clouds above and below as well as on all four sides, providing them protection from all directions.

The source of the *sukkah* as a place of separation is found in the

21. ותקרבון ותעמדון תחת ההר וההר בוער באש עד לב השמים חושך ענן וערפל.

22. וסוכה תהיה לצל יומם.

Torah's account of the revelation at Har Sinai. The Torah states, *And you approached and stood at the foot of the mountain and the mountain was burning with fire up to the heart of heaven, darkness, cloud, and thick cloud.*

This verse describes the barrier that Hashem set up between Himself and the Jewish people as they stood at Har Sinai, ready to accept the Torah. But how does this image fit that of the *sukkah* as a place of light and shelter?[23]

In reality, the protection the *sukkah* provides is identical to the protection the clouds and darkness provided at Har Sinai. The *sukkah* keeps us safe by creating a barrier that keeps away all negative influences. As we mentioned, the *sukkah* is a place of refuge from the Satan.

Mechitzah

Chazal refer to a wall or barrier as a *mechitzah*. The purpose of a *mechitzah* is to separate two sides, just as the *mechitzah* in a shul separates the men's section from the women's section. The *mechitzah* function of the *sukkah* is to provide a barrier against all that needs to remain outside its holy interior; thus, the walls make the *sukkah* a place of both light and protection. This precisely reflects the purpose of the cloud barrier Hashem created between Himself and the people at Har Sinai.

The same concept emerged when the Jewish people sinned and the Beis Hamikdash was destroyed. In *Megillas Eichah*,[24] Yirmiyahu laments, "You have enveloped (סַכֹּתָה—*sakosah*) yourself in a cloud that no prayer can pierce." Here again, we see the usage of

---

23. See "The *Sukkah*: A Place of Refuge" in Chapter 2.

24. סכתה באף ותרדפנו הרגת לא חמלת.

sukkah as a cloud that forms a barrier, this time in a way that is detrimental to the Jewish people. Nevertheless, whether as protection or barrier, in the *sukkah's* role as a *mechitzah*, it functions only in relation to the Jewish people. Even when the clouds protected us in the desert, the Bnei Yisrael alone dwelled on the inside. The *erev rav* remained outside.

Yitzchak and the *Sukkah* as a *Mechitzah*

The *sukkah's* function as a *mechitzah* is an expression of the trait called *gevurah* or *middas hadin*, which is identified with Yitzchak.[25] We can understand that Avraham, who hosted travelers in his tent (see Day One), created the shade of the *sukkah*, while Yitzchak provided the walls.

On a deeper level, we find this connection of *mechitzah* in the structure of the word *sukkah*: *samech-vav-kaf-hei*. Let's make the connection by returning briefly to a *gematria* we learned earlier for *sukkah*. The numerical value of the letters, which is 91, equals the value of two names of Hashem: The *Shem Adnus—Adonai*—is 65, and the *Shem Havayah—Yud-hei-vav-hei*—is 26. In the word *sukkah*, the outside letters (*samech-hei*) equal 65, and the inside two letters (*kaf-vav*) equal 26. These two Names of Hashem represent two different ways in which Hashem interacts with us: *Yud-hei-vav-hei* indicates His attribute of love, while *Adonai*, which means "my Master," signifies our submissive relationship with Hashem, characterized by awe and fear.

These are fused together in the *sukkah*, creating a

25. For an elaboration of the seven *middos* and how they connect to the seven guests, see introduction to *Ushpizin*.

coexistence of love, protection, and light for those on the inside, with darkness and separation for those on the outside. This explains the usage of *sukkah* in *Megillas Eichah* when the Jewish people were outside the cloud in which Hashem had enveloped Himself.

This balance and fusion of the two opposite forces is Yitzchak's attribute. His relationship with Hashem was based on knowing how to draw very close to Him while still keeping a respectful distance. The ability to respect boundaries and thrive within them defines the *middah* of *gevurah*. This is Yitzchak's personal connection to our *sukkah*; it is therefore appropriate that he is the preeminent guest on Day Two.

The *Sukkah*: An Admission Test for the World to Come

This perspective offers a new appreciation of the Gemara (*Avodah Zarah*) we learned earlier about the nations of the world asking Hashem for an opportunity to earn a portion in the World to Come. He tested them by giving them the mitzvah of *sukkah* on a brutally hot day, and they failed the test. Although they were permitted according to halachah to leave the *sukkah* because it became uncomfortable, they went one step further and kicked the *sukkah* on the way out. The *Talmud Yerushalmi* states that in this scenario, the *sukkah* itself filtered out those who were unworthy to dwell in it. The devotion and complete submissiveness to Hashem that Yitzchak had built within himself was a prerequisite for belonging within the *sukkah's* walls. This necessary commitment is beyond the ability of the nations. By proving themselves unworthy of the *sukkah*, they prove themselves inherently unworthy of a portion in the World to Come.

The Laughter of Yishmael

We return now to the subject of laughter, this time through the prism of the *sukkah's* role as a filter that removes those who do not belong within. There is a type of laughter, which we discussed earlier, that marks a person as one who is disconnected from Hashem. It was this type of laughter, exhibited by Yishmael, that "filtered him out" of Avraham's spiritual legacy and gave Yitzchak the status of Avraham's only child.

As the Torah (*Bereishis* 21:9-10) relates, *And Sarah saw the son of Hagar [Yishmael]... whom she had borne to Avraham, laughing* (metzacheik), *and Sarah said to Avraham, "Drive out this maid and her son, for the maid's son will not inherit with my son, with Yitzchak."*

What was so wrong with Yishmael's laughter that it demanded banishment? Rashi explains with a midrash that cites a similar type of laughter. This occurred when the Jewish people finished making the Golden Calf, and as the Torah (*Shemos* 32:6) relates, *They arose early the next day and offered elevation offerings and peace offerings. The people sat to eat and drink and then got up to enjoy* (l'tzacheik).

The Sages explain that the expression of *l'tzacheik* after serving the Golden Calf was no laughing matter. Rather, it is the Torah's description of how the Jewish people had transgressed through idolatry. Their laughter was a mockery of everything Bnei Yisrael stood for. Likewise, this same kind of mockery was at the heart of the laughter Sarah saw coming from Yishmael. He demonstrated that he had become too corrupt to have a place in the house of Avraham and that he could have no role in the future of the Jewish people.

It is no coincidence that the term used is *metzacheik* (which begins with the letter *mem*). The letter *mem* in the Hebrew language expresses the idea of being "removed" or "taken from." Because of his derisive laughter, Yishmael is no longer a part of the lineage of Avraham, which is defined by Yitzchak, who is named for laughter that rejoices in Hashem.

Day Three: Welcoming Yaakov (Nighttime)

Yaakov's connection to the *sukkah* is one of the clearest among all the *Ushpizin*, as it is mentioned explicitly in *Parshas Vayishlach*. The Torah (*Bereishis* 33:17) relates, *And Yaakov journeyed to Sukkos and built himself a house, and for his livestock he made booths* (sukkos). *He called the name of the place Sukkos.*

We see that Yaakov built both houses and booths, and yet he named the location only for the booths. Furthermore, Yaakov placed all his livestock in the *sukkos* rather than just fencing off an area and building a corral for the animals. Clearly, Yaakov has a unique connection to the *sukkah*. Understanding this connection reveals both the holiness of the *sukkah* and Yaakov's spiritual achievements, specifically at this stage of his life.

The *Sukkah* Yaakov Built

The next verse in the Torah (*Bereishis* 33:18) states, *And Yaakov arrived complete.* Rashi quotes the Gemara (*Shabbos* 33b) which explains that the word complete means that Yaakov was intact in all aspects of life: his physical body, his wealth, and his Torah.

It would seem that Yaakov's arrival in Sukkos is the end of the story of his struggles with his brother Eisav. However, the next *pasuk*, *And Yaakov arrived complete*, begins with the letter *vav*, meaning "and," which implies that the *pasuk* is connected to the previous one. Yaakov has successfully evaded Eisav and arrived "complete" at the outskirts of Shechem. A new chapter of his life has seemingly begun, and yet there is the *vav*—the "and," which connects the two statements.

In light of this connection, we would read the verse as, *And Yaakov journeyed to Sukkos and built himself a house, and for his livestock he made* sukkos. *He called the name of the place Sukkos* ***and*** *Yaakov arrived complete* (shalem). This indicates that his completeness—*shleimus*—was a prominent factor in his naming the location Sukkos and placing his possessions in those *sukkos*. What is the connection between the *sukkah* and Yaakov's *shleimus*?

The answer can be found by acquiring a new understanding of the holiness of the *sukkah*. This is derived from a *Zohar* that quotes a *pasuk* in *Tehillim* (76:3): *And in Shalem was His* sukkah *and His dwelling place in Tzion.*

Shalem: The Original Yerushalayim

The midrash on *Tehillim* explains this *pasuk* with the following lesson from Rav Brachya: "From the beginning of the creation of the world, Hashem made a *sukkah*, placing it in Yerushalayim. And there He would pray, saying, 'May it be My will that My children should do My will, so I should not destroy My house in My Temple.'" The midrash goes on to explain that the original name of Yerushalayim was Shalem, which was given to it by Shem, Noach's son. When Avraham went to sacrifice his son Yitzchak, Avraham prayed to Hashem saying, "*B'har Hashem yeira'eh*—May Your presence, Hashem, be seen on this mountain." To honor both Shem and Avraham, Hashem combined the two names, *er'eh* (be seen) and Shalem, creating the name Yerushalayim. Thus, Shalem in the *pasuk* from *Tehillim* refers to Yerushalayim; it is the place of the Beis Hamikdash.

The *Zohar* tells us that this *pasuk* refers to a *sukkah*, thus connecting the place Shalem to Yaakov's achievement of *shleimus*. This *Zohar* informs us that by building the *sukkos* and calling the name of this place Sukkos, Yaakov didn't just build a shelter for all his possessions. Rather, he brought all his life's accomplishments to a *sukkah* that was a prototype of Yerushalayim, a temporary dwelling place where Hashem is found. This was the achievement of his *shleimus*.

Yaakov's *Shleimus*

As we mentioned, Rashi quotes the Gemara (*Shabbos* 33b), which explains that the word "complete" means that Yaakov was intact in all aspects of life: his physical body, his wealth, and his Torah. Elaborating on this, the Maharal says that Yaakov was completely loyal to Hashem, never wavering from his belief that Hashem had watched over all these aspects of his life. This was the key to Yaakov's completeness because these three parts of a person—body, wealth, and Torah—are those which we dedicate to Hashem as we recite, in the Shema, that we must love Hashem *b'chol levavcha, u'v'chol nafshicha, u'v'chol me'odecha*—"with all your heart, with all your soul, and with all your resources."

Further, says the Maharal, a person who serves Hashem with all these aspects of himself is considered completely devoted to Him. Since the Torah informs us that Yaakov was complete in all these categories, we understand that Yaakov had perfected himself not only with his heart and soul, but with all his resources. He had achieved a level of righteousness so perfect that the Torah testifies to this wholesomeness. Not only was Yaakov complete, but all his possessions were elevated to the level of wholesomeness attained by their owner. This is *shleimus*!

The midrash says that Yaakov did not leave this world before seeing 600,000 of his descendants. Yaakov's accomplishments were the *shleimus* needed for the foundation of the entire Jewish nation. This wholeness culminates when there is a nation descended from him that expresses his achievements. The qualities of Yaakov, who journeyed from his parents' house and single-handedly created a wholesome family amid the most immoral and dishonest surroundings in the world, who fought with the Angel and was rewarded with the name Yisrael, were now shared by every one of his descendants. He created the identity of all children who are called Bnei Yisrael.

At this stage of his life, after successfully surviving his encounters both with his father-in-law Lavan and his brother Eisav, Yaakov needed a place to safeguard all that he had created. Where could he find this impermeable place?

The answer is in *sukkos*!

Shalom and *Sukkah*

Through the lens of this *pasuk* in *Tehillim*, the *Zohar* views the Torah's description of Yaakov as *shaleim* (complete and spiritually whole) as a testimony to his success in his life's mission to establish the foundation of the Jewish people. Throughout his encounters with Lavan and his brother Eisav, Yaakov maintained his connection to Hashem, an achievement worthy of bringing the *Shechinah* into his life. Yaakov had reached the level of wholeness that Hashem required from him.

The memorialization of this accomplishment is described in the Torah as *sukkos*. As it says, *Yaakov established for his belongings* sukkos. By passing his tests,[26] Yaakov reached a state of *shleimus* that was embodied in the *sukkah*.

Day Three: The Tent of Yaakov (Daytime)

The Torah exclaims, *How great are your tents, Yaakov!* One of the names for the *sukkah* is *ohel*, which means a tent. The connection between a tent and a *sukkah* is quite simple, since both structures are temporary. They are both the type of "flimsy structure" the Torah requires a *sukkah* to be. But what is the connection to Yaakov?

The answer is found in a midrash on *Parshas Toldos*, which is quoted by Rashi. On the *pasuk*, *and the children crushed [struggled] within her*, Rashi explains that Yaakov and Eisav were struggling with one another in their mother's womb, fighting over the inheritance of this world and the world to come. While Yaakov wanted the next world, Eisav desired this world. From Yaakov's perspective, this world was a transient existence, a waystation that a person enters with the intention to exit. To Eisav, however, this world held everything he wanted, and the next world was of no concern.

This World and the Next World

During Sukkos, the choice that Yaakov made while still within his mother's womb becomes our reality. We often pass through our house to enter the *sukkah*. This creates a sense that this world and all its belongings are merely an entry hall into the *sukkah*, a place beyond this world. The *sukkah* is not only a mitzvah; it is a

26. The Gemara (*Sanhedrin* 107a) states that Yaakov was tested by Hashem and passed the test.

recognition of what this world really is, a chance to see our life through the pristine lens of Yaakov at the very inception of his life.

We can now build on the theme we have developed over the previous two days of Sukkos, with each forefather—through his preeminent *middah*—supplying a component of the *sukkah*. Avraham, through his *chessed*, provides the shade of the *sukkah*. Yitzchak, through his *middah* of *gevurah*, provides the walls. However, we have yet to define what type of structure is being built. What function is it meant to fulfill? That is Yaakov's contribution. Through his trait of *shleimus*, he defines the *sukkah* as a space in which we, in our state of completeness, dwell securely and contentedly with Hashem: *Ma tovu ohalecha Yaakov!*

Day Four: Welcoming Moshe (Nighttime)

Moshe Rabbeinu, our next guest, seems to appear out of order. Chronologically, Yosef should follow Yaakov.[27] Even if there is a reason to skip to Yosef's generation at this point, Aharon, the elder brother, would seem to be the most appropriate choice. Why does Moshe "skip the line" and announce himself on Day Four?

The reason for the order of the *Ushpizin* is that it follows the order of the seven *sefiros*,[28] each of which is exemplified by one of these illustrious guests. We learn of these *sefiros* from Dovid Hamelech, who lists them in the *tefillah* of *Va'yevarech Dovid*, which we say each morning in *Pesukei D'zimrah*:

---

27. According to some traditions, the seven guests appear in chronological order with Yosef following Yaakov, then Aharon, Moshe, and Dovid.

28. The same order is found during the seven weeks between Pesach and Shavuos as mentioned in the *tefillah* of *Ribono Shel Olam* said after *sefiras ha'omer*.

Yours Hashem is the greatness (hagedulah), *the strength* (hagevurah), *the splendor* (hatiferes), *the triumph* (ha'netzach), *and the glory* (ha'hod), *even everything in heaven and earth* (yesod).[29] *Yours, Hashem, is the Kingdom* (ha'mamlachah) *and the sovereignty over every leader* (malchus).

The seven guests correspond to these seven attributes:

Avraham brings out the greatness of Hashem; Yitzchak exemplifies His strength; and Yaakov reflects His splendor. *Netzach*—triumph—corresponds to Moshe Rabbeinu who taught the people of the world to conduct themselves with recognition of man's obligation to his Creator. *Hod*, which can be translated as glory or gratitude, is embodied in Aharon Hakohen (see the *dvar Torah* for Day Five below for explanation). Yosef corresponds to *yesod* (see Day Six), and Dovid Hamelech, the eternal King of Israel, represents *mamlachah*—kingship.

So That You Should Know

The Torah instructs us to fulfill the mitzvah of *sukkah*, *So that your generations will* know *that I caused the children of Israel to dwell in booths when I took them out of the land of Egypt. I am Hashem your G-d.* The key word here is *knowledge*; the Jewish people were commanded to not *merely remember* the booths and the clouds that their ancestors experienced in the desert, but rather to know about them; *to know* means to forge a live emotional connection to the mitzvah of *sukkah*, reliving the experience.

To fulfill this commandment, someone had to impart this knowledge to the people. That is where Moshe Rabbeinu takes center stage. He is the *rebbi*, the teacher

---

29. The *middah* of *yesod* is the attribute that connects heaven to earth. Therefore, it is referred to in the verse as, *Everything in heaven and earth.*

of all Jews, universally known as Rabbeinu, our (personal) teacher.

Moshe Rabbeinu

The *mekubalim* inform us that the role of the *Avos* in relation to Moshe is similar to the model of *derech eretz* in relation to Torah. *Derech eretz* means conducting ourselves properly, and it is a prerequisite to the study of Torah, as reflected in the verse, *Derech eretz kadmah l'Torah*. This model of refined behavior was the accomplishment of our *Avos* and *Imahos*. They fashioned the Jewish people's nature.[30] Once this was done, the nation was prepared to absorb the wealth of knowledge of Hashem and His Torah. Teaching this knowledge is the crucial role of Moshe.[31] This is why Moshe follows the *Avos* in the roster of *Ushpizin*. Simply stated, the *Avos* created a nation that *could* connect to Hashem, and Moshe made that connection.

The *Rebbi* Is Also a Father

A *rebbi* is a teacher; he imparts knowledge to his students. But in a sense, a teacher is like a father, for both figures are a source of life for the child. The father gives the child physical life and sustains him as he grows to adulthood. He equips the child to live his life in this world and profoundly influences how the child will live it. The teacher too exerts tremendous influence on how his students will live.

---

30. The Maharal explains that the attributes that describe the Jewish people as רחמנים ביישנים וגמלי חסדים (merciful, humble, and of a giving nature) are the three attributes of the *Avos*: Avraham, גמלי חסדים; Yitzchak, ביישנים; and Yaakov, רחמנים.

31. We see a similar pattern in the blessings of the *Shemoneh Esrei*. The first three blessings represent Avraham, Yitzchak, and Yaakov. The fourth blessing is the request for knowledge, and that is the realm of Moshe Rabbeinu.

Further, the Gemara[32] states that there is one way in which a *rebbi's* role exceeds that of the biological father; the father brings a person into this world to live a finite life, while the teacher gives him what he needs to merit a place in the Next World so that he can live on for eternity. It is precisely for this reason that Moshe comes immediately after the *Avos* in the order of the *Ushpizin*. Because of his role in giving the Jewish people the knowledge to earn eternal life, he is honored together with the fathers.

Day Four: Experiencing *Hashgachah Pratis* (Daytime)

Now that we have established Moshe as the "Father of Knowledge," let us connect this to the *sukkah*.

The Knowledge of the *Sukkah*

As we mentioned, the commandment of *sukkah* is unique in that we don't just remember the event (as we are told with the mitzvah of *tzitzis* to *remember* the exodus). Rather, we need to internalize this mitzvah, *So that your generations will know that I caused the children of Israel to dwell in the booths when I took them out from the land of Egypt. I am Hashem your G-d.*[33]

The key message is "I am Hashem." In some way, our performance of this mitzvah teaches us the knowledge of Hashem. Therefore, the *sukkah* itself

---

32. *Bava Metzia* 33a.

33. By way of example, although we declare on the Seder night of Passover that "one must see himself as though he has left Egypt," there is certainly no need to go back to Egypt to fulfill this order; rather one can fulfill this in the privacy of his own home for the declaration is "as though," meaning it is a state of mind. On Sukkos, however, we are responsible to physically leave our homes and live in the *sukkah*. There are no shortcuts. This is the practical meaning of **knowing** how the Jews lived in tents when they left Egypt.

performs the role of Moshe Rabbeinu, as we will now see.

The *Emunah* of *Hashgachah Pratis*

Hashgachah pratis means that Hashem is intimately involved in our daily lives. We experience this by recognizing how Hashem leads us on our path, opens certain doors for us, and arranges certain encounters and "coincidences" that create the story of our lives. As we learned in Chapter One,[34] the three *regalim* form the foundation of our connection to Hashem, and especially on Sukkos, we celebrate our *emunah* that Hashem is involved in every part of our lives. How do we achieve this faith? **By living it!**

When we leave our homes and spend a week outside in the *sukkah*, we are meant to feel that we are entirely in His hands. Indeed, in the desert, the Jewish people had no choice but to completely rely on Hashem. To achieve this *emunah*, we need to relive the experience of the *sukkah*. In the *sukkah* we are learning the knowledge of Hashem, and therefore, Moshe Rabbeinu receives a place of honor.

---

34. See Chapter 1, "The Three *Regalim*."

Day Five: Welcoming Aharon (Nighttime)

The Torah states, *All citizens should sit in the* sukkah.[35] The Gemara derives from this that the whole nation should be united in one *sukkah*. The problem arises when there is a lack of unity. How will the Jewish people be able to reconcile their differences?

Welcome Aharon Hakohen!

Aharon is characterized in the mishnah as one who "loves peace and pursues peace." The Midrash relates that whenever Aharon saw two people in conflict, he took it upon himself to try to restore peace between them. He accomplished this by bending the truth. Aharon would approach one party and tell him that the other party was distressed by the rift. If that bit of information elicited a positive response, he would go to the second party and tell him the same thing. Because Aharon was a man of stature, the adversaries would readily believe him, and when they met again, their hearts would be softened toward each other. They would then be able to reconcile their differences.

Peace among the Jewish people creates an environment that draws the *Shechinah* into this world. As we have mentioned in the previous chapters regarding Clouds of Glory, Hashem manifests His presence through clouds. Hence, the clouds surrounding the Jewish people testified to their spiritual bond with each other, a blissful relationship that merited Hashem's presence.

Through his ardent pursuit of peace among the Jewish people, Aharon set the stage for the Clouds of Glory, the manifestation of the *Shechinah*, to descend. Peace among the Jewish people is an integral part of the mitzvah of *sukkah*; the Torah commands that *Every native in Israel shall dwell in booths*, meaning that the *sukkah* should serve as a place in which everyone is gathered

---

35. כל האזרח בישראל ישבו בסוכות.

together. Without peace—without Aharon—this would not be possible.

Day Five: Aharon and the *Middah* of *Hod* (Daytime)

The Rambam (*Hilchos Chanukah, Perek* 3, *Halachah* 12) makes what at first seems like a cryptic connection between Aharon and the recital of the Hallel. He writes that the custom in the days of the early Sages was for the congregation to recite Hallel by repeating the word *Hallelukah* after every declaration of the *chazzan*. For example, the *chazzan* would recite the blessing for Hallel and say "*Hallelukah*," and all the people would respond "*Hallelukah*." Then he would say "*Hallelu avdei Hashem*," and they would again answer "*Hallelukah*," and so on throughout the *tefillah*. In that type of recitation, the word *Hallelukah* would be repeated 123 times. One way to remember this, says the Rambam, is to remember Aharon, who lived for 123 years.

Rambam apparently saw a connection between Aharon and Hallel. In fact, "The House of Aharon" is mentioned in Hallel several times, as in *Beis Aharon Bitchu b'Hashem* and *Yomru na Beis Aharon*.

Total Submissiveness

The message in the connection between Aharon and Hallel lies in the various forms of recitation. The Gemara records several customs. The first of those methods is the one followed today: Hallel is recited as a group, but each person says the words for himself. Another way mentioned is to repeat each verse after the *chazzan* recites it. The third version is that which was cited above: The *chazzan* recites the verses and the congregation responds "*Hallelukah*."

These three methods carry a deep significance, for each demonstrates a different shade of gratitude. The variable among them is the degree of submissiveness embedded in each method. In general, the extent of our gratitude mirrors the extent of our willingness to humble ourselves, to admit we owe a "debt of gratitude" to the giver.

When the members of a congregation recite Hallel along with the *chazzan*—or recite it responsively, they are participating, taking an active role in giving thanks. They present themselves as people who have "something to offer" to Hashem. However, when the congregation simply repeats "*Hallelukah*," they indicate that they are incapable of offering sufficient praise. This form—the one that corresponds numerically to Aharon's lifetime—represents submissiveness so total that there is no sense of self involved.

Total submissiveness is the purest level of the attribute of *hod*. The word *hod*, which means to praise, is also the root of the word *modeh*—to admit. Conceptually, these two concepts are intertwined because a person will only say thank you if he admits that he has received something, and admitting to having been helped by another person requires submissiveness. Aharon's total devotion to the Jewish people exemplified this trait. This is the Rambam's rationale for linking the years and the life of Aharon to the method by which the Jewish people recite Hallel. Aharon devoted his life to bringing peace to the people, mediating and reconciling differences between husbands and wives, among families, and among members of the nation. He was the pillar of peace who served the Bnei Yisrael selflessly for his entire life. How appropriate it is, since Aharon was *niftar* on Rosh Chodesh, that on his *yahrtzeit*, the Jewish people recite the Hallel.

Therefore, Aharon represents the form of Hallel that

gives us no input other than to say "*Hallelukah.*" On Sukkos, the only Yom Tov on which we recite the entire Hallel all seven days, thereby offering Hashem an especially abundant amount of praise, we humbly welcome Aharon, whose life reflected the utmost recognition of our debt to Hashem.

Day Six: Welcoming Yosef (Nighttime)

One of Yosef's links to Sukkos is based on this Yom Tov's identity as "The festival of the ingathering (*ha'asif*) at the conclusion of the year." As we mentioned, Sukkos is the time when the ripe produce is gathered and stored for the lean months of winter. This was precisely the accomplishment of Yosef in his role as Pharaoh's viceroy.

The Torah tells the story of Pharaoh's dreams, which Yosef interpreted as a warning that there would be seven years of bounty followed by seven years of famine. Yosef, appointed to manage the situation, gathered all the produce during the seven years of plenty. He excelled in the most righteous manner, as the one and only person with the attributes necessary to squeeze the maximum benefit out of the blessings of the good years. Yosef accomplished what we are meant to accomplish annually. Therefore, he visits us, for indeed he has a place in our *sukkah*.

Yosef: The *Middah* of *Yesod*

There is, however, a much deeper link between Yosef and the *sukkah*, which is based on the *middah* he represents. He is the one who gathers all the attributes of the previous five *sefiros* and unifies them into one power. This *middah* is known as *yesod.*

In the words of our Sages, there are righteous people upon whom the world rests, and such a person is called a *tzaddik yesod olam.* In the Torah's description of Yosef's role in Egypt, we see that he indeed became the foundation and source of life for everyone. Anyone who wanted food had to come to Yosef. The same was true for anyone who wanted to bear arms or be granted the privilege of riding a horse; Yosef was in control of all of it. In short, the honor, power, and sustenance of Egypt, the world's superpower at the time, was in the hands of one person: Yosef. However, Yosef responded to all the praise and honor heaped upon him by disclaiming any credit—he constantly responded by attributing his success to Hashem. This is the truest representation of the attribute known as *yesod*.

The Seventy Bulls

On Sukkos, the time of ingathering and storing the abundant harvest that Hashem has bestowed upon us, we also connect our blessings to all the nations of the world. We do this by sacrificing a bull for each of the seventy nations. We are empowered on the Yom Tov of Sukkos with the attribute of *yesod*. This aligns with the accomplishment of Yosef, who gathered Egypt's harvest and distributed Hashem's bounty to Egypt and the surrounding nations.

Day Six: Yosef, the Satan's Nemesis (Daytime)

Sukkos is celebrated after Yom Kippur, the precise time on the calendar when the Jewish people are cleansed of sin and most distant from the Satan. Our daily Ma'ariv prayer articulates this connection in the words of *Hashkiveinu*, which ask Hashem *to remove the* Satan *from in front of us and behind us, and spread upon us Your* Sukkah *of Peace.*

The *sukkah's* simplicity provides us with a haven from our constant pursuit of possessions. *Hashkiveinu* evokes a time in the future when Hashem will ensconce us in His protective shelter, and we will be permanently free of the pernicious Satan.

Yosef and the Satan

Once a year, however, we physically leave our homes and live in the *sukkah*, so that we actually dwell under Hashem's protection right now, in this world. Although we lived in the *sukkah* for the entire forty years we spent in the desert, it is most appropriate to enter the *sukkah* after we have been cleansed from our sins and have separated ourselves from the evil inclination. The *sukkah* is meant to keep the Satan away.

Indeed, overcoming the Satan was Yosef's signature achievement. Rashi cites a midrash that states that Yosef's birth gave Yaakov the confidence to leave Lavan's home and travel back to Eretz Canaan. Rashi calls Yosef "the Satan's Satan," meaning that just as the Satan tests and opposes us, Yosef tested and opposed the Satan. Indeed, Yosef proved Yaakov's assessment correct; he withstood temptation after temptation, rising with each test to a higher plateau of righteousness. In this sense, Yosef fashioned the *sukkah* as a safe haven where we are protected from the Satan.

Day Seven: Welcoming Dovid (Nighttime)

Dovid Hamelech's connection to Sukkos is quite clear, for we identify the *sukkah* with him in the prayer *May the Merciful One raise the fallen* sukkah *of Dovid.* It is obvious that the *sukkah* in this verse refers to the Beis Hamikdash, but why is it associated with Dovid, who never fulfilled his hope of building Hashem's home? (Hashem told Dovid that he would not be the one to build the Beis Hamikdash because he had "blood on his hands" from his life as a warrior.) Why is the Beis Hamikdash called a *sukkah*, and specifically, Dovid's *sukkah*?

The midrash (*Tehillim*), which we discussed earlier regarding Yaakov, states: *From the beginning of the creation of the world, Hashem made a* sukkah, *placing it in Yerushalayim, and He would pray in it, saying "May it be My will that My children should do My will, so I shall not destroy My house, My Temple."* The point of this midrash is that even before the Beis Hamikdash was built, the desire for it created an everlasting connection.

That connection is referred to as a *sukkah*. Just as Hashem desired a dwelling place in this world that the midrash calls a *sukkah*, Dovid's efforts to actualize this dwelling is referred to as a *sukkah*. Thus, the Beis Hamikdash is *Sukkas Dovid*.

But why is the desire for a Beis Hamikdash—"a place of heaven in this world"—known as a *sukkah*?

Eternal *Sukkah*

A *sukkah* is like a tent, in that when it falls, it can be reassembled. The Maharal explains that the difference between a house and a tent or *sukkah* is that when a house is destroyed, it is called a *churban*, which means complete obliteration. After the *churban* of a building, it cannot be restored; it can only be rebuilt from the ground up. With a *sukkah* or tent, however, even when the structure collapses, it retains its original identity. It is not "lost forever" or obliterated just because it is no longer standing. In this sense, a *sukkah* is everlasting. It remains a *sukkah* even when it is dismantled or has fallen.

This would seem to indicate that although there has been a *churban* of the "Beis" Hamikdash—the aspect of the edifice that is defined as a house—this destruction does not affect its status as a *sukkah*.[36] Rav Moshe Shapiro *zt"l* points out that the prayer

---

36. The *Zera Shimshon* writes that the day after the *churban*, Hashem was ready to build another Beis Hamikdash had the Jewish people repented. The *pasuk* (*Eichah* 1:12) laments, "Behold and see if there is any pain like my pain, which has befallen me, with which Hashem has afflicted on me on the day of His burning wrath." Note that the verse says, "on the day." The next day, Hashem would have

referring to the "fallen *sukkah* of Dovid" does not ask that it be rebuilt, but rather, that it be "raised." This implies that it hasn't been destroyed, but rather, it lies dismantled, waiting to be assembled once again.

The prayer of *Sukkas Dovid* expresses our deep faith that although the Beis Hamikdash is not presently standing, in its essence it is impregnable and everlasting, like a *sukkah* that maintains its integrity even when it lies folded and waiting to be assembled.

Day Seven: Dovid, the *Tikkun* of Adam Harishon (Daytime)

Adam and the Beis Hamikdash

Continuing the night's theme of the connection between the *sukkah* and the Beis Hamikdash, the Maharal in *Sefer Derech Hachaim* (*Pirkei Avos*) draws a further parallel that exists between the Beis Hamikdash and man. The source of this connection is the following mishnah (5:21):

> *He used to say: A five-year-old begins Scripture, a ten-year-old begins Mishnah, a thirteen-year-old becomes obligated in mitzvos, a fifteen-year-old begins Talmud, an eighteen-year-old enters the wedding canopy, a twenty-year-old begins pursuit [of a livelihood], a thirty-year-old achieves strength, a forty-year-old achieves understanding, a fifty-year-old achieves counsel, a sixty-year-old reaches old age, a seventy-year-old attains extreme old age, an eighty-year-old attains might, a ninety-year-old begins to stoop, and a one-hundred-*

---

replaced the Beis Hamikdash, indicating that the *sukkah* concept was never affected. Although the people lost their Temple, they did not lose their Father in heaven or their relationship with Him.

year-old is as if he has passed and is gone from the world.

"Behold," explains the Maharal, "that the span of human life encompasses a hundred years." Although the general lifespan is seventy years, through merit a person can reach one hundred. The Maharal continues, **"And just as the life of a man spans a hundred years, so too the height of the chamber in the Beis Hamikdash is a hundred cubits."**

This correlation, the Maharal explains, illustrates that man is like a Mikdash, because the essential function of both man and the Mikdash is to house the *Shechinah.* Moreover, man is responsible for the building of the Beis Hamikdash and unfortunately, for its destruction as well. Further, says the Maharal, the Gemara (*Sanhedrin*) states that originally, Adam stretched from the earth to the heavens. When he sinned, Hashem placed His "hand" upon Adam's head and compressed his stature, reducing him to one hundred cubits. This too corresponds to the height of the Beis Hamikdash. But there is far more to this comparison than height.

Divine Intelligence

The Maharal's point is that like the Beis Hamikdash, a human being has the capacity to fill himself with Hashem's presence. Indeed, the Gemara (*Brachos* 33a) says that a person who has developed the attribute of knowledge and understanding of Hashem—*da'as*—causes the Divine presence to rest upon him, and it is as if the sanctuary were rebuilt in his days. The basis for this idea, says the Gemara, is that in a verse in *Shmuel* 1 (2:3), the word *da'as* appears between two Divine Names; and in *Shemos* (15:7), the word Mikdash appears between two Divine Names.

On a deeper level, through the insight and intellect of a person who has attained Divine knowledge, Hashem's presence is brought into this world. We can say of such a person, "Hashem lives together with him." As the Maharal (*Nesiv HaTorah* Chapter 9) writes, intellect gives a person *d'veikus* to the *Shechinah.*

The word *d'veikus* is first used in the beginning of *Bereishis* after Hashem creates the first woman. The Torah says, *Therefore a man shall leave his father and mother and cling (*davak*) to his wife, and they shall become one flesh. D'veikus* is the most complete and intimate connection. Thus, by successfully internalizing the knowledge of Hashem and His Torah, a person connects intimately with the Almighty; he is considered, as the Gemara stated, to be surrounded by the Names of Hashem.

The Maharal has provided us with a deeper understanding of what it means for a human being to be like a Mikdash—a place built to serve as a dwelling place for the Divine presence in the physical world. Just as the Beis Hamikdash was a place where heaven met earth, a human being can connect heaven to earth within himself.

Adam in the Garden

When Hashem placed Adam and Chava in the Garden of Eden, their concept of "knowledge" encompassed only that which was good. As the Torah states, the spirit of Hashem manifested itself in the Garden. The first man and woman were warned not to eat from the Tree of Knowledge of Good and Evil, for the Divine intellect—the interface by which a person can intimately connect with Hashem—can only be absorbed by a mind that is untainted by evil. Once

Adam and Chava had eaten from the Tree of Knowledge, they had corrupted their minds and polluted the entire world. Therefore, Hashem drove them out of the Garden.

Dovid Hamelech

One person arose in Klal Yisrael who was able to rectify much of the damage done by Adam and Chava. That was Dovid Hamelech. (See introduction to Hallel for an extensive explanation of the connection between Dovid and Adam.) By preparing the foundation of the Beis Hamikdash, Dovid was able to bring Hashem's presence back to this world in a permanent way, essentially building an earthly throne for the King of Kings. This corresponds to Dovid's *middah* of *malchus.* This dwelling place of Hashem is also known as the *sukkah—Sukkas Dovid.*

Sukkos

We may now have a better appreciation for the *pasuk* commanding us to observe the mitzvah of *sukkah, so that your future generations will* ***know*** *[have the understanding and knowledge] that I have placed you in the* sukkos.[37] To know Hashem means to have *d'veikus* with Him, which means to build Him a Mikdash. This is precisely what is expected of the person who dwells in the *sukkah.*

In conclusion, with the *sukkah* providing each person the opportunity to connect his entire self—body and soul—to Hakadosh Baruch Hu, it becomes a place of sanctity similar to the Beis Hamikdash. In such a place, the seven *Ushpizin* feel at home as they come to visit every day, for the entire duration of the Yom Tov.

---

37. למען ידעו דרתיכם כי בסכות הושבתי את בני ישראל.

CHAPTER 6

Simchas Beis Hasho'evah

The Joy of the Waters of Creation

The custom of the *simchas beis hasho'evah* revolves around music, dancing, and festivities. The mishnah in *Sukkah* tells us, *The flute [played for] five or six days [depending on where Shabbos and Yom Tov fell in the week]. This was the flute of the* beis hasho'evah, *which means "the house of the [water] drawing."*

Rashi explains that the music played because of the happiness that was associated with the pouring of the water, as the *pasuk* states, *And you shall draw water with happiness.*

Simchas Beis Hasho'evah

The happiness was vivid and wholehearted. During the Chol Hamoed of Sukkos, the holy city of Yerushalayim would be alive with the sound of music, singing, and dancing. The sounds emanated from the Beis Hamikdash, turning our words of prayer and the declaration of *zman simchaseinu* into a palpable reality.

As the mishnah states, *Whoever did not witness the happiness of the festival of the* simchas beis hasho'evah *never experienced happiness in his life.* Even today, 2,000 years since the destruction of the Beis Hamikdash, on each evening of Chol Hamoed Sukkos, the streets of Yerushalayim are bursting with music as people of all ages dance and rejoice together.

Maximum Happiness

Let us take a moment to reflect on the words of the mishnah, *Whoever did not witness the happiness of the festival of the* simchas beis hasho'evah *never experienced happiness in his life.* This is a bold statement! Imagine all the events in your life that have brought you happiness: family gatherings, birthdays, engagements, weddings, the birth of children, awards, or successful achievements. None of these compare to the happiness of *simchas beis hasho'evah*!

To understand how this could be, let us first define happiness. Happiness is a completely subjective emotion. Can one person tell another person what they should feel? How can the author of the mishnah tell us where the *simchas beis hasho'evah* ranks on our personal happiness scale?

There is an expression in Hebrew[1] that translates, "On taste and smell, there is no argument." The general meaning of this is, "To each his own." We cannot tell another person what he does or does not enjoy. We cannot tell him that he should prefer chocolate over vanilla because that is a personal preference. In truth, we cannot share our experience of any sensation or event with another person. For example, can anyone explain to another person what a banana tastes like, or what the color orange looks like? The best we can do is to let the person have the experience himself, and even then, he will surely experience it at least slightly differently than we did.

So, what does the mishnah mean by declaring the *simchas beis hasho'evah* to be the universal peak experience of happiness?

---

1. על טעם וריח אין להתווכח.

The Joy of Life

Rav Moshe Shapiro *zt"l* explained that the essence of happiness is ingrained in the life force, while the core of sadness is rooted in death. When we engage in an activity we enjoy—whether physical or intellectual—we feel good, happy, and alive, even if this activity is strenuous. Indeed, the experience of happiness is very personal, and it depends on each person's individual values. However, the principle is the same. The degree to which we find meaning and satisfaction in the activities we undertake in life is the barometer of our happiness. While each of us has our individual "likes and dislikes," this is the universal common thread.

Sadness, on the other hand, is rooted in the feeling of being "devoid of life." The most common form of sadness is the loss of a loved one. Whether that loved one is a family member, a friend, or even a pet, the void a person feels is the source of his sadness. This idea extends to the loss of a job or an opportunity, for the concept remains the same; the more a person senses the pulsing of the life force within himself and his world, the happier he will be. The weaker this sensation is, the less happiness he feels.

Hashem: The Source of Life

The Source of all life is, of course, Hashem, the Creator of everything. We can therefore conclude that a person is happiest when he is connected to Hashem, for he cannot feel more alive than he does when connected to the Source of life. Therefore, the closer the connection, the greater the feeling of happiness—and the weaker the connection, the weaker the feeling of happiness.

Nevertheless, we see many people who have very little to do with Hashem and are arguably very satisfied and happy. The answer to this paradox lies in their value system. A person who neither believes in G-d nor has any appreciation for Him will find happiness in his own world. However, if at any time he becomes aware that his world has no intrinsic value, how can he maintain his happiness? He will realize that all his happiness was an aberration—a temporary misconception on which he built his life. A person can be happy living a lie, but when the lie is revealed, the emptiness is devastating, and the sadness is crushing.

In Western civilization, the principles of a "good life" have been fabricated through a culture that values all sorts of entertainment—food, movies, sports, music, vacations. All this brings happiness to those who are a part of it. But if at any point in a person's life he recognizes that these experiences and efforts they entail lack any real meaning, he feels tremendous emptiness. According to our Sages, this recognition of emptiness is one of the definitions of Gehinnom. It is the painful regret of a person living his life in a fabricated reality, and then waking up one day to discover that he spent his allotted days running hard and fast in the wrong direction. In the *tefillos* of Rosh Hashanah and Yom Kippur, we declare, *All of the evil will disappear like smoke when the wicked regime*[2] *dissipates.* Evil is like smoke—something without substance. Just as smoke appears to have a form, but disperses on its own, the false principles of a life devoid of Hashem disappear the moment the truth is perceived.

Beis Hamikdash, *Beis Chayeinu*

The world has yet to come to this reality, but the truth will be recognized when the Third Beis Hamikdash is built, and the world acknowledges Hashem's sovereignty. The Beis Hamikdash is Hashem's dwelling place on earth, and it provides the world with an epicenter of genuine values and absolute truth. Dovid Hamelech (*Tehillim* 73:2) expresses this idea when he writes, *But as for me, my feet were almost turned astray; my steps were very nearly washed aside. For I envied the perverse when I saw the peace of the wicked.* But

---

2. The conventional understanding of "wicked regime" would refer to the nations that deny Hashem's existence. In this context, Rav Moshe Shapiro *zt"l* explains it to mean the culture of Western civilization.

he only entertained these thoughts *until I came to the sanctuaries of Hashem* (*Tehillim* 73:17). That encounter turned his mind toward truth; the wicked people will come to a bitter end, and their realization will be "like a dream upon awakening." The Beis Hamikdash is referred to as *Beis Chayeinu*—"the House of Our Life," life as it is meant to be according to Hashem. It is a house of a healthy, well-balanced life. It is a place of *simchah*.

Nisuch Hamayim

So far, everything we have discussed about happiness applies to every day of the year. Let us now zero in on the specific relationship of these concepts to Chol Hamoed Sukkos and the water libations ceremony known as *nisuch hamayim*. The basis of this relationship is that *nisuch hamayim* is connected to the ultimate Source of life. But that connection revolves around several concepts:

- the mitzvah of *nisuch hamayim*
- the creation of Adam
- the separation of waters during creation
- the role of Sukkos as the holiday of the ingathering

Let us explore these one by one.

The Mitzvah of *Nisuch Hamayim*

The mitzvah of *nisuch hamayim*—pouring of the water—is mentioned in the Gemara (*Sukkah* 48a).[3] The mishnah describes the process by which golden bowls were filled with water from the river of Shiloach. Shofar blowers would then escort the *kohanim* who carried the water to the *Mizbei'ach*. There, the *kohanim* poured the water into two bowls fashioned with openings in them, which were affixed to the *Mizbei'ach*. The poured water

---

3. במוצאי יום טוב הראשון של חג ירדו לעזרת נשים ומתקנין שם תיקון גדול, ומנורות של זהב היו שם וכו׳ חסידים ואנשי מעשה היו מרקדים לפניהם באבוקות של אור שבידיהן ואומרים לפניהן דברי שירות ותשבחות.

would flow down to the *shittin.*[4] The celebration began the night before the pouring, with music and dancing that continued throughout the night until sunrise, when the *kohanim* poured the water.

Sho'evah or *Chashuvah*

The Gemara (*Sukkah*, ibid.) explains that there are two descriptions of this festive event. One description is *simchas beis hasho'evah*, which identifies the event with the *sho'evah*—the drawing of the water—which must be performed before fulfilling the mitzvah of pouring the water. The other version is *simchas beis hachashuvah*, which identifies the event as *chashuvah*—a time of distinction and importance. Those who favor the name *sho'evah*, says the Gemara, base their opinion on the verse, *You shall draw waters with joy from the wells of salvation* (*Yeshayah* 12:3). According to the second opinion, the word *chashuvah* refers to the same event but emphasizes its importance: It is a mitzvah that interacts with the world at its very core.

Mitzvah Chashuvah

The Gemara, citing Rav Nachman, states that this mitzvah arises directly from the six days of creation. Rashi explains that Hashem fashioned the *shittin*—the deep cavities beneath the earth into which the water libation was poured—when He created the world. Thus, the groundwork was laid for this mitzvah at the very beginning of time. So integral were the *shittin* to creation that they are even hinted at in the first word of the Torah: *Bereishis*. This word can be divided into two: *bara* (He created) and *shis* (*shittin*).

The fact that the mitzvah was embedded in creation is surely enough of a distinction to give it the status of *chashuvah*. However, the same Gemara goes further; it describes the water libation as a

---

4. *Shittin* was an underground crater beneath the *Mizbei'ach*. We will discuss the *shittin* separately.

mitzvah that brings peace between the upper and lower worlds of creation. On the second day, when the world was nothing but water, Hashem created a division by separating the upper waters from the lower waters. This created a reality of separation from Hashem, and because it was a day of separation, it is the only day of creation that the Torah does not describe with the words *ki tov*, and it was good.[5]

But this deficiency is not permanent; it is corrected through the pouring of the water, as we will now explain.

Upper Waters and Lower Waters

Our Sages (*Rosh Hashanah* 16a) teach that Hashem instructed the Jewish people to bring water before Him on Sukkos so that we would be blessed with rain in the upcoming rainy season.[6] Why does the pouring of the water on the *Mizbei'ach* trigger this blessing for the entire year? The answer lies in the interplay of the upper waters and the lower waters.

Rabbeinu Bachya (*Vayikra* 2:13) quotes a midrash that teaches that the water libation is connected to the separation of the waters on the second day. When Hashem commanded this separation, the lower waters wept, pleading, "We too wish to be close to our Creator!" Hashem noted that their distress arose from a true yearning for holiness, and this would ultimately be a pillar of the world's survival. Hashem consoled the water by commanding that all *korbanos* be salted (the salt comes from the sea), and that on Sukkos the Jewish people would perform the mitzvah of pouring

---

5. Separation without connection creates "another side" known as "*sitra achra*," a reference to the dark and evil side of the world.

6. ומפני מה אמרה תורה נסכו מים בחג, אמר הקדוש ברוך הוא נסכו לפני מים בחג כדי שיתברכו לכם גשמי שנה—*And why did the Torah say to make water libations during the festival of Sukkos? Because Sukkos is the time for the judgment of water. The Holy One blessed be He said, "Pour water before Me on the festival so that the annual rains will be blessed for you."*

the water. How is this a consolation? This can be answered on many levels.

Sukkos *Chag Ha'asif*

As we have discussed, Sukkos is the time of ingathering, when the world returns to its Source. Ultimately, every separation can be rectified through connection and return to the Source. Regarding Day Three of creation, when Hashem finished separating the waters and the earth brought forth its vegetation, the Torah states the phrase *And it was good,* twice. One time applies to Day Two, and the other applies to Day Three. The praise was given on the same day because the purpose of the division Hashem created on Day Two was to bring about the connection of heaven and earth on Day Three. Since this is the holiday of the ingathering, it is the appropriate time to rectify everything in creation.

The Origin of Adam

Our Sages explain this on a deeper level, connecting this rectification back to the origins of creation. As we learned, the wine and water libations were poured into two holes in the *Mizbei'ach.* They would flow under the *Mizbei'ach* into the *shittin.* Rav Moshe Shapiro *zt"l* explains that the "dust of the earth" that was used to form Adam created the crater known as *Shittin*[7]. The *Mizbei'ach* was built above this crater. His source is found in the Rambam.

The Rambam explains:

> The location of the *Mizbei'ach* is extremely exact and can

---

7. Since this *shittin* crater is **the earth that was used to form the creation of man**, it is ultimately the place of origin of the purpose of creation. It was there that Hashem breathed into the nostrils of man, embodying him with his soul. Subsequently, any *avodah* (*nisuch hamayim*) done at this place is significant in that it accesses the place of man's origin.

> never be moved. According to tradition, Dovid and Shlomo built the *Mizbei'ach* at the exact location where Avraham offered Yitzchak his son as a sacrifice. This is the same place where Noach, upon exiting the ark, brought sacrifices to Hashem. It is also where Kayin and Hevel brought their sacrifices and the original Adam brought his. Indeed, the *Mizbei'ach* is the location of the earth from which Adam was created. The Sages have taught us that man was created from the place of his atonement.

The Rambam's words reveal that because man was created from the place of the *Mizbei'ach*, the place where *korbanos* were brought, he was created with the potential for atonement. No matter how distant a person is, since his core comes from the source of atonement, he never loses his built-in capacity to reconnect to Hashem.

The Maharal, in a commentary on the Haggadah, says that because the Jewish people have a venue at which they can bring sacrifices to achieve forgiveness, they can maintain an unobstructed connection to Hashem. The Beis Hamikdash and its *avodah* guarantee the everlasting bond between man and Hashem, insuring it against the corrosive effects of human error.

But the earth from the place of the *Mizbei'ach* was not the only substance from which Hashem made man. The waters from the depths of the earth played an essential role as well.

The Water of Creation

The Torah (*Bereishis* 2:6) describes Adam's formation: *And a mist ascended from the deep and watered the whole surface of the soil.* Rashi explains that this was Hashem's preparation for creating man. He brought the water up from the deep and absorbed it into the clouds so that it would rain down and saturate the soil. Rashi concludes, *and man was created, as a baker who puts water [in the flour] and afterwards kneads the dough.*

The Gemara describes the lower waters as the "crying waters," for they longed to reconnect back to Hashem. From this water, the "water of longing," He created man so that he would have within himself a natural desire to reconnect. By drawing up this "lower water" and pouring it on the *Mizbei'ach*, we celebrate the uniquely human capacity to bring G-dliness and good to the world.

We can see from the above that whether we stress the *sho'evah* or the *chashuvah* aspect of this celebration, we are describing the same event—the creation of man. The only difference is whether we are emphasizing Hashem's act of creation, when He poured the water over the earth, or we are emphasizing the central, crowning importance of this creation. Once again, the significance of this prominent act of *nisuch hamayim* is that it is part of the greater ingathering.

There is yet one more facet of the *simchas beis hasho'evah* that "connects the dots" between this celebration and the creation of man. The Sages teach that the two openings in the *Mizbei'ach* simulate human nostrils. By pouring the water into these openings, we re-enact the Torah's description of Hashem's final step in creating man: *And He breathed into his nostrils the breath of life.* Further, coming right after the atonement of Yom Kippur, this ceremony captures the vast opportunity we have for attaching to Hashem and thereby starting a new life.

The lower waters thus achieve complete consolation. Their longing to connect to their Source comes to fruition as they are poured upon the *Mizbei'ach* and connect mankind and all of creation back to the Source of life.

CHAPTER 7

Hoshana Rabbah

Sweetening the Judgment

The day of Hoshana Rabbah is perplexing. Some of its prayers are reminiscent of Rosh Hashanah and Yom Kippur. In fact, the *shaliach tzibbur* wears a *kittel*, a sign that the day is similar to the Yamim Nora'im. But how is it possible in the middle of Sukkos to suddenly find ourselves in a time of judgment? Wasn't the judgment sealed at *Ne'ilah*, at the conclusion of Yom Kippur? Before we discuss Hoshana Rabbah, an introduction is necessary that explains the connection of the days of judgment to the Yom Tov of Sukkos.

Sukkos is "The Time of Our Joy." The Torah describes it as days of happiness, which is the antithesis of Days of Awe! How are we to reconcile *Zman Simchaseinu* with the *Yom Din*?

My *rebbi*, Rav Moshe Shapiro *zt"l*, answered these questions based on the Vilna Gaon's commentary. The Gaon discussed a mishnah (*Sukkah* 28b) that states that rain on Sukkos is a negative omen (since it prevents us from fulfilling the mitzvah of *sukkah*), signaling that Hashem is not interested in our service to Him. The mishnah gives a parable of a servant who serves his master a cup of wine, and the master throws it back at his face. This is generally understood to mean that the master throws the entire cup of wine back onto the servant.

The Gaon gleans an explanation from Rashi far different from the conventional meaning. Rashi says that the master spills water, not wine, onto the face of his servant. This is the water that was brought to dilute the wine to make it drinkable. Based on this conclusion, Rashi derives a message that is very different from that of Hashem's rejection of our service.

Meziga

Why does it matter if the master throws the entire cup of wine or he throws the water and is left holding the undiluted wine? It is relevant because in the times of the mishnah, wine was produced in a very concentrated form. Only when it was watered down—a process called *meziga*—did it become drinkable. According to the Kabbalists, the act of *meziga* holds a hidden message. Wine represents strict judgment while water represents *chessed*. Therefore, *meziga* represents the mitigation of strict judgment. When we add water to wine, the Kabbalistic meaning is that there is no strict judgment against the Jewish people. This is known as *Hametakas Hadin* (Sweetening the Judgment). The timing of Sukkos, a period of happiness that comes directly after the Days of Awe, serves a purpose similar to that of *meziga*.

Therefore, when Rashi interprets the mishnah to mean that the master spilled out the water and is left holding pure undiluted wine, he is telling us that there has not been any "sweetening of the judgment." This is the connection between the Days of Judgment of Rosh Hashanah and Yom Kippur (the days of wine) and Hoshana Rabbah, the seventh day of Sukkos (the day we pray for rain). Throughout Sukkos, we serve Hashem through happiness, which can sweeten the judgment. Then on the final day, Hoshana Rabbah, we have the opportunity to pray once again in a tone similar to that of Yom Kippur for the purpose of requesting abundant blessings from heaven to mitigate and sweeten the judgment.

To summarize, if we can sit in our *sukkos* and fulfill the mitzvah of *simchas Yom Tov*, we are sweetening the judgments rendered on the days of the Yamim Nora'im. If, however, we are unable to sit in our *sukkos* and cannot serve Hashem with joy during this *Zman Simchaseinu*, we are left only with the *din* of the Yamim Nora'im.[1] With this, we can begin understanding the concept of Hoshana Rabbah.

Hoshana Rabbah: Fear Born from Love (*Yirah Mi'ahavah*)

There is still a deeper level of connection between *Zman Simchaseinu* and the *Yom Din*. This can be found in the midrash (*Tanna D'vei Eliyahu* 3:1) on Dovid Hamelech's words, "I fear Hashem through my happiness and my happiness emerges from my fear."

What is "fear through happiness"? Sometimes, we are intimidated by a great person, which causes us to be very careful of how we speak and act in that person's presence. This is pure *yirah*, unadulterated awe. In another type of relationship, our love for the other person causes us to be careful not to say or do anything that will damage the relationship or upset the person. In both scenarios, we are careful about what we say. However, in the first case, we act out of fear; in the second case, we act out of love. From this explanation, we can understand that even days permeated by love and happiness contain an element of fear.[2]

---

1. It is interesting to note that while the only way to fulfill the commandment of Sukkos is if there is no rain, at the end of the Yom Tov on the seventh day, we pray for a year of rain. This of course is not a contradiction. It is only after the holiday that the planting season begins again, and it is at that time that we need the heavens to shower us with rain.

2. We have only explained the first part of the verse, the "fear through happiness." The second part of this statement, "happiness through fear," can be

This is the essence of Hoshana Rabbah, a day of happiness that is mixed with the awe-inspiring awareness that we are so close to our King. It is a day of awe installed within the "Time of Our Joy."

---

understood as follows: The respect one shows to a great person allows him to maintain that relationship, which brings contentment and happiness. This is a connection for the Yom Tov of Sukkos that is rooted in and follows the Yamim Nora'im. (We should not construe the happiness of Sukkos as merely a product of the Yamim Nora'im, for then Sukkos would not have the title of *Zman Simchaseinu*, and its joy would be curtailed. Rather, since Sukkos has its own self-generated mitzvos—*lulav, sukkah, simchas beis hasho'evah*, it is indeed a time of joy, based on the *middah* of *ahavah*.

CHAPTER 8

Shemini Atzeres

The Yom Tov of Now

This dvar Torah *is from my oldest son Reb Binyomin, presently a* rosh chaburah *in Beth Medrash Govoha, Lakewood, New Jersey.*

Pesach, Shavuos, and Sukkos commemorate three different events in the desert. During each of these holidays, we are commanded to remember and relive these past events. The Sages have taught that the spiritual energy created during those original events is invested in that time of year and returns to us on an annual cycle. We don't just celebrate an event that happened in the past; we live the holiday.

What event happened on Shemini Atzeres? What holiness and energy has Hashem invested in these twenty-four hours that we can tap into?

The Holiday of Now

The answer is simple and somewhat astonishing; nothing happened on this day in history that we commemorate! Unique among the holidays, Shemini Atzeres does not include a historical remembrance; rather, it is the holiday of the present. Even Rosh Hashanah and Yom Kippur are days of the present rooted in the past; Hashem judges the world annually on this day because Adam, the first man, was created on Rosh Hashanah. Yom Kippur is rooted historically in the day that Moshe descended from the mountain with the second set of *luchos*, marking Hashem's forgiveness of the sin of the Golden Calf. Shemini Atzeres is different. Its only purpose is to enable Hashem to connect to His children, generation after generation, year after year.

The One Bull

Over the seven days of Sukkos, the Jewish people sacrificed seventy bulls. These bulls correspond to the seventy nations of the world. The sacrifices shielded all nations from adversity, but their protection was in the merit of the Jewish people.

On Shemini Atzeres, we bring just one bull.

Rashi, quoting the Talmud, explains that this individual bull, which is brought after all the nations have been represented, corresponds to Israel. The message from Hashem is, although we have finished the Yom Tov and completed all the sacrifices that represent all the nations, "I still want one more day exclusively with you. Therefore, remain with Me a little longer." Through this singular sacrifice, Hashem expresses His affection for Israel. Rashi continues, citing the Gemara (*Sukkah* 55b), *It is like children taking leave of their father, who says to them, "It is difficult for me to part with you; stay one more day."*

Every year, Hashem requests that His people spend just one more day with Him. This is not a day for commemorating the past but for celebrating and appreciating the present. This holiday is for *us*. It belongs to each one of the Jewish people in his/her unique way, forever.

Shemini Atzeres

As Shemini Atzeres is a distinct Yom Tov, it has a distinct message. The Maharal (*Sefer Gevuros*) reveals that this day represents a time in the future when we, Hashem's children, will be safe and secure. This comes appropriately after spending seven days in the *sukkah*—the structure that represents a place of protection for the Jewish people. We have recognized the rest of the world with the seventy bulls we have sacrificed, but once that is done, we stand alone, as if these nations no longer exist. In that case, there is no longer a need for any protection.

The Maharal elaborates: Shemini Atzeres celebrates the Jewish people, a nation different from all others. Rather than a festival commemorating an event in time or place, Shemini Atzeres is a celebration for a people, Hashem's people. How do we show the importance of the "people"?

Simchas Torah

On the eighth day, we read the last *parshah* of the Torah—*V'zos Habrachah*—and celebrate the conclusion of all the Torah portions. This custom is mentioned in the *Shulchan Aruch*, and dates back to the times of the *Midrash Rabbah*. The *Anaf Yosef* cites this as the source for the custom of making a *siyum* at the completion of a tractate. In addition, every Jewish male, regardless of age, is called up to the Torah for an *aliyah*. Even infants who are not capable of making the blessing over the Torah, and those who are not capable of understanding the words of the Torah, are gathered together under the canopy of outspread *talleisim* and are thereby adjoined with the person who is honored with the *aliyah* known as *Kol Hane'arim*.

The message is quite clear: Every Jewish person should be honored on this day, regardless of age or capacity. We are all special in the eyes of Hashem, not merely because of our history, but for the fact that we are His children.

The Limitless Blessings

There is one final point to take note of regarding the custom of reading *Parshas V'zos Habrachah*. If someone were to ask how many times on Simchas Torah the portion of *V'zos Habrachah* is read in synagogues and yeshivos around the world, the answer would be "countless times." Even if just one person did not get an *aliyah*, the entire portion is read for that person. There's no way of knowing before Simchas Torah how many times that portion will be read—even in a single shul, let alone in a town, a city, or among all the Jewish people together. Indeed, we get the feeling that the blessings bestowed on the Jewish people are endless. The words of the prophet ring true: *V'harikosi brachah ad bli dai*—"And I shall bless you until you say it is enough!" We read the Torah portion of *V'zos Habrachah* until we say it is enough!

As the Torah proclaims, *And these are the blessings that Moshe blessed the Jewish people!*

CHAPTER 9

Hallel and *Hodayah*

Giving Thanks to Hashem

In our relationship with Hashem, communication is one of the main components. We find ourselves talking to Hashem both in formal prayer and at random times throughout the day. And as in any healthy relationship, we need to communicate not only our needs but also our gratitude and appreciation.

Indeed, our *tefillos* are structured to accomplish this. In our daily *Shemoneh Esrei* (meaning "eighteen" for the eighteen blessings[1]), the prayer is divided into three sections of blessings. We begin with three blessings that praise Hashem. We then recite twelve blessings in which we request everything that is important to us, and in closing, we recite three blessings of *hoda'ah*—gratitude.

On certain special days, we continue our praises with Hallel. It

1. The word *chai* in Hebrew means life and has a numerical value of 18. This is obviously not coincidental. Nowadays there are actually nineteen blessings in the *Shemoneh Esrei* because the blessing of ולמלשינים was added. Since this occurred a few generations after the codification of the *Shemoneh Esrei*, the name remained. Indeed, we live through our connection to Hashem, which we establish through the *Shemoneh Esrei*. It is our source of life.

is interesting to note that there is no Kaddish between the "thank you" said at the end of *Shemoneh Esrei* and the beginning of Hallel. It therefore seems that Hallel is a continuation of the *Shemoneh Esrei.* Indeed, the blessing of *tiskabel* said in Kaddish, which indicates the conclusion of the prayer, is only said after we finish Hallel. This underscores and reinforces the understanding that the Hallel is not a different *tefillah* but rather an expansion of the expression of gratitude we recite daily in the *Shemoneh Esrei.*

Why do we reserve this expansive show of gratitude for special occasions? Why not communicate our most expansive expression of thanks every day?

Let us begin to answer this question by comparing the various methods by which we praise and give recognition to Hashem. What factors determine when various forms of thanks are most appropriate?

Thanking Hashem: Daily versus Periodically

When analyzing our daily *tefillos* as well as the *tefillos* of Shabbos and holiday services, we see differences in the types of praises we offer. For example:

In our daily Shacharis prayers, we begin with *Pesukei D'zimrah*, in which we praise and thank Hashem using various verses of *Tehillim* composed by Dovid Hamelech. These focus on all of Hashem's creations and how the world naturally does Hashem's work. We also give gratitude in the *Shemoneh Esrei* in the affirmation of *Modim,*[2] in the section of *Hoda'ah*. There, we say, "We thank You and retell Your praises for our lives that are in Your hand, and our souls that are remembered by You and for the miracles that You do with us daily—morning, afternoon, and evening." By recognizing Hashem's daily miracles, we remind ourselves that He is involved

---

2. נודה לך ונספר תהילתך על חיינו המסורים בידך ועל נשמותינו הפקודות לך ועל נסיך שבכל יום עמנו ועל נפלאותיך וטובותיך שבכל עת ערב בוקר וצהרים.

with every aspect of our lives; that even our normal, natural functioning is the result of *hidden Divine miracles.*

Shabbos: The Gratitude of the *Neshamah Yeseirah*

On Shabbos, we expand our declaration of praise by including *Hallel Hagadol* and *Nishmas* in our *Pesukei D'zimrah.* Why do we add these praises?

Our Sages teach that on Shabbos, we receive a *neshamah yeseirah*, an additional soul. This Shabbos soul not only expands the person,[3] but also, all of his senses. This opens within him a deeper appreciation of Hashem's world. A person who connects to his Shabbos soul can sense the handiwork of Hashem within creation at a level he does not and cannot access during the weekdays. As we say at the beginning of the Shabbos *Pesukei D'zimrah* (from *Tehillim* 19), *The Heavens recount the glory of Hashem and the firmament proclaims His handiwork.* It's a story of glory that we can grasp only on a holy day like Shabbos or Yom Tov.[4]

Since Shabbos is the day of the week about which the Torah states, *The world has come to rest,* it represents the completion of the world's weekly cycle. This allows our praises to take on a more expansive perspective. On Shabbos, we are offering the all-inclusive gratitude that a person can only appreciate at the conclusion of a project. This sense of completion applies also to spirituality; the Torah says *shavas vayinafash*—the world rested (from creation) and received a greater spiritual acuity. Therefore, we add *Hallel Hagadol* and *Nishmas* to our praises.[5]

---

3. Rashi (*Maseches Shabbos*) says that the *neshamah yeseirah* allows a person to enjoy the Shabbos and all its delicacies beyond his/her weekday capacity.

4. We have a *neshamah yeseirah* on both Shabbos and Yom Tov.

5. *Nishmas* is the prayer of the *neshamah yeseirah* and is therefore only recited on Shabbos and Yom Tov.

The Praise of Hallel

Hallel is different. Only periodically do we praise Hashem with Hallel. We recite Hallel on three different kinds of special days: Rosh Chodesh, Yom Tov, and Chanukah. In addition to reciting Hallel, on Yom Tov we praise Hashem with the expanded Shabbos version of *Pesukei D'zimrah*. Before we discuss the Hallel we recite on these days, let us introduce the Maharal's insight into why we *do not* recite Hallel in our daily prayers.

The Maharal provides a penetrating insight based on the statement in the Gemara (*Shabbos*)[6] that says, *One who says Hallel every day is thereby belittling and blaspheming Hashem.* Why is it blasphemous to offer a daily "thank you" in the form of Hallel?

The Maharal explains with a mishnah that recounts a discussion recorded in the Talmud (*Avodah Zarah*)[7] between the Jewish elders of Rome and the philosophers. The philosophers ask, "If Hashem really disapproves of idolatry, why doesn't He use His power to stop it from happening?" The elders respond that since idolators serve the sun, the moon, and other celestial forces that are necessary for the world to survive, Hashem chooses to allow the world to run its natural course. As for those who have sinned, He will deal with them according to their deeds. Let us note that this Gemara reveals the Torah's rationalization of "Mother Nature."

Mother Nature versus Miracles

With this answer, says the Maharal, the elders clarify that Hashem runs the world according to a system that operates

6. שבת קיח.: הקורא הלל בכל יום הרי זה מחרף ומגדף.

7. שאלו את הזקנים ברומי אם אין רצונו בעבודת כוכבים למה אינו מבטלה, אמרו להן אילו לדבר שאין צורך לעולם בו היו עובדין היה מבטלו, הרי הן עובדים לחמה וללבנה ולכוכבים ולמזלות, יאבד העולם מפני השוטים, אמרו להם אם כן יאבד דבר שאין צורך לעולם בו ויניח דבר שצריך העולם בו, אמרו להם אף אנו מחזיקים ידי עובדיהם של אלו. ובגמרא הוסיף, 'אלא עולם כמנהגו נוהג והולך, ושוטים שקלקלו עתידים ליתן את הדין' (עבודה זרה נד:).

regardless of human sin or error; the world runs its natural course. The reason for this is that while indeed Hashem desires that the world be a place of peace and positivity, His *deeper desire* is for this state to be achieved through the free will of human beings. Therefore, Hashem chooses to not openly involve Himself. Rather, He allows nature to run its course.

This concept is quite logical. If Hashem would allow nature to react to human behavior—whether good or bad—people would not be able to exercise their free will. It would be futile to do something wrong because it simply wouldn't work. Therefore, Hashem "steps back" and allows humanity to choose and create their own destiny.

The Gemara (*Avodah Zarah* ad loc.) gives a few examples of this argument. For instance, if a person stole grain and planted it in the ground, it would be appropriate that it should not grow, for benefiting from stolen items violates Hashem's laws. Instead, Hashem allows the stolen grain to grow because the world follows the course of nature; Hashem deals with the wrongdoer at the appropriate time. Miracles that interrupt the course of nature reveal Hashem's personal involvement and *directly contradict* the concept that the world runs according to the laws of nature. But if we are not meant to live with a constant, daily recognition of Hashem's supervision of nature, why is it *ever* appropriate to say Hallel?

Hallel: Recognizing Hashem's Periodically Revealed Involvement

Praising Hashem with Hallel signifies that Hashem has deviated from the normal routine of nature and altered the natural course of the world. Since this happens only periodically, it does not disrupt the regular, natural course of the world. However, if we were to say Hallel every day, we would be expressing an expectation that Hashem will involve Himself in a miraculous way every day. This would undermine the entire basis of nature and raise the following questions: If Hashem is performing open miracles on a daily basis, why isn't He putting a stop to all the bad that exists in the world? Also, why do good people suffer while wicked people seem to live in tranquility? Is it possible, heaven forbid, that there are things beyond Hashem's capacity?

Therefore, explains the Maharal, the Gemara (mentioned earlier) says that in our daily prayers, we must praise Hashem in terms of the world's natural events. If we were to say Hallel every day, it would be a form of blasphemy for it would lead to the questions stated above. The daily glory we offer to Hashem reflects His hidden, behind-the-scenes involvement. By limiting Hallel to special days, we signify our understanding that Hashem alters the course of nature only periodically, for specific occasions. These are the occasions marked by the Yamim Tovim. Since these open miracles happen infrequently, we can retain the perspective that the world runs its natural course, yet at the same time, we understand that when Hashem deems it appropriate, He alters nature.[8] To summarize, while it is obligatory to recite Hallel at its appropriate time, it is completely unsuitable when it is not warranted.

With this overview of when we *do not* recite Hallel, we can begin to explore the Hallel that we *do* say.

Hallel Hagadol versus Hallel

The Gemara (*Pesachim* 118a) asks, *Since the purpose of reciting Hallel is to recognize the kindness of Hashem, would it not be more appropriate to recite* Hallel Hagadol, *for that declares the kindness of Hashem twenty-six times with the words* Ki l'olam chasdo*–"His kindness is forever"*? The Gemara provides three answers from

---

8. This idea is presented in the Ramban at the end of *Parshas Bo*, where the Ramban explains the reason for all the miracles at the time of exodus. He writes that from the great miracles, we can and are obligated to believe in the small daily miracles.

Rabbi Yochanan, Rabbi Nachman bar Yitzchak, and Rabbi Chizkiyah. The Maharal elaborates on each.

The Five Components of Hallel

Rabbi Yochanan states that the standard Hallel was chosen for Rosh Chodesh and Yom Tov because it mentions five miraculous occasions that are not mentioned in the *Hallel Hagadol*.[9]

These are: the exodus from Egypt, the splitting of the sea, the giving of the Torah, the resurrection of the dead, and the travails of Mashiach.

The Maharal (*Gevuros*, Chapter 61), commenting on this Gemara, points out that Rabbi Yochanan not only lists the miracles that Hashem performed for us, but focuses on the fact that there are five different miracles. This hints that the number five itself reflects a higher reality of existence.

The Letter *Hei*

The Marahal derives this from the *pasuk* (*Bereishis* 2:4): *These are the generations of the world when they were created* (בהבארם). *Chazal* expound that in addition to the literal meaning of the verse, a deeper meaning emerges by dividing בהבארם into ב ״ה״ בראם, which means "They were created with the letter *hei*."

The Maharal comments that the letter *hei* is considered the most spiritual letter of the *aleph-beis*, for we pronounce it not only with the mouth but primarily with the soul (see footnote).[10] Therefore, explains the Maharal, the *pasuk* that tells us that the letter *hei* was

---

9. וכי מאחר דאיכא הלל הגדול אנן מאי טעמא אמרינן האי, משום שיש בו ה׳ דברים הללו, יציאת מצרים, קריעת ים סוף, מתן תורה, תחיית המתים, וחבלו של משיח.

10. The letter *hei* is pronounced with the least amount of involvement of the body compared to any other letters. All other letters require the body to be involved in pronouncing the letters. However, the letter *hei* can be said without the movement of lips, tongue, teeth, or throat—just by a person's breath. This gives the *hei* an aspect of spirituality not found in any other letters.

a primary tool in creation is also telling us that through the *hei*, the physical world is connected to the higher realm of spirituality.

Furthermore, says the Maharal, Rabbi Yochanan is revealing that since Hallel contains *these* five specific miracles, it is describing these specific connections between the world and its inherent spirituality. Through Hallel, we retell and recognize how the world reacts to its connection with Hashem. This means that when we praise Hashem through Hallel, **we recognize how the letter *hei*, acting as a force in creation, manifested itself through these five events and created the three *regalim* that are described in the Hallel**.

The Three *Regalim* and the Letter *Hei*

The Maharal elaborates that these five connections are divided into three main events: the beginning, middle, and end of the world's connection to its higher reality. Taken together, the first two events, the exodus and the splitting of the sea, represent the beginning of this connection. Although the world had been created more than 2,000 years earlier, only with the birth of the Jewish nation, which brought into the world a people that could identify as Hashem's children, was the channel to the spiritual realm opened. By virtue of the emergence of the Jewish people, the entire world was elevated to this new reality, reflected by the world's creation with the letter *hei*. These two events—the exodus and the splitting of the sea—encapsulated the birth of our nation, and they are celebrated as the first and last days of Pesach. Therefore, we recite Hallel on Pesach.

Each year, when we reach the fifteenth of Nissan, we recognize and praise Hashem as He raises us—His children—and the entire world above a natural physical existence. The matzah and the entire Seder are the uplifting products of the letter *hei* that created the world. This is precisely why Hallel is an integral part of our Seder.

The same is true with Shavuos. Rabbi Yochanan's third reason for reciting Hallel is that it records the giving of the Torah. This is the miracle commemorated on the Yom Tov of Shavuos.

Sukkos, the Completion of the World

The Hallel with which we praise Hashem on Sukkos represents the transformation that the world will undergo at the end of 6,000 years. This will happen through the coming of the Mashiach and the resurrection of the dead. These events will complete the world's transformation from its present state of existence to its higher reality.

The Gemara (*Sukkah* 2a) quotes the *pasuk, And there will be a* sukkah *as a shade from the heat in the daytime and as a protection and refuge from storm and rain.*[11] The Gemara explains that this verse refers to the days of Mashiach. Furthermore, we identify the *sukkah* as our protection in the evening prayer of *Hashkiveinu*. There, we pray for Hashem to rid the world of all negative forces—including the Satan—and all forms of illness, pestilence, violence, and war. We ask that He spread over us His *sukkas shaleim*—His complete *sukkah*. Sukkos represents the world in its eventual state of *shleimus*, another miracle that justifies the recitation of Hallel.

It is fascinating to note that we find that not only are all three Yamim Tovim the sources of these five miraculous occasions, but also, the letter *hei* is in a primary position in all three.

The *Hei* in Pesach

Chazal explain that *chametz* and matzah, the two words that define what we may and may not eat on Pesach, differ from each other by only one letter. Both words include a *mem* and a *tzadi*. However, *chametz* includes a *ches*. The word matzah replaces the *ches* with a *hei*. The *Zohar* (*Parshas Bo*) states that the

---

11. וסוכה תהיה לצל יומם מחורב ולמחסה ולמסתור מזרם וממטר.

difference between *chametz* and matzah is that *chametz* is identified with the *yetzer hara*, the evil inclination—while matzah represents the *yetzer tov*, a person's desire to do good. Indeed, the letter *ches*, when spelled out, means sin. Therefore, when the *ches* is turned into a *hei*, bad is changed to good. We see a hint at this meaning of the letter *hei* as we begin the Seder with the declaration ***Ha*** *Lachma Anya*. The letter *hei* is what makes this bread humble.[12]

The *Hei* in Shavuos

The next miracle that Hallel commemorates is the giving of the Torah, which we celebrate on Shavuos. The giving of the Torah gave human beings the power—by performing the mitzvos—to connect with Hashem and the World to Come. This gives us an entirely new perspective on Rashi's famous statement at the beginning of *Parshas Bereishis*[13] that Hashem added the letter *hei* to the sixth day of creation as a hint that the Torah would be given to the Jewish people on the sixth day. Once again, we can appreciate the words of Rabbi Yochanan, that the most appropriate letter to use as a hint of the miracle of Shavuos is of course the letter *hei*! As we mentioned earlier, the giving of the Torah is rooted in the power of the *hei*. Therefore, we say Hallel on Shavuos.

The *Hei* in Sukkos

The Gemara (*Sukkah* 6b) teaches us the laws of the structure of the *sukkah*. We learn that we need three

---

12. Humility is the character trait singled out by the Torah when it describes the greatness of Moshe.

13. יום השישי, הוסיף ׳ה׳ בששי בגמר מעשה בראשית לומר שהתנה עמהם על מנת שיקבלו עליהם ישראל חמשה חומשי תורה.

walls, two of which must meet a certain minimum size and be placed perpendicular to each other. The third wall can measure a mere *tefach*, but where should that *tefach* be placed? The Gemara answers that it belongs opposite the extension of either end—and provides an illustration.[14] The figure it shows is the letter *hei*. This means that the structure of the *sukkah* is a replica of the letter *hei* that it represents.

To summarize, Hallel shows recognition and gratitude for Hashem's active involvement in the world. Rabbi Yochanan related that Hallel records a total of five miraculous events that Hashem revealed for all to see. These open miracles *created* the three holidays of Pesach, Shavuos, and Sukkos. Therefore, we recite Hallel on these three holidays.

The Praise of Rosh Chodesh

Now that we have explained why Hallel is appropriate for the Yamim Tovim, we are left with a question. Why *do* we say Hallel on Rosh Chodesh, which does not mark a miracle? The Torah does not call it a "sanctified day" on which we refrain from our daily activities. It would seem, therefore, that Rosh Chodesh would not be a day for praising Hashem with Hallel. While *Chazal* say that this practice falls into the category of a *minhag*, why is it even permitted?

The Shelah answers that the Jewish calendar is comprised of lunar months, and the holidays are observed exclusively through the calculation of these lunar months. The beginning of each month is called Rosh Chodesh, which identifies it not only as the first day of the month, but also as the head of the month. The Shelah explains that this means that the rest of the month is encapsulated in the first day. Rosh Chodesh is the catalyst for

---

14. See Ritva ad loc.

the observance of that month's holidays. It is appropriate to say Hallel on Rosh Chodesh because this day carries within it the seeds of all the holidays and the miracles contained within each month.

Greeting the *Shechinah*

A second reason for saying Hallel on Rosh Chodesh is because it has its own status as a holy day. The special character of Rosh Chodesh can be gleaned from the Gemara (*Sanhedrin* 42a) that explains that *Kiddush Levanah* constitutes Israel's recognition of the greeting of the *Shechinah*.

Indeed, when we recite *Kiddush Levanah*, we quote the statement of Rabbi Yishmael: "Had Israel not been privileged to greet the countenance of their Father in heaven except once a month, it would have sufficed." Therefore, Abaya adds, "We must stand," for we are in the presence of the *Shechinah*!

What is so momentous about this blessing that it is considered an experience of the *Shechinah's* presence? Why does greeting Shabbos not carry this same status? Although we formally greet Shabbos and refrain from work on that day, we still do not recite Hallel on Shabbos. To understand why this is so, let us explore a fundamental difference between Shabbos and our other holy days.

Shabbos versus Yamim Tovim

The Maharal says that we have two types of holy days: Shabbos and the Yamim Tovim. Although they are different, they certainly have much in common. Indeed, the *parshah* that commands us to observe the *mo'adim* begins with the mitzvah of Shabbos, indicating that there is a connection between Shabbos and Yom Tov. Both Shabbos and the Yamim Tovim are holy days in which we are restricted from engaging in our regular daily routine and thus freed from life's mundane activities. Nevertheless, the processes through which we arrive at these distinct states of holiness are, in essence, complete opposites.

The fundamental difference between these two types of holy days is that the Yamim Tovim clash with the physical world while Shabbos complements it. Shabbos occurs weekly; observing it depends on the counting of days of the week. Yamim Tovim, on the other hand, are not bound to a specific day of the week, but rather, they are dependent on the new moon.

This means that Shabbos is in sync with the world; it is a consistently occurring holy day that is the culmination of six days of work. Shabbos is, by definition, a day of rest from work: Six days you will labor and do all your work. Then comes Shabbos.

The name for Shabbos reflects this definition: *For He rested* (Va'yishbos) *on the seventh day from all His work that He completed.* This tells us that the physical world advances to the *kedushah* of Shabbos. By the end of the week, the physical world has "rested," and therefore ascended to a state of holiness. Not only is Shabbos the holiness that enters at the end of the week, but Shabbos is also *the source* of the physical world in the week to come.[15] Shabbos is always one of seven days, and as such, it depends on the weekdays.[16]

In contrast, Yamim Tovim are never linked to the days of the week. This is because they derive from specific miraculous events that happened at a particular time—events that clashed with nature and altered the sequence of an orderly world. These events superimposed the world with a realization that there exists a

---

15. This holiness is both at the end of the week and before the week begins. The power and energy of Shabbos at the end of the week is rooted in the Shabbos before the week. This concept is known as סוף מעשה במחשבה תחילה—*What is revealed at the end is first in thought.* We say this every Friday before sundown as we accept the Shabbos in *Lecha Dodi*.

16. The Talmud teaches us that if a person were to be lost in a desert and forget what day of the week it was, therefore not knowing what day Shabbos is, the person should count six days and the seventh will be Shabbos. This underscores the concept that Shabbos is the Seventh Day.

higher reality. Yamim Tovim are an "out of this world experience." Yom Tov, created through miracles, takes a weekday, mundane as it is, and *transforms* it into a holy day.

The Time of the Sun, the Time of the Moon

If we delve deeper, we find that these two types of holy days are each connected to different luminaries. Shabbos depends on the passage of seven days, which are marked by the rising and setting of the sun. The sun governs our days in the sense that the length of each day is dependent upon it. The moon, however, has no visible effect on our daily life; its connection is hidden. The Yamim Tovim are rooted in months of the year, which are marked by the phases of the moon. For example, the Torah informs us that Pesach and Sukkos are on the fifteenth of their respective months, and Rosh Hashanah is on the first of the month. The Yamim Tovim are identified not through the physical world below, but rather by signs from heaven above.[17] Yamim Tovim are not tied to a specific day of the week because *they have no inherent* link to creation. Rather, they are an infusion of holiness from above. The moon is the source for this higher spiritual involvement.

The Moon's Role

The first mitzvah Hashem gave the Jewish people was to maintain the Jewish calendar. In the words of the Torah (*Shemos* 12:2), *This month is to you the head of the months...* This commandment created the possibility of declaring the Yom Tov of Pesach fifteen days later. Rashi, commenting on the *pasuk* (*Bereishis* 1:14) that says the luminaries *shall be for signs and for appointed seasons* (mo'adim), sees this as a reference to the Yamim

---

17. The exception is Shavuos, for which no calendar date is designated. Rather, it is fifty days after the beginning of Pesach. Indeed, the Gemara quotes two opinions as to the date of the original Shavuos: either the sixth or the seventh of Sivan.

Tovim that Hashem would eventually command the Jewish people to observe. What quality does the moon possess that makes it worthy of heralding the holy times in the world?

Waxing and Waning

The Maharal observes that the moon is the only heavenly power that seems to have peaks and low points in its appearance.[18] As we perceive the moon waxing and waning, we see a parallel to the world of *ruchniyus*. There are times of growth and *shleimus* and times of stagnation and even withdrawal. We, in our own personal growth, are exactly the same. While our physical self remains in a relatively stable and consistent state, our inner self is constantly fluctuating. We have the capacity to rise up—motivated by energy and positivity—sometimes for days or weeks at a time. But we are unable to maintain the constant momentum; eventually, we stagnate or even slip backward.

We as the Jewish people identify with the moon. We declare this connection in *Kiddush Levanah* when we say, "The Jewish people are like the moon for we are destined to be renewed like her [the moon]." This is why the moon symbolizes *ruchniyus*. It is heavenly, for it is up in heaven, but it also shares the waxing and waning of earthly humans. This makes it the ideal interface between heaven and earth.

A Glimpse of Heaven

Every new moon initiates a renewed flow of energy and holiness from above. Furthermore, this signal of renewal is in relative proximity to the earth and can be perceived naturally by the naked eye. Therefore, explains the Maharal, the beginning of every month carries the seeds of the higher reality of heaven. Here

---

18. The sun, on the other hand, is constant. It rises in the East and sets in the West. The subtle changes in its path (a more northern route in the summer versus a southern route in the winter) are not perceived on a day to day basis.

again is a hint to the spiritual energy of the letter *hei* that is the source of *ruchniyus* with creation. The moon infuses us with the energy integral to the five events that were the source of the Yamim Tovim. Rosh Chodesh gives us a rare glimpse of Hashem as He uses heaven to interact with us in our lives. When Rabbi Yishmael says, "Had the Jewish people only been privileged to greet the countenance of their Father in heaven except for once a month, it would have sufficed," he tells us that the infusion of spiritual energy we receive on Rosh Chodesh is enough to sustain us. The rest of our *ruchniyus* flows from there.

No specific miracle occurs on Rosh Chodesh, nor does weekday activity cease. Yet the new month provides access to Hashem that allows us to reach the yearly times of holiness. Therefore, we recite Hallel on Rosh Chodesh.

Hallel and the Righteous

In addition to five miracles mentioned earlier, the Gemara (*Pesachim* 118a) gives an alternative reason for reciting the standard Hallel on Yamim Tovim in lieu of the *Hallel Hagadol.* Rabbi Nachman bar Yitzchak points out that Hallel mentions the escape of the righteous souls from Gehinnom: *I beseech You, Hashem, deliver my soul* (*Tehillim* 116:4). This verse refers to the righteous being delivered from Gehinnom because of the purity they have attained.

Why does Rav Nachman connect these two ideas? What does reciting Hallel have to do with the deliverance of the righteous?

Tzaddikim

The Maharal explains that Rav Nachman bar Yitzchak is teaching us *why* Hashem makes miracles for the Jewish people. A *tzaddik,* according to the Maharal, is a person who conquers his or her negativity, physical as well as emotional. The Hebrew word *tzaddik* also means correct and virtuous. *Tzaddikim* live in a manner that elevates them above the lowliness of this world**. Since these virtuous people have conquered their personal, natural**

limitations, they have created a miracle within themselves; therefore, Hashem provides miracles on their behalf.[19]

The Maharal (*Gur Aryeh, Bereishis*)[20] explains that this is known as "rising above one's physicality" and is an exalted accomplishment. The Hallel that the Sages chose to recite expresses recognition that Hashem performs miracles for those who raise themselves above the lowliness of this world.

The Maharal's explanation of Rabbi Nachman bar Yitzchak's words casts a new light on the praise offered in Hallel. Uniquely, Hallel identifies Hashem's goodness and praises Him for His personal, individual deliverance of *tzaddikim*, rather than His elevation of the world (as we discussed in the first approach). The Maharal thus teaches us that when we recite Hallel, we are showing gratitude to Hashem for assisting the righteous to attain a level of spirituality that raises them above any deficiency, making them worthy of all the miracles that Hashem performs.

Gehinnom

Since rescue from Gehinnom figures prominently in our discussion, let us examine what exactly is meant by this term. In general, our superficial understanding of Gehinnom is that it is the place where wicked people must go after their passing. But that is an incomplete picture.

---

19. The Maharal (*Pirkei Avos*) brings proof for this idea from two adjacent mishnayos in the fifth *perek*. The mishnah writes that Hashem tested Avraham ten times and he successfully passed all of them. The next mishnah states that Hashem made ten miracles for the Jewish people in Egypt. The Maharal explains that the correlation between these two mishnayos are as follows: Since Avraham was successful in rising above his own nature to do Hashem's will, Hashem reciprocated and brought supernatural events (the ten plagues) to benefit Avraham's children.

20. *Perek* 28, *pasuk* 11: The Maharal explains Rashi's account of when Yaakov gathered twelve stones and then lay his head on them, and the stones began to quarrel as to which would merit being the stone upon which the *tzaddik* would rest his head. This happened because of Yaakov's מעלת הנבדלת.

The Maharal tells us that Gehinnom is much more inclusive than we think. It is a vacuum, a place of emptiness for those who did not actualize their mission in this world and failed to fulfill their *neshamah's* potential. The *neshamah* is the energy source that allows us to do good in the world. However, the trivialities and distractions of the world can easily steer us away from that calling, leaving us with many wasted hours, days—or even a wasted life.

This is a universal human struggle. We all are created with both a body and a soul, each pulling in a different direction. A person who solely heeds the dictates of his or her body and ignores the soul creates an emptiness—a personal Gehinnom. Simply possessing a physical body with its needs and desires puts us at risk of this outcome. The only solution is to proactively push back against the demands of the physical self.

The Maharal defines a *tzaddik* as someone who succeeds in tapping into his soul's energy, which he can only achieve through the constant battle to rise above the distractions of his physical self.

Regarding the Jewish people, the introduction to *Pirkei Avos* declares that they are inherently righteous: *All Israel has a portion [awaiting] in Olam Haba, as it says (*Yeshayah *60:21), "And your nation are all righteous. They will eternally inherit the [eternal] land."*[21]

These are the righteous people who escape from Gehinnom. They rise above the physical part of themselves and attach themselves to their own souls. When this occurs, says the Maharal, a person is not bound by his own limitations. Therefore, he deserves Hashem's miracles and has much reason to praise Him. Indeed, his praise goes beyond the daily praise of the world; it is the praise of the righteous who have incorporated Hashem into their lives. This is why Rabbi Nachman bar Yitzchak identifies

---

21. ועמך כולם צדיקים לעולם יירשו ארץ.

escape from Gehinnom as a reason we should praise Hashem for His miracles by reciting Hallel.

Chananyah, Mishael, and Azariah

A third reason for saying this version of Hallel is stated in the same Gemara (mentioned earlier) by Rabbi Chizkiyah. It is because the verses of Hallel mention the occurrences for the specific miracles that Hashem performed to benefit the righteous.[22] An episode mentioned twice in Hallel is the descent of the *tzaddikim* (Chananyah, Mishael, and Azariah) into the fiery furnace, and their subsequent salvation from it. This episode, explains the Gemara, is the background of the *perek* of Hallel that begins, *Lo Lanu*—"not for our sake."

Perek 115 begins, *Not for our sake, Hashem, not for our sake; rather for the sake of Your Name give honor, for Your kindness and for Your truth.* Although this verse seems to emanate from one speaker, Rav Chizkiyah informs us that there are three voices involved, each expressing thanks for a different miracle. The background to his explanation is rooted in the story of Chananyah, Mishael, and Azariah. Here is a short synopsis of the event.

Chananyah, Mishael, and Azariah in *Bikas Dura*

When the Jewish people were exiled to the Babylonian Empire, King Nevuchadnezzar demanded that every person bow down to a particular idol that he established in the valley of Dura. The Jews unfortunately succumbed and bowed, but Chananyah, Mishael,

---

22. Herein lies the difference between the second and third reasons for reciting this form of Hallel. In Rabbi Nachman's explanation, there are no specific miracles that were done on behalf of the righteous. Rather, Hallel is praising Hashem for the general system in which the righteous can lift themselves above this world. In Chizkiyah's approach, however, Hallel is the praise given for the specific events that happened to these three righteous men, as will be explained in the next paragraph.

and Azariah refused. When the situation came to a head, they were given the choice of bowing or being thrown into a fiery furnace. In their loyalty to Hashem and His commandments, they chose to be thrown into the raging fire. Miraculously, **amid the flames that did not extinguish**, they called out to Hashem, as mentioned in the *pasuk*, and they remained unharmed. In contrast, when Avraham was thrown into a fiery furnace by Nimrod for refusing to bow to an idol, the fire extinguished itself. The Maharal explains that the fact that the fire had no power to harm these *tzaddikim* reveals that the righteous can rise to the level of angels, who cannot be burned by flames.

Returning to the Gemara, it elaborates: Chananyah said, "Not for our sake, not for our sake." Mishael said, "For Your Name's sake give honor." Azariah said, "For Your kindness and for Your truth." This portion of Hallel describes their *descent* into the furnace.

All Nations Praise Hashem

Hallel also alludes to their *ascent* from the fiery furnace in *Tehillim* 117: *Praise Hashem, all nations. Praise Him, all the states. For His kindness has overwhelmed us, and the truth of Hashem is eternal.*[23]

Once again, this seemingly single declaration is divided into parts: Chananyah said, "Praise Hashem, all nations." Mishael said, "Praise Him, all the states," and Azariah said, "For His kindness has overwhelmed us." The concluding statement, "and the truth of Hashem is eternal," was proclaimed by all of them.[24]

The Maharal finds a deep meaning in this Gemara, which gives us insight into Hashem's methodology for performing miracles. He reveals that Chananyah, Mishael, and Azariah were not just

---

23. הללו את ה׳ כל גוים שבחוהו כל האמים. כי גבר עלינו חסדו ואמת ה׳ לעולם הללוקה.

24. חזקיה אמר מפני שיש בו ירידתן של צדיקים בכבשן האש ועלייתן ממנו, ירידתן דכתיב לא לנו ה׳, לא לנו אמר חנניה, כי לשמך תן כבוד אמר מישאל, על חסדך ועל אמיתך אמר עזריה, למה יאמרו הגוים אמרו כולם. עלייתן מכבשן האש דכתיב הללו את ה׳ כל גוים אמר חנניה, שבחוהו כל האמים אמר מישאל, כי גבר עלינו חסדו אמר עזריה, ואמת ה׳ לעולם הללוקה אמרו כולם.

invoking the merit of the *Avos*. Rather, each one merited to awaken the power of the *Avos* so that it was as though the *Avos* had come back to life. (See below regarding the relationship between the names of Chananyah, Mishael, and Azariah and the names of the *Avos*.)

Three Motives for Miracles

According to the Maharal, the Gemara is informing us that Chananyah, Mishael, and Azariah forged a connection to Hashem that paralleled that of Avraham, Yitzchak, and Yaakov.[25] Hashem saved these righteous, devoted followers through the three different attributes of the *Avos—chessed, gevurah,* and *tiferes*—which we delved into in detail in an earlier chapter. If we review the statements of Chananyah, Mishael, and Azariah, we find that each reflects one of these *middos*.

Yitzchak and *Gevurah*

In requesting from Hashem, "Not for our sake, not for our sake," Chananyah asked Hashem to save the three *tzaddikim* through the *middah* of strict judgment, which is rooted in *gevurah*. The Maharal explains that in the struggle between good and evil, Hashem uses strict judgment to save the righteous from the hands of the wicked. This is not "for our sake," because the merit of the righteous justifies Hashem's miraculous salvation, but rather, so *that the wicked should not triumph*. Because Chananyah's own righteousness paralleled that of Yitzchak's, the request expressed the attribute of *gevurah*, and was fulfilled in the merit of Yitzchak.

Yaakov and *Tiferes*

Mishael, who said, "For Your Name's sake give

25. This will be discussed later in the chapter devoted to לא לנו.

honor," asked Hashem to save him and the other two men to bring glory to His Name. This is an entirely different reason from that of Chananyah. The impact of *tiferes* (honor and glory) is that Hashem honors His followers since their glory reflects Hashem's glory. Therefore, Hashem granted Mishael's plea and delivered a miracle in the merit of Yaakov, whose *middah* of *tiferes* Mishael emulated.

Avraham and *Chessed*

Finally, Azariah prays, "For Your kindness and for Your truth," calling upon Avraham's *middah* of *chessed.* This tells us that sometimes, Hashem grants a miracle based solely on His kindness.

The same pattern also holds true for their ascent from the furnace. "Praise Hashem, all nations" was exclaimed by the nations who recognized their defeat. This reflects the *middah* of *din,* called upon by Chananyah. The nations received what they deserved—strict judgment. The word *shabechuhu* used in the *pasuk* means to bring praise to Hashem, and connects to Mishael's request for Hashem's help in the merit of Yaakov and *tiferes*. "His kindness has overwhelmed us" corresponds to Azariah's request in the merit of Avraham.

In summary, the declarations of Chananyah, Mishael, and Azariah reawakened the exclusive relationship the *Avos* had with Hashem and were the impetus for Hashem to save them.[26]

---

26. On a side note, I once heard from Rav Moshe Shapiro *zt"l* that the sacrifice of Chananyah, Mishael, and Azariah was the catalyst for building the second Beis Hamikdash. The first Beis Hamikdash was given to Bnei Yisrael in the merit of our three patriarchs. Indeed, after the *akeidah* at the site of the future Beis Hamikdash,

The Maharal now explains why each of these *tzaddikim* corresponds to a certain Patriarch. The secret is in the names Chananyah, Mishael, and Azariah.

Three *Tzaddikim* and Three *Avos*

The Gemara (*Sanhedrin* 93a) quotes a *pasuk* in *Zechariah*: *And I saw in the evening and behold a man was riding upon a red horse and he stood among the myrtles.* The Gemara explains that this vision refers to Hashem as a "Man" in the same way the Torah, in *Az Yashir*, calls Him a "Man of War."

It means that at that time, the Almighty was ready to go to war to destroy the world because the Jews in Bavel had deserted Him and bowed to Nevuchadnezzar's idol in Dura. With the Beis Hamikdash destroyed and the exiled Jews completely embracing idolatry, they deserved annihilation. Furthermore, if there were no Jews in the world, there would be no purpose for the world's continued existence. However, when Hashem noticed the refusal and self-sacrifice of Chananyah, Mishael, and Azariah, He was pacified. The *Maharal* (*ad loc.*) explains that the spiritual power of each of these men replicated the merit of the *Avos* and saved the world! Their efforts guaranteed that the world would continue until it reaches its ultimate purpose.[27]

Avraham proclaims, "*Behar Hashem yira'eh*—In this mountain Hashem will be seen." The Talmud says that we learn that Yitzchak prayed at the place of the future Beis Hamikdash from the Torah's words that "Yitzchak went to pray in the field." Yaakov's dream of the ladder also occurred at the Beis Hamikdash, identified as the *Beis Elokim*—the House of Hashem. This reference to the Beis Hamikdash prophetically foretold of the house of worship in Yerushalayim. This is known as *zechus Avos*, the merit of our forefathers. When the first Beis Hamikdash was destroyed, we lost that merit. However, the self-sacrifice of Chananyah, Mishael, and Azariah provided us with a second Beis Hamikdash, for just as the *Avos* were the catalysts for the first Beis Hamikdash, Chananyah, Mishael, and Azariah were, like the *Avos*, a catalyst for the second Beis Hamikdash.

27. Nothing less than the foundation of the *Avos* could have merited this accomplishment.

The way in which each of the three men correspond to the *Avos* is revealed by analyzing their names:

Mishael is rooted in the word *she'eilah*, which means to ask or make a request. A request is evidence of friendship and connection, for we only request favors and kindness from those we feel are inclined to comply. This is parallel to Yaakov's *middah* of *rachmanus*—mercy.[28] Azariah's name is rooted in the word *ozer*, which means [Hashem's] help. This emanates from the *middah* of *chessed*, drawn from the *zechus* of Avraham.

The name Chananyah is based on the word *chein*, which is Hashem's favor. The Maharal points out that we pray, "*Chaneini, Hashem, chaneini*," because *chein* mitigates the *middah* of *din* with which Chananyah is associated.

To summarize, the Maharal explains the three reasons for the unique supplication of Hallel:

1. Rav Yochanan states that Hallel reveals a higher reality that was embedded in the world at the time of creation.
2. Rav Nachman bar Yitzchak explains that Hallel praises Hashem for the opportunity given to the righteous to rise above the physical world.
3. Chizkiyah reveals that Hallel was enacted for Chananyah, Mishael, and Azariah, who saved the world.

---

28. Up until this point, Yaakov has been *tiferes* or *emes*. How does *rachmanus* enter the picture? The answer is that *rachmanus* (mercy) is the product of *emes*. We only have mercy when we feel a connection to the person or animal that needs our help. Yaakov awakens mercy because he is always connected to Hashem; as the Gemara states, *Yaakov didn't die*. He is inextricably bound to the Source of life—a status he achieved through his unwavering devotion to truth. The Maharal explains that the source for Yaakov's connection to *rachmanus* comes from *Bava Basra* (9b), which says, *Anyone who gives* tzedakah *to the poor is blessed with six blessings*. The Maharal explains that these six *brachos* are "Yaakov's blessings."

Hallel and Sukkos

The Hallel we recite on the Yom Tov of Sukkos is unique in that it is the only Hallel that is incomplete without the performance of an accompanying *avodah*, which is the *arba'ah minim* and its *na'anuim*. How do the *arba'ah minim* enhance our Hallel?

As we learned earlier, reciting Hallel connects us to five miraculous events, one of which is "the name of the Mashiach." The Maharal (*Sefer Hanetzach*, Chapter 62, and *Derashos for Shabbos Hagadol*, p. 63) explains, from the Gemara in *Pesachim*,[29] that *In the merit of three we are* zocheh *to three*. One of those three is the mitzvah of *lulav*, with which we will merit to receive the name of Mashiach.[30] For Hallel to connect us to the name of the Mashiach, who will come at a future time, we must elevate ourselves to a level even higher than that which we can reach through the normal recitation of Hallel.[31] This elevation is activated by reciting Hallel with the *lulav*, for in doing so, we attach ourselves to Hashem; as the Torah says, *seven days in front of Hashem*. Further, as we mentioned earlier, the *na'anuim* have the power to ward off all evil spirits. This brings us to a state of happiness that expresses a higher state of wholesomeness. With our connection to a greater level of wholesomeness, we can identify the name of Mashiach.[32]

---

29. As we discussed in "The *Arba'ah Minim* and Mashiach."

30. See above, "The *Arba'ah Minim* and Mashiach."

31. Note: The recitation of Hallel on Pesach and Shavuos praises Hashem for episodes that happened in the past: the exodus and the receiving of the Torah. And although Sukkos is also a holiday that celebrates a previous experience, it is, as we have mentioned many times, an "out of this world existence" that is linked to a more perfect world. As such, it requires an added connection.

32. To "identify the name of Mashiach" means that although Mashiach has not yet arrived, we can connect to him through the understanding of what his arrival will mean to the world. Simply stated, we might not yet know who Mashiach is and when he will come, but it is possible to understand the impact that he will make on the world.

The Eight Days of Hallel

Sukkos is unique amongst the other Yamim Tovim in that we recite the Hallel for eight days in a row. The number eight signifies an elevated state of being. It represents the unique bond that the Jewish people have with their Creator. (*Bris Milah* is on the eighth day, a bond that identifies the Jewish people as His children.)

Although the first seven days require the *lulav* and its *minim*, the final day of the Hallel requires nothing other than our recitation. On this day, we are able to bring all of the spiritual energy back with us into our homes. This is the unique eighth and final day of the recitation of Hallel.

CHAPTER 10

Dovid Hamelech: The Composer of Hallel

The word Hallel means to praise and to glorify. Dovid Hamelech is not only the king of the Jewish people, but he also reigns as the premier voice of praise for Hashem, the King of Kings. Dovid's *Sefer Tehillim* is the source for so many of our prayers. *Tehillim* is also the source of Hallel, but there are other forms of praise to Hashem as well.

The Gemara (*Pesachim* 117a)[1] says that in composing *Sefer Tehillim*, Dovid used ten different praises of Hashem. The Maharsha observes that the Gemara uses the term "*ma'amoros*"—utterances—to describe Dovid Hamelech's words. This is also the term the mishnah uses to describe Hashem's acts of creation.[2] From this connection, the Maharsha draws the conclusion that Dovid's ten forms of praise correspond to the ten utterances that Hashem used to create the world.

What is this connection? I heard from my *rebbi*, Rav Moshe Shapiro *zt"l*, that through *Sefer Tehillim*, Dovid Hamelech was able to tap into the same energy that Hashem used to create the world. How did he reach this level of spirituality?

---

1. אמר רבי יהושע בן לוי בעשרה מאמרות של שבח נאמר ספר תהילים בניצוח בנגון במשכיל במזמור בשיר באשרי בתהלה בתפלה בהודאה בהללוקה.

2. *Perek* 5 mishnah 1: For every act of creation, Hashem says ויאמר.

Adam and Dovid

The Midrash (*Yalkut Shimoni, Remez* 41) writes that when Adam was created, Hashem showed him every generation that was to be born, and He disclosed their contributions to the world. When Hashem showed Dovid Hamelech to Adam, Adam saw that he was allocated only three hours of life.[3] Adam asked Hashem if it was possible to give a gift in heaven, for Adam desired to donate a portion of his life to Dovid. Hashem confirmed that it was possible, and Adam gave Dovid seventy years of his life.

This means that Dovid's life came from the source of all human life. The man who was created directly by the Creator, and was the purpose of creation, shared his life with Dovid. With the power of this astounding connection, Dovid was able to tap into the original *ma'amoros* of creation. Adam's heavenly gift endowed Dovid with the opportunity to be the king of the Jewish people! In this capacity, Dovid was able to influence mankind in an everlasting and unending manner never seen before or after.

I would like to share a personal story that allowed me to

---

3. Why was Dovid Hamelech only allocated three hours? The answer can be found in the Talmud (*Avodah Zarah* 3b) that explains that one of Dovid's accomplishments was that he taught the world how to repent. The idea of repentance is only possible after sin; therefore, whether Dovid would live a short life or a long life depended on whether man would sin. It was possible that Adam wouldn't sin, and Dovid's soul would just need to make an appearance rather than having the job of leading the world in repentance.

But why the number three? The Gemara in *Maseches Sanhedrin* 38a describes the sixth day of creation and the first day of Adam's life. In the ninth hour he was commanded to refrain from eating from the Tree of Knowledge. In the tenth hour he sinned, in the eleventh he was judged, and in the twelfth and final hour he was sent out of the Garden of Eden. It is evident that Adam was given three hours as his test with regard to the Tree of Knowledge. Had he stayed strong and refrained from eating from the tree, he would have needed to do so for three hours. Those were the three hours Dovid would have lived, and it would have been sufficient. However, since Adam sinned, Dovid's *neshamah* needed to go into service. It needed to develop and rectify Adam's mistake.

understand the influence of Dovid Hamelech as an offshoot of Adam Harishon—the source of all humanity.

Dovid Hamelech

First, a short disclaimer. As Jews who adhere to the laws of the Torah, we are careful to distance ourselves from exposure to other religions and their services. Indeed, it is prohibited for a Jew to enter a church, and under no circumstances may one participate in any form of prayer with anyone else other than their fellow Jews. Therefore, the prayers of Gentiles are and should be totally foreign to an observant Jew. In light of that, I was completely ignorant as to the nature of the prayers of the Gentiles of the world.

Several years ago, I was asked to lead the benediction for the inauguration of the Mayor of Bridgeport. I found myself in the Chamber of the City Council, a room full of hundreds of people from a wide range of religions and ethnicities. When I began quoting *Tehillim* (in English) I was astounded to hear **that practically everyone in the room was able to recite the words of King David**.

Actually (since I never say *Tehillim* in English), they were quicker than I was in quoting the words verbatim! I was shocked! How did they know the words of Dovid Hamelech so perfectly that they would roll off their tongues? I came to realize that while Dovid Hamelech is the king of the Jews, we do not have a monopoly on his prayers. In fact, millions, if not billions of people are familiar with the words of *Tehillim*, which they know as Psalms. Dovid Hamelech has successfully been able to motivate and enrich the lives of *all of humanity* in their service of the Almighty.

Where did he get this world renown?

The midrash reveals that he received it directly from Adam, the first man, and the source of all of humanity. Based on this midrash, we understand that Dovid's worldwide influence is due to the unique connection that Dovid and Adam shared.

On a deeper level, while all of humanity is traced to Adam, **no one's life (except for Dovid Hamelech) in this world is composed of years *taken* directly from Adam, thus reducing Adam's lifespan.** Rather all human beings are an extension of Adam Harishon. Dovid, however, did possess years *from* Adam, which means that *Dovid replaced Adam and lived in Adam's stead*. He was a partner with Adam in the role that Adam Harishon played in the world. Dovid Hamelech completed the original *tzuras ha'adam*—the form of man.

Mashiach Ben Dovid

Dovid was thus uniquely suited to become the king, but not just the king of the Jews; he is the father of the person who will bring all humanity back to its proper *tzurah*; that person is Mashiach. Although Mashiach is not a child of Dovid, he is the heir to Dovid's power to unite people and gather them into one kingdom—the Kingdom of Hashem.[4] The Rambam writes that Mashiach's task is to teach the world that Hashem is the only true G-d; he will repair the entire world. This is the task that Dovid performed in his time, bringing Klal Yisrael together into one kingdom under Hashem. But the *Zohar* writes that Adam's years of life were not the only asset he used for this purpose. He was also empowered by the purest people in the world: Avraham, Yaakov, and Yosef.

Dovid and the *Avos*

The *Zohar* in *Parshas Vayishlach* gives more insight into Dovid's origins. It states that some of the patriarchs also gave him years from their lives. Avraham, who could have lived 180 years, gave

4. רמב״ם הלכות מלכים פרק י״א הלכה ד׳ ;ואם יעמוד מלך מבית דוד הוגה בתורה ועוסק במצות כדוד אביו, כפי תורה שבכתב ושבעל פה, ויכוף כל ישראל לילך בה ולחזק בדקה, וילחם מלחמות ה׳ הרי זה בחזקת שהוא משיח. אם עשה והצליח ובנה מקדש במקומו וקבץ נדחי ישראל הרי זה משיח בודאי, ויתקן את העולם כולו לעבוד את ה׳ ביחד, שנאמר כי אז אהפוך אל עמים שפה ברורה לקרוא כולם בשם ה׳ ולעבדו שכם אחד.

Dovid five years and died at 175. Yitzchak, who lived a complete 180 years, did not give Dovid any years because, as the *Zohar* cryptically explains, Yitzchak's life was not compatible with Dovid's.[5] Yaakov, who lived 147 years, gave twenty-eight years to Dovid. We derive this from the assumption that Yaakov should have lived as long as Avraham, which would bring him to the age of 175, but he passed away twenty-eight years short of that. Thus, between Avraham and Yaakov, Dovid gained thirty-three years. Yosef provided the remaining thirty-seven years. Yosef should have lived to 147 like his father Yaakov,[6] but instead, he passed away at 110. The other thirty-seven years went to Dovid, which granted him a lifespan of seventy years (5+28+37=70).

The Chida asks, if Dovid received seventy years from Adam and seventy from the *Avos* and Yosef, why did he not live 140 years? He provides a few answers that center on the fact that Adam's years were bequeathed after he had sinned. This left Dovid in need of untainted years, which he received from the pure lives of the *Avos* and Yosef.

Dovid Melech Yisrael Chai V'kayam

Alternatively, says the Chida, Dovid needed seventy years for the days of his life and seventy years for the nights. This idea is based on the Gemara (*Sukkah* 26b) that explains that sleep is one-sixtieth of death. The Chida's explanation can be understood as follows: Since Dovid Hamelech was empowered to rectify the mistake of Adam, Dovid never allowed himself to sleep for any

5. The explanation that the *Zohar* provides is beyond the scope of this work.

6. The *pasuk* states אלה תולדות יעקב, יוסף—*These are the generations of Yaakov, Yosef.* Rashi explains that everything that happened to Yaakov happened to Yosef. Yaakov was hated by his brother and Yosef was hated by his. Yaakov's brother attempted to kill him, and Yosef's brothers attempted to kill him. So too, the years of their lives should have been identical.

length of time. The Gemara says Dovid slept only for short intervals. He lived a life full of *chaim*.

Mashiach

As we stated earlier, Dovid could only fix the sin of humanity and reunite the world because he was empowered with the years that came from the source of all human life; those are Adam's years. This explains why only Dovid could bring the lineage of Mashiach to the world.

Herein lies a very deep and fundamental concept. Both Adam and Dovid exerted the influence of oneness in the world:[7] Adam, as the source of all of humanity, connects human beings to each other. The dream of humanity is that all people should be at peace with each other, and indeed we have the potential to unite because we come from one man.

Dovid Hamelech, whose years come from Adam, possesses this same influence; he too can unite all people. This is what the Jewish people believe the Mashiach will do. But this unity will not be cobbled together out of peace treaties or other physical causes. Rather, Mashiach will unite humanity under the sovereignty of Hashem. This crucial element comes from the purity of Avraham, Yaakov, and Yosef, whom Dovid also embodies.

Dovid, as a partner with Adam and with the *Avos* and Yosef, has the energy and the wherewithal to unite all of humanity under the rulership of the Almighty.[8]

---

7. The Maharal (*Gevuros*, Chapter 31) explains the dual concept of the number one. The number one represents both an exclusive beginning and a unified, consolidated end. As we mention in our morning prayers, אמת אתה הוא ראשון ואתה הוא האחרון ומבלעדיך אין לנו מלך גואל ומושיע—*It is true that You are the first and You are the last and other than You we have no king, redeemer, or savior.*

8. In the upcoming section *Hashem Echad*, we will develop the concept of the duality of the number one.

The Power of *Tehillim*

We now can begin to appreciate the contribution of *Sefer Tehillim*. My *rebbi*, Rav Moshe Shapiro *zt"l*, explained that Dovid Hamelech's praise of Hashem encapsulates the praises of all humanity. As an extension of Adam Harishon, Dovid has the capacity to be the source of spiritual inspiration for all those who are willing to follow his lead. The heartbeat of the king sets the beat of all his followers. Like Adam, who is the source of oneness for all humanity, Dovid too is a unifier.

So significant is *Sefer Tehillim* that its five books are considered parallel to the five books of the Torah. The Torah's five books encapsulate all of Hashem's commandments to man, thereby establishing a relationship between Hashem and humanity. Likewise, the five books of *Tehillim* embody the entire realm of man's response to his relationship with Hashem.

This similarity between Torah and *Tehillim* can be explained as follows: As the King of the World, Hashem decrees His commandments to His subjects. That is the role of the Torah. *Kesuvim*, which includes *Tehillim*, portrays humanity's response to these decrees. This means that not only have we accepted His Torah, *Kesuvim* expresses our *reaction* to this relationship with Hashem, and our wholehearted acceptance of His Kingship.

In *Tehillim*, Dovid expresses all the emotions a human being experiences in his connection to Hashem: the joy and the sorrow, the longing for hope and the feeling of despair, the fear and the trust. How was Dovid able to understand and feel all these emotions?

He had this power because he had Adam's *neshamah*—the original *neshamah* Hashem breathed into Adam. Dovid became the *ruach memale'la* of creation.[9] Indeed, the *sefer Zera Shimshon*

9. The *pasuk* describing the creation of man states, ויצר ה' אלקים את האדם עפר מן האדמה ויפח באפיו נשמת חיים ויהי האדם לנפש חיה. ובתרגום לרוח ממללא—*And Hashem*

(*Parshas Bereishis*, Chapter 25) states that Adam and Dovid shared the same *neshamah*, and together, they lived 1,000 years. This clarifies the statement in the Gemara (*Sanhedrin* 98b) that *The world was created for the sake of Dovid Hamelech*. Adam's sin caused Hashem to veil His presence in the world to a greater degree,[10] but Dovid, by providing a way to reach out to Hashem, brought Him back.

Adam and Prayer

Embedded in the name "Adam" is a new layer of appreciation for his connection to Dovid Hamelech and *Tehillim*. We will start by recognizing that every word is a combination of letters, and each letter is also a word. The word Adam—אדם—has three letters, *aleph, dalet,* and *mem*. Each of these three letters is also a word.

---

formed the person from dust of the ground and He breathed into him the breath of life. This "breath of life" is interpreted as man's capacity to speak. On a deeper level, the power of speech is the source of leadership since the act of speaking signals the speaker's desire for the listener to follow his words. When a speaker wants to share a thought, the words that express the idea are spoken one by one, allowing the listener to put the words together and follow the statement. In essence, the speaker is the leader of all those who are listening. This is why a leader is known in *Lashon Hakodesh* as a דבר, which means *word, speech,* and *leader*. Dovid Hamelech didn't merely receive his years from Adam, he also acquired the role of the leader of the world, the spokesman for humanity. Indeed, every day before we begin פסוקי דזמרה, we recite the prayer of ברוך שאמר and we say, "And with the songs of Dovid Your servant we praise You and glorify You." This statement means that we, who pray to Hashem, stand in the footsteps of Dovid as we repeat his words to Him. On a deeper level, our power to address Hashem has been made possible by Dovid, for without him, we would be at a loss as to the proper words to use to offer our prayers.

10. *Midrash Rabbah* (*Parshas Bereishis* 19) explains that when Hashem created Adam and Chava and placed them in Gan Eden, Hashem's presence was there with them. However, after they sinned, the *Shechinah* rose up from the world to dwell in the lowest level of heaven. When Kayin killed Hevel, the *Shechinah* ascended to the next level. The midrash continues that with the sins of the ensuing generations, the presence of Hashem departed to the seventh and highest heaven. This all started with Adam.

Aleph is אלף, *dalet* is דלת, and *mem* is מם. The letters that make up the unspoken part of a word are known as the "hidden part—the *chelek nistar*—of a word.

Let us look at the word Adam and its hidden part.

אלף

דלת

מם

The hidden parts are the letters מתפלל—*mispallel*—which means to pray. They represent Adam's hidden power to be *mispallel*—to pray to Hashem. It is noteworthy that when we look at the list above of the letters in Adam's name, we can find the word מתפלל by reading from the bottom to the top—*mem, saf, peh*—and then around the top and downward—*lamed, lamed.* This structure provides a "diagram" of a vital development in creation: The Torah says that the vegetation did not sprout because there was no one to work the land. Rashi (*Bereishis* 2:5) explains this to mean that since man had yet to be created, there was no one to pray for rain. The message is that rain, the source of life for the world, is activated through prayer. Adam embodied this power, but it was his "hidden part." That is the part of Adam that Dovid developed and thereby completed and rectified through *Sefer Tehillim.*

The Five Books of *Tehillim*

At the conclusion of *Sefer Tehillim*, there is a prayer that starts, *May it be Your will, Hashem our G-d and G-d of our fathers, in the merit of the five books of Tehillim that correspond to the five books of the Torah...* Of all the holy writings, only *Tehillim* is seen as a counterpart to the Torah. The Torah is Hashem's communication to man, and *Tehillim* is man's communication to Hashem. *Sefer Tehillim* acquired its similarity to Hashem's Torah by bringing the ultimate *tikkun* to the world and rectifying the *tzuras ha'adam*—the original form of Adam—from whom Dovid Hamelech received the years of his life.

One of the sources cited for the name of the first man—Adam—is the word *adameh*, which can be translated as "I resemble Hashem." When we address Hashem in *Tehillim*, we are doing so just as Dovid Hamelech did, for he is the bearer of this resemblance at its very source; therefore, he is the most appropriate human being to teach the world how to respond to Hashem. Born of the original relationship that Hashem created with man, Dovid Hamelech is responsible for the prayers that will bring the *tikkun* of the world; he is the father of Mashiach.

This explains the unique connection that all people have with *Tehillim*. Just as Dovid experienced the entire spectrum of human emotions in his relationship with Hashem, and he articulated those feelings by putting them into words, songs, praises, and supplication, so too does all humanity. This is the power of *Tehillim* and the basis of praising Hashem through the words of Hallel.

CHAPTER 11

Hallel

What Is Hallel?

Hallel is composed of six chapters of *Tehillim*, from 113 to 118. While each verse has its own individual message, the Maharal reveals a theme that is conveyed throughout the entire Hallel.

In the first chapter, which begins, *Give praise, you servants of Hashem*, we praise Hashem for His involvement with all the world's inhabitants. For although He is above all creation, He reaches into this world and involves Himself in everyone's lives. As we proclaim, *He raises the poor from the dust, He lifts the destitute from the rubbish heaps... He establishes the barren woman into a joyful mother of children.*

In the next chapter, which begins, *When Israel went out of Egypt*, we praise and thank Hashem for delivering the Jewish people from bondage in Egypt. However, the focus of the *perek* is not on our rescue and relief from suffering; rather, it details the reaction of the world to Hashem's revelation of His power and glory. It describes the splitting of the sea and the mountains that shook and trembled like rams. Hashem showed His mastery over nature and revealed that there is a higher reality that He applies to help those who are devoted to Him.

The third chapter is yet another step in our recognition and appreciation of Hashem. Here we explain *why* Hashem involves Himself in the physical world. The *perek* begins, *Not for our benefit, Hashem, not for our benefit but to give glory to Your Name.* With these words, we declare that Hashem showers us with His goodness not because we deserve His involvement and miracles, but rather because His Name is glorified when the world witnesses the good that He does. We conclude with the declaration that *Those who fear Hashem and trust in Hashem, He is their help and their shield.*

We continue with the *perek* that begins, *Hashem Who has remembered us will bless [us].* The Maharal notes that until this point, we have not requested a blessing from Hashem. Now that we have declared that His involvement with us is for His honor, it is appropriate that He bless us, for just as Hashem is blessed, so too are His servants.

The next *perek* opens with the words, *I love Him, for Hashem hears my voice, my supplications, as He has inclined His ear to me.* Here, explains the Maharal, Dovid Hamelech expresses the unbreakable bond between Hashem and the Jewish people. This bond means that Hashem always listens to our prayers. Further, not even death can break the bond. The Maharal explains that this *perek* contains the promise of the resurrection of the dead with the words, *I shall walk before Hashem in the land of the living,* meaning the land of eternal life.

The next *perek* opens with the question, *With what can I repay Hashem for all His kindness to me?* In the text of *Sefer Tehillim*, these words are part of the previous paragraph—because once we've recognized that we will never be separated from Hashem, there is nothing left to do but thank Him. The Maharal explains that Dovid Hamelech asked, "With what can I repay Hashem?" because he felt that Hashem had showered him with the maximum amount of good. His gratitude was so intense that he felt incapable of offering an adequate thank you.

Hallelukah! The Ultimate Praise

Hallel opens with the praise *Hallelukah!* The Maharal, in his commentary on the *Haggadah shel Pesach*, explains the significance of this common yet exalted praise. The Gemara (*Pesachim*) refers to this word as "the tenth praise that includes both the Name of Hashem and His praise merged into one word." Therefore, it is the ultimate, most complete, and inclusive form of praising Him.

At the Pesach Seder, toward the end of *Maggid*, we raise a cup of wine and introduce the Hallel with the following declaration from the paragraph of *Lefichach*:[1]

> *Accordingly, it is our duty to thank, to laud, to venerate, to glorify, to elevate, to esteem, to bless, to acclaim, and to honor the One Who carried out all these miracles for our fathers and for us... Therefore, let us recite a new song before Him.* Hallelukah*! Sing forth the praises of G-d.*

This paragraph contains ten different praises, and the tenth one is *Hallelukah*. What is the significance of the number ten, and what is the value of being the tenth praise? To answer, we must understand the Kabbalistic energy of the number ten.

The Number Ten

In the Torah, the number ten represents holiness. For example, the tenth animal that comes out of the pen needs to be tithed. Also, the amount of *ma'aser* is ten percent. Further, the Gemara states that when ten men are gathered, Hashem's presence rests among them, and therefore, ten men are needed for a *minyan*. The Torah (*Vayikra* 27:32) provides a basis for all of this: *Asiri yihiyeh kodesh*—"The tenth shall be holy."

The Maharal explains that the number ten symbolizes completeness. When counting numbers up to the number ten,

---

1. לפיכך אנחנו חייבים להודות להלל לשבח לפאר לרומם להדר לברך לעלה ולקלס... ונאמר לפניו שירה חדשה הללוקה.

each number is a new entity. Each is distinct with no resemblance to the other. But from ten upward, the numbers are reused.[2] This, says the Maharal, teaches us that ten is a complete number.

The above reveals why the *Shechinah* is not found in groups of less than ten. Hashem's Divine presence does not connect to an incomplete or deficient reality, known as *chisaron*. Only where there is wholeness, as the number ten expresses, is there a place for a higher presence to attach.

On a slightly deeper level, ten as a unit creates a "higher reality" for each specific individual of the group. Thus, the nine sheep that come before the tenth one, which is designated for tithing, are elevated by the presence of the tenth sheep. They have made tithing possible.

Likewise, the nine men who gather for a *minyan* are brought to a new level of *kedushah* by the arrival of the tenth. Unified as a group of ten, they become something above and beyond any single one of the group's members. This unity creates a level of holiness that is suitable for the *Shechinah*.

We can now appreciate the difference between the first nine praises of *Lefichach* and the tenth. Just as the tenth element raises sheep and men from a mundane gathering to a medium for the *Shechinah*, the tenth praise, *Hallelukah*, consolidates and completes the holiness of the nine other praises. As the tenth praise, it transforms the *tefillah* into a magnet for the *Shechinah*, enabling us to cleave fully to Hashem.

---

2. There are two lessons to be learned here: the incompleteness until nine and the wholeness of the number ten. Since every number until nine adds to the count, each number brings more, which allows us to complete what was conceptually deficient. However, once the number ten is reached and there is a complete unit of ten, everything that follows—while it certainly adds—does not make it more complete. For example, once a *minyan* has ten men, additional participants cannot change the essence of the *minyan*. Indeed, the *minyan* is more respectable with a larger crowd; this is known as ברוב עם הדרת מלך. However, that critical reality of having or not having a *minyan* is decided with ten men.

Hallelukah, Praise Hashem

הללוקה הללו עבדי ה׳ הללו את שם ה׳. יהי שם ה׳ מבורך מעתה ועד עולם. ממזרח שמש עד מבואו מהולל שם ה׳. רם כל גויים ה׳ על השמים כבודו. מי כה׳ אלוקינו המגביהי לשבת המשפילי לראות בשמים ובארץ. מקימי מעפר דל מאשפות ירים אביון. להושיבי עם נדיבים עם נדיבי עמו. מושיבי עקרת הבית אם הבנים שמחה הללוקה.

Hallelukah! Give praise, you servants of Hashem, give praise to the Name of Hashem. May the Name of Hashem be blessed from now until forever. From the rising of the sun until its setting, the Name of Hashem shall be praised. Exalted over all the nations is Hashem, above the heavens is His glory. Who is like Hashem our G-d Who is enthroned on high, yet He lowers Himself to look upon the heavens and earth. He raises the poor from the dust, He lifts the destitute from the rubbish heaps to seat them with the noblemen, with the noblemen of His people. He establishes the barren woman into a joyful mother of children, Hallelukah.

Dovid Hamelech begins and concludes the first paragraph of Hallel with the word "*Hallelukah.*"[3] The Maharal explains the meaning of this structure: It represents a level of faith in Hashem that brings us to praise Him with the same enthusiasm at the beginning of our various journeys in life as we feel when we get to our destination. It indicates that we fully comprehend, despite our limited intellect, that everything that Hashem does from start to finish is praiseworthy. While anyone can feel gratitude to

3. The Maharal notes that this form of praise is also found again in Hallel in the paragraph that begins with the praise הודו לה׳ כי טוב כי לעולם חסדו and concludes with הודו לה׳ כי טוב כי לעולם חסדו. The same is true with *Hallel Hagadol*, as the praise begins with כי לעולם חסדו and concludes with כי לעולם חסדו.

Hashem when he sees the results he has been hoping for, Dovid Hamelech's words express the belief that the entire process is worthy of exuberant praise, even when we experience bumps along the way.

When a difficult task or momentous event comes to fruition, there is a moment of jubilation and gratitude that is amplified by the recognition of having come "full circle"—the goals at the inception have become the reality of the present. For example, when parents marry off all their children, the feeling of gratitude is not limited to the current wedding but includes "meriting to marry them all off." That is the lower level of gratitude.

However, there exists an even greater level, expressed by the praise of *Hallelukah* at the beginning and at the conclusion. With this praise, we perceive not only that we have come full circle, but that Hashem's actions are perfect and complete. The parents can make peace **and be thankful for all the ups and downs, and all the rejections and disappointments throughout the entire *shidduch* process. To express the same enthusiasm at the end as at the beginning is to show ultimate faith in Hashem**. In the words of *Chazal*, it is the understanding of Hashem's "*Echad* moment."

Hashem Echad: Hashem's Complete Objective

The Gemara (*Pesachim* 50) quotes the conclusion of our daily prayers, where we proclaim ביום ההוא יהיה ה' אחד ושמו אחד—*On that day, Hashem will be One and His Name will be One.* This means that a day will come when everything in this world will unite in perfect, total devotion to one purpose, which is to connect to Hashem. This will be the ultimate revelation of Hashem's Oneness, in both Name and purpose. It is the future we hope and pray for every day as we declare in our daily prayers that Hashem is One. Yet when we look a little deeper into this concept, we can find that there are two different ways of understanding it.

One concept arises from Hashem's identity as the Source of creation; everything emanates from the One. As we say, "*Shema Yisrael Hashem Elokeinu Hashem Echad.*" Hashem is the Creator and the beginning of all that exists.

The second concept of Oneness identifies Hashem as the *tachlis* or purpose for which creation exists. Everything in the world will ultimately find its purpose with Hashem. That is the meaning that arises from the statement, *On that day, Hashem will be One and His Name will be One.*[4]

The message conveyed by beginning and ending our praises with the word *Hallelukah* is that when we reach the level of true and complete gratitude, we recognize that everything from Hashem is good; that which we perceived as bad and evil was a misconception, for when it comes from Hashem, nothing is bad.

This is an *Echad* moment—the type of awareness that we will acquire at the End of Days.

And this is *Hallelukah!* As we learned earlier, it is a praise into which one of the Names of Hashem (*yud-hei*) is incorporated. Let's now explore why this particular Name was chosen for this purpose.

Hallelukah

This word of praise expresses the essential truth that everything Hashem brings about in creation emanates from His Name. We see this idea reflected in a verse from *Yeshayah* (26:4), which we

---

4. On a deeper level, both aspects of "one" are connected to the statement of "the Shema." The Maharal explains that there is a fundamental difference between the Shema recited in the morning and the Shema recited at night. The daytime Shema is said when it is light outside, and we can perceive the world and declare that it all comes from Hashem, the Source of creation. However, when we say the evening Shema, we're in the darkness. Everything we perceived during the day seems to have disappeared. At that point, says the Maharal, we declare that Hashem is the ultimate and final "One" at the conclusion of creation.

say in our daily prayers:[5] *Because in Hashem* (yud-hei) *is the strength of the worlds.* This means that Hashem created the world with the letters *yud* and *hei*. Therefore, when we praise Him by exclaiming *Hallelukah*, incorporating the letters of this Name into the word *Hallelu* (we praise), we're expressing our recognition of Hashem's capacity as Creator, Who exclusively is capable of making miracles, and our gratitude for our own existence.[6] The essence of *Hallelukah* is, "Only You, Hashem, Who created the world, could have saved us. Thank You!"

When we are aware of the true and complete goodness of Hashem and are bursting with the desire to express our gratitude, this is the word that comes forth from us: *Hallelukah!*

הללו עבדי ה׳ הללו את שם ה׳—*Give praise, you servants of Hashem, give praise to the Name of Hashem.*

The opening praise of Hallel calls upon one and all to praise Hashem. The Maharal notes that by *repeating* the word *Hallelu*—"give praise," this declaration turns into two statements when it could just as easily have conveyed the message in one combined statement. Why does it not simply say, "Give thanks to Hashem, you servants of Hashem"?[7]

The Maharal explains that this verse highlights two separate points:

1. First, we claim our identity. We are servants of Hashem, who are praising Him.
2. Second, we are praising His Name.

Our role as Hashem's servants, says the Maharal, is the most appropriate position from which to praise Him, for it encompasses

---

5. כי בקה ה׳ צור עולמים.

6. This will be explained in the upcoming statement of הללו את שם ה׳.

7. הללו עבדי ה׳ את שם ה׳.

the "background story" behind the praises. This, he says, is that we have been saved from some *tzarah*, such as illness, persecution, or a dire situation. We therefore express gratitude to Hashem for redeeming us. We are indebted to the One Who has freed us from our troubles. In the words of *Chazal*, we are *meshubad* (literally, indentured servants) to Hashem.[8] Therefore, those who praise Hashem are identified as His servants, not His children.

הללו את שם ה׳

This second praise is distinctive because we directly praise the *Name* of Hashem. This expresses recognition that only Hashem could have brought about our redemption—no angel, nor any other intermediary, could have done it. The reason that only Hashem could perform the redemption, explains the Maharal, is that taking slaves and turning them into free men is a transformation that is on the level of creation itself. This is something an angel cannot accomplish; only Hashem, the Creator of reality, can alter it.[9] As we say in the *Unesaneh Tokef* prayer on Rosh Hashanah, Hashem decrees, "Who will live and who will die, who will be impoverished and who will prosper." While there are messengers that carry out Hashem's decree, certain decrees can only be fulfilled by Him. Therefore, the praise we give Hashem for redeeming us from our *tzarah* is directed exclusively to His Name.

---

8. The significance of identifying ourselves as His servants comes at a critical point in *Yetzias Mitzrayim*, when Pharaoh released the Jewish people. The midrash describes the incident as follows: In the middle of the night, during the plague of the firstborn, Pharaoh located Moshe and Aharon and declared, "Until now you have been my servants, and now you are the servants of Hashem." Having been released from bondage and suffering, the Jewish people were no longer slaves to anyone other than the Almighty.

9. See Maharal Haggadah in the section of אני ולא מלאך for multiple reasons why it could only have been Hashem and not an angel that took the Jews out of Egypt.

Now that we have mentioned Hashem's Name, Hallel goes on to bless it.

יהי שם ה׳ מבורך מעתה ועד עולם.
ממזרח שמש עד מבואו מהולל שם ה׳.
רם על כל גוים ה׳ על השמים כבודו.

At this point, having defined ourselves as Hashem's servants and designated His Name as the object of our praise, Dovid Hamelech proclaims three glorifying phrases that encompass three worlds: an upper, middle, and lower world.

Upper World

His first praise: *May the Name of Hashem be blessed from now until forever.* The first word, *yehi*—may it be—is in the future tense, indicating that our blessing continues on into eternity. This refers to *Olam Haba* and represents Hashem's eternal world. The Maharal compares this phrase to the response we make to a person saying Kaddish: *May His great Name be blessed forever and ever.* Here too we are blessing Hashem for all eternity, thereby recognizing the higher world.

Middle World

The next part of the verse, *From the rising of the sun until its setting*, focuses on the world of celestial bodies, known as the middle world.

Lower World

The praise that follows, *Hashem is high above all the nations*, refers to the lower world of mankind. Taken together, these three phrases recount three praises emanating from three different worlds. The Maharal reveals that these three verses comprise one unit, containing three parts. They correspond to the three times we say in Aramaic translation (*targum*) *kadosh kadosh kadosh* in our daily prayer of *Uva L'tzion*.

Kadosh Kadosh Kadosh

The three words *kadosh* are a description of three different realities.

קדיש בשמי מרומא עלאה בית שכנתיה **קדיש** על ארעא עובד גבורתיה **קדיש** לעלם ולעלמי עלמיא

- An upper eternal world that is both limitless in power and endless in time
- The middle world where the sun and the moon dwell
- The lower world, which is identified by its inhabitants

In these verses of *Hallelukah hallelu avdei* we praise Hashem as the sole Ruler of all three worlds, underscoring the theme discussed above. Since this paragraph begins and ends with the same all-encompassing statement of *Hallelukah*, our praise expresses a complete fusion of all three worlds working cohesively to do Hashem's will.

The Maharal (*Sefer Nesivos*)[10] adds that it is through this fusion that the world is maintained. Citing the Gemara (*Maseches Sotah* 49), he explains that when the Beis Hamikdash was destroyed, the blessings it radiated out to the rest of the world ceased. Nevertheless, a connection between the upper world and the world below still exists. To summarize, the three statements of יהי שם, ממזרח שמש, and רם על כל גוים express the unity of Hashem over the three parts of the universe. Next, we laud the goodness that comes through this connection in the next five expressions of praise, each of which ends with the letter *yud*.

---

10. *Nesiv Ha'avodah* (Chapter 11) quotes the Gemara ,ואלא עלמא אמאי קא מקיים אקדושא דסדרא—*Since the destruction of the Beis Hamikdash, the world survives on the order of the* kedushah. The Maharal explains that when we sanctify Hashem's Name, there is a remnant of the holiness of the Mikdash.

מי כה' אלוקינו המגביהי לשבת המשפילי לראות בשמים ובארץ מקימי מעפר דל מאשפות ירים אביון להושיבי עם נדיבים עם נדיבי עמו מושיבי עקרת הבית אם הבנים שמחה—Who is like Hashem our G-d Who is enthroned on high, yet He lowers Himself to look upon the heavens and earth. He raises the poor from the dust, He lifts the destitute from the rubbish heaps to seat them with the noblemen, with the noblemen of His people. He establishes the barren woman into a joyful mother of children.

Hashem's Involvement

Having declared that we are His servants and He is the ultimate Source of power in all worlds, we now turn our focus to the good that we receive from Him. Dovid Hamelech identifies five different attributes that relate to Hashem's involvement with us, His children. They are:

המגביהי, המשפילי, מקימי, להושיבי, מושיבי. Each ends with a *yud* to emphasize that each is a separate action. The Maharal explains these five points and how they are interconnected:

1. המגביהי—*Enthroned on high.* Although there are heavenly powers in the world, Hashem's dwelling is above all of them, which means that there is nothing above Him. All powers are under His domain. This is the *middah* of Hashem as the Omnipotent. It describes the belief that was crystallized for the Bnei Yisrael at the splitting of the sea.
2. המשפילי—Yet, He does not forsake the lowly, for *He lowers Himself to look upon* (and involve Himself in) all that is below. This tells us that Hashem sees what we need in the world below and takes it upon Himself to organize all these necessities. This is Hashem's attribute of supervising and managing the world. It corresponds to the *emunah* that the Jewish people acquired in Egypt when they saw

Hashem afflicting the Egyptians with plagues that left the Bnei Yisrael untouched.

The next three *yuds* reveal *the three attributes with which Hashem manages* the world.[11] They are *chessed, din,* and *rachamim*—kindness, judgment, and mercy. The verse refers to these *middos* with the words מקימי להושיבי מושיבי.

3. מקימי—*Hashem raises the poor from the dust, He lifts the destitute from the rubbish heaps.* This verse portrays Hashem acting with *din*—judgment. The Maharal explains that the attribute of *din* advocates for a person who is so demoralized and destitute that he dwells in rubbish heaps. The *middah* of *din* objects to this hopeless condition, saying, "It isn't fitting for a human being to be so low that he is this downtrodden." Therefore, Hashem lifts him up.
4. להושיבי—*To seat them with noblemen, with the noblemen of His people.* This goes further than justice demands; it is an act of kindness. For justice, it would be enough to relieve the person of his suffering and let him live like a normal person. But out of *chessed*, Hashem goes much further, raising him to a place of high honor.
5. מושיבי—*He transforms the barren woman of the house into a joyous mother of children.* When Hashem wondrously transforms a barren woman into a mother, it is considered an act of mercy, which is the balance between *din* and kindness.

Thus, with these five expressions of praise, Dovid Hamelech gratefully recognizes Hashem's involvement with every level of the entire world.

11. This means that after we have declared that Hashem is both the most powerful and also the most involved, we go on to describe the method of His involvement.

Hashem's Appearance

בצאת ישראל ממצרים בית יעקב מעם לועז. היתה יהודה לקדשו ישראל ממשלותיו. הים ראה וינס הירדן יסב לאחור. ההרים רקדו כאילים גבעות כבני צאן. מה לך הים כי תנוס הירדן תסב לאחור. ההרים תרקדו כאילים גבעות כבני צאן. מלפני אדון חולי ארץ מלפני אלוק יעקב. ההופכי הצור אגם מים חלמיש למעינו מים.

When Yisrael went out of Egypt, the House of Yaakov from a people of a foreign tongue. Yehuda became His sanctuary, Yisrael His dominions. The sea saw and fled, the Yarden turned backwards, the mountains skipped like rams, the hills like lambs. What happened to you oh sea that you flee, the Yarden that you turn backward? The mountains that you skip like rams, the hills like lambs? Before the L-rd does the earth tremble, before the G-d of Yaakov, the One Who turns the rock into a flowing stream, the flintstone into a fountain of water.

בצאת ישראל ממצרים בית יעקב מעם לועז—
When Yisrael went out of Egypt, the House of Yaakov from a people of a foreign tongue.

When reading the second *mizmor* of Hallel, we notice that every idea is written in double language:

> *When Yisrael went out of Egypt* is another way of saying *the House of Yaakov from a people of a foreign tongue.*
>
> *Yehuda became His sanctuary* is echoed in the words *Yisrael, His dominions.*
>
> *The sea saw and fled* is echoed by *the Yarden turned backwards.*

This pattern continues until the end of the *mizmor*, with the words *Who turns the rock into a flowing stream, the flintstone into a fountain of water.*

The Maharal explains this pattern by relating it to the first *mizmor*, which praises Hashem for His supervision of an organized, cohesive world that suits our needs, and does not deviate from its natural course represented by "the rising of the sun to its setting." This second *mizmor* exalts Hashem for His actions that are above nature. Everything it describes happens in a supernatural way, revealing that there is more to the world than what we see. Rather, it is all connected to a higher reality.

With the exodus and the birth of the Jewish nation, we perceive the world not only as Planet Earth, but as a higher realm, a place in which Hashem interacts with His children. The praises recounting these interactions are therefore fittingly stated in two ways. Beyond this general explanation, the Maharal delves into the specific choice of the splitting of the sea as the iconic event through which we grasp Hashem's greatness.

Yisrael and Yaakov: The Identity of the Jewish People

The Jewish people have two names in this *mizmor—Beis Yaakov* and Yisrael. These are the two names with which the Torah identifies our forefather Yaakov, as well as the Jewish people. Although we have three patriarchs, Yaakov is the one whose name we carry.

This is because Yaakov was the father of twelve sons, all of whom were true and loyal to the traditions of their father. During their lives and for all of eternity, they were the seminal twelve Tribes of Israel—the entire Jewish nation. Unlike Avraham who had Yishmael, and Yitzchak who had Eisav, Yaakov's children were complete and pure offspring. It is therefore appropriate that Yaakov is the forefather with whom we identify as a nation.

The Maharal explains that these names also represent the Jewish people on two levels. Yaakov, the name given at birth, refers to the fact that he was born holding on to the heel (*eikev*) of his brother Eisav; this is the lower name. The term *Beis Yaakov* identifies the Jewish people as a distinct and separate nation among the other nations. Yisrael, however, is the name Yaakov earned by triumphing over the angel with whom he wrestled. This name represents the Jewish people's higher reality.[12]

Egypt and *Am Lo'ez*

Indeed, the Egyptians are also given two names in this verse, Mitzrayim and *Am Lo'ez* (a nation that speaks a foreign tongue). The first name in the verse, Mitzrayim, is its higher name. It

---

12. A deeper understanding of the difference between the name Yaakov and the new name Yisrael is found in the commentary of the מקנה in *Maseches Kiddushin, Daf* 30. He bases his idea on the *gematria* of the names. יעקב has the numerical value of 182 and ישראל is 541. The difference is 359 (541-182=359), which is the numerical value of the word שטן—*Satan*. How are we to understand this?

Let us examine the episode that led up to the name change from Yaakov to Yisrael. The Torah (*Parshas Vayishlach*) relates that Yaakov was alone when he was attacked by an angel: ויותר יעקב לבדו ויאבק איש עמו. After a fight that lasted the entire evening, the angel admitted defeat. Yaakov asked the angel for a blessing. The angel responded by informing Yaakov that his name is now Yisrael. Later in the Torah, after Yaakov returned to Eretz Canaan, Hashem informed him that his name was Yisrael. Since the angel already changed his name, why did Hashem need to change it as well? If, on the other hand, only Hashem has the power to change a name, what was the purpose of the angel's blessing?

The answers to these questions revolve around the role that Yaakov assumed after purchasing the right of the firstborn from Eisav. Yitzchak's plan was for Eisav and Yaakov to be "partners" in advancing the mission of their fathers Avraham and Yitzchak. Eisav's job was to go out into the material world and glorify Hashem by elevating the physical and the mundane. Yaakov would remain undefiled by the outside world, dedicating himself purely to the non-physical and the heavenly spheres. However, Yaakov keenly recognized that Eisav was not willing to do the job, and he resolved to accomplish both tasks. When Yaakov responded to his father's question as to his identity, Yaakov maintained, "I am, Eisav your firstborn." This had become his new role. *Chazal* teach that the angel who fought with Yaakov was Eisav's Guardian Angel. The fight was about the nature of Yaakov's new mission. The angel did not change Yaakov's name but rather, he begrudgingly affirmed that the additional name was warranted. This new name was achieved by conquering the powers of Satan, hence the total numerical value of Yisrael is Yaakov plus Satan. Indeed, Yaakov had synthesized both roles to become Yisrael. It was due to this admission by the angel that Hashem changed his name.

represents Egypt as a distinctive and unique nation, and it also represents the *Sar* (heavenly power) that interacts with it from above. Every one of the seventy nations has its own *Sar*, or higher power.

The second name, *Am Lo'ez*, is a generic name that could apply to any nation. The name identifies the Egyptians as a mundane and lowly nation, a people that speaks gibberish. Thus, both Yisrael and Egypt have two names. Is there any correlation?

Two Forms of *Galus*

We can understand the two aspects of the nation by comparing it to a human being, who has a body—its lower part, and a soul—its higher part. Since every nation is a collection of individuals, it too can be divided into higher and lower parts. The soul of the nation is like the human *neshamah*; this is one way of identifying a nation. Mitzrayim is the name that describes that nation's soul. Its body, the lower, more basic level, is the *Am Lo'ez*.

Although both the Jewish people and Egyptians have a connection to a higher power, there is a fundamental difference between the heavenly power of Yisrael and that of Egypt. The Jewish people's Divine connection is solely Hashem, the Source of holiness. We are completely connected to Him, receiving His influence without any intermediaries. The Egyptians, and all other nations, lack this direct connection. Rather, they have their own *Sar* or heavenly power.

By stating *When Yisrael went out of Mitzrayim and Yaakov from* Am Lo'ez, we imply that we were in two different types of exile: one where we are identified as Yisrael and the other as Yaakov—meaning that both the body and the soul of the nation were enslaved.[13]

---

13. This parallels the statement in the Haggadah עבדים היינו לפרעה במצרים. The Jews were in a double state of exile: Their bodies were forced to work for Pharaoh,

Let us delve deeper to understand these forms of exile. From this explanation, we can appreciate why Hallel is associated with the splitting of the sea.

Mi'Mitzrayim* and *Me'am Lo'ez

We've now established that each nation exists on two levels. From there, we can perceive that the Jewish people, under their identity as Yisrael—their higher identity—were subjugated to Egypt's higher level, conveyed by the name *Mitzrayim. Beis Yaakov*, the Jewish people's lower identity, was oppressed by the *Am Lo'ez*, the lower aspect of Egypt, characterized by its foreign tongue.

What is meant by this description of Egypt as a nation of an alien tongue, and how does this trait directly subjugate the House of Yaakov? Also, which is the higher level of servitude?

***Arel Sefasayim*—Uncircumcised Lips**

The Maharal explains that from the Jewish people's perspective as *Beis Yaakov* exiled in an *Am Lo'ez*, they became incapable of communicating with Hashem[14] because their ability to articulate through speech was also in exile. The alien tongue served Hashem's purpose by creating a barrier between the Jews and the idol-worshipping Egyptians, but it also hampered their power of speech. The Torah relates that Hashem heard the "cries" of Bnei Yisrael, not their prayers, for their prayers were not able to ascend to Hashem.

This "exile of speech" was so great an issue that when Hashem assigned Moshe the mission of leading the Jewish people and speaking to Pharaoh on Hashem's behalf, Moshe demurred

---

and their souls identified themselves as slaves. See *Divrei Simchah: Maharal on the Haggadah Shel Pesach* (pp. 54-56) for further explanation of the double level of slavery.

14. The Torah writes that the Jewish children cried out to Hashem. The *Zohar* explains that they were incapable of praying; they could only cry.

because he lacked the ability to articulate. He described his state as uncircumcised lips—*arel sefasayim.*[15] The *Zohar* explains that Moshe's power to speak was also in exile within the *Am Lo'ez* of Egypt. On a practical level that meant Moshe could not lead the Jewish people out of Egypt.

The Maharal cites two verses that identify two levels of servitude:

In *Devarim* (4:34), Moshe says, "Or has any god performed miracles to come and take for himself a nation from a nation?" This refers to the exile described by the words עבדים היינו—*We were slaves*, for the Jewish people's only identity during their exile was that of a nationless people enslaved within another nation. They had no national identity at this point. They had no voice in their day-to-day lives, no way of expressing their nationhood, and no way to receive or act upon any of Hashem's commandments.

A different level of servitude is defined in *Devarim* (4:20) when Moshe tells the Jews that "Hashem took you out from an iron crucible." (A crucible is a vessel in which iron or gold is melted to separate the ore from impurities.) The metalsmith cannot easily reach into the intense heat of the fire to remove the metal. Likewise, Pharaoh's oppression was so intense that it prevented the Jewish people from leaving. No human agent could draw them out of the fire. This is a higher level of subjugation.

However, both levels of servitude relate to the concept of *avadim hayinu* because we had no other identity than that of

---

15. The term ערל, used to describe Moshe's inability to speak for Hashem, is the same term used to mean "foreskin" in relation to circumcision. This term is also used to describe stubbornness and an inability to comprehend. As the Torah states in *Devarim* (*Parshas Eikev* 10:16), ומלתם את ערלת לבבכם וערפכם לא תקשו עוד—*I shall cut away the barrier (lit. foreskin) of your heart and you will no longer stiffen your neck.* This indicates that Moshe's inability to speak for Hashem was not just a speech impediment, but rather an obstruction that prevented Moshe from revealing what was really behind his words.

slaves until we left Egypt. All of this is included in the plight of *Beis Yaakov*, exiled within an *Am Lo'ez.*

The Forty-Ninth Level of Contamination

In addition, even the higher status of the Jewish people—Yisrael—was subjugated by its higher-level Egyptian equivalent—Mitzrayim. Egypt was recognized as a place where the presence of Hashem was unknown and unwanted. After spending over 200 years as slaves to the Egyptians, the Bnei Yisrael had almost completely forgotten the Name of Hashem. The Jews were as idolatrous as the Egyptians. This is the higher level of contamination and slavery.

Krias Yam Suf and Hallel

Once the Jewish people reached the Yam Suf, outside the borders of the *Am Lo'ez*, their capacity to speak returned to them. The Torah relates that at the Yam Suf, Moshe and Bnei Yisrael were finally able to address Hashem and praise Him for all that He had done for them. At that moment, for the first time in history, the Jewish people sang the exultant song of praise to Hashem known as *Az Yashir.* With this new form of *avodah*, the seeds of Hallel were planted. At the moment the people reached the other side of the sea, our nation was born. With our power of speech returned, the first thing we did with it was to sing Hashem's praises. That is why Hallel is so closely linked to the splitting of the Yam Suf.

היתה יהודה לקדשו—*Yehuda became His sanctuary.*

The exodus was a moment of transformation! Upon entering the water, the Jewish people became identified with Hashem. They were now imbued with *kedushah*.

In all the world's history before the splitting of the Yam Suf, there had never been a concrete occurrence that could be identified as the work of the Creator. This monumental event shook the mountains and transformed all the oceans and rivers into masses of solid water. The Jewish people, now a nation, were ready for their own hierarchy. Appropriately, this *mizmor* proclaims that the tribe of *Yehuda became His sanctuary*. The Maharal explains that since the tribe of Yehuda provides the Jewish people's leaders and monarchy, Yehuda emerged from the exodus as "the exalted one," identified with Hashem and His monarchy.

As we have mentioned, the power of a leader is his power to speak. One of the Hebrew words for leader is *dabar*. *Dabar* is also a "speaking entity," which is the name of the fourth and highest level of existence after inanimate objects, plant life, and moving creatures. Having emerged from Egypt, the Jews regained their ability to speak and simultaneously acquired the leadership of Yehuda, thus connecting to Hashem as a holy nation.[16]

ישראל ממשלותיו—*Yisrael, His dominions*

The Maharal explains the depth of the next phrase in the *mizmor*, which means *Yisrael, His dominions*. Not only are the Jews attached to Hashem through the exodus, but Hashem also identifies Himself exclusively through us.[17] We state in our daily prayer, כי הוא ה׳ אלוקינו ואנחנו ישראל עמו—*For He is Hashem our G-d and we are Yisrael, His nation.* This, explains the Maharal, is why Hashem didn't allow any intermediary to have a hand in the exodus; rather Hashem Himself made the miracles that took us out of slavery. Because of His direct act of creating our freedom, our departure from Egypt was not just a redemption from slavery but the forging of our connection to the Source Himself. In this light, we see that the splitting of the sea was the birth of a spiritual reality that

---

16. It's fascinating to note that the Talmud refers to a certain Rebbi Yehuda as *Rosh Hamidabrim*. Since Yehuda is the leader in general, he is the one designated to be the first speaker.

17. In contrast to the forty-ninth level of contamination, the Jews were now completely out of that mindset and were firmly with Hashem.

extended far beyond the finite and limited world in which this one-time miraculous event occurred.

Everything in this mizmor *is mentioned twice because the Jewish people at the Yam Suf embodied the duality of the lower and the upper worlds. All that happened to and through the Jews fused the world of nature to a higher reality.*

הים ראה וינס הירדן יסב לאחור—*The sea saw and fled, the Yarden turned backwards.*

Adding to the miracle at the Yam Suf, this phrase recounts that the water of the Jordan River turned backwards. The Maharal explains, citing the midrash, that when the Yam Suf split, so did all the waters in the world. Why was it necessary to split *all the waters* in the world? Furthermore, why is it necessary to mention this in Hallel?

ההרים רקדו כאילים גבעות כבני צאן—*The mountains skipped like rams, the hills like lambs.*

Dovid Hamelech informs us that even the mountains and hills felt the impact of the splitting of the sea. Why were they affected?

The *Tzurah* of Man

The Maharal[18] explains that when *Krias Yam Suf* ushered in the birth of Hashem's children, this amplified Hashem's presence in the world, for the Jewish people are the conduit of His holiness. The Jewish people's emergence from Egypt is compared to the birth of a child. The gestation period was the 210 years in Egypt. Labor pains began with the commencement of the plagues, and the birth was the crossing of the Yam Suf. On the seventh day of Pesach, the day of *Krias Yam*

18. *Gevuros* 41 and 42.

Suf, the Jewish people were finally free from Pharaoh and Egyptian slavery.

The birth of Bnei Yisrael had such a powerful impact on the world that all the waters split; no liquid flowed, anywhere in the world.[19] The Maharal compares this birth of Hashem's children with the creation of Adam: At the beginning of creation, water covered the earth, but on the third day Hashem commanded the water to constrict, thereby revealing the dry land. Adam would not be created for another three days but the waters retracted in anticipation of the creation of Adam. Hashem's *tzurah*—the image of Hashem that Adam bore—caused the water to congeal, and this *tzurah* ultimately gave the world its form.[20] Likewise, the Jewish people's emergence on the scene was a representation of the spirituality of G-d—Hashem's *tzurah*—in this world.

Hashem's presence was the force that affected the water and the world. Since it was specifically His image that caused all the waters to split, we see clearly why Hashem didn't allow any angel or other power to enact this miracle.

רוקע הארץ על המים

Rav Moshe Shapiro *zt"l* explains that this is the meaning of the morning *brachah*, רוקע הארץ על המים—Hashem *spreads the earth over the water*. As we just discussed, Hashem made room for the world to exist

---

19. The Maharal explains that water represents a state of *chomer* that has no *tzurah*. It is incapable of having its own *tzurah*, but rather, it takes on the form of the vessel that contains it. If water is in a cup, it takes the shape of the cup. When there is no vessel to hold the water, it just spreads.

20. If we understand this correctly, it means that the world, like Adam, parallels the image of Hashem.

through His *tzurah*. At the time of Creation, His *tzurah* was in the form of man, and it was that form that made the world sustainable. After ten sinful generations, the *tzurah* of Hashem was no longer discernible in man. The result of this was a reversion to the conditions that preceded Hashem's initial congealing of the water. There was a flood, and the face of the earth was once again covered with water.

The *mizmor* is true to form, as it continues highlighting the theme of duality. However, this time the message is more profound; it is the Jewish people themselves who are reflected in the higher reality of Hashem, as the verse says, מלפני אדון חולי ארץ מלפני אלוק יעקב—*Before the Master, the Creator of the earth, before the G-d of Yaakov.*

מה לך הים כי תנוס הירדן תסב לאחור ההרים תרקדו כאילים גבעות כבני צאן—*What happened to you oh sea that you flee, the Yarden that you turn backwards, the mountains that you skip like rams, the hills like lambs?*

Why is Dovid Hamelech asking the waters and the mountains these questions? The Maharal explains that he wanted to emphasize the process through which the waters altered their form and the mountains shook to their core. These unnatural events were not the result of overt acts by Hashem. Rather, His presence evoked the natural reaction of any physical entity when it is bathed in a powerful emanation of holiness. This is what caused the waters to congeal as if the state of liquidity no longer existed.

מלפני אדון חולי ארץ מלפני אלוק יעקב—*Before the Lord does the earth tremble, before the G-d of Yaakov.*

The Maharal explains that the appropriate name for the intense holiness that alters nature is *Elokei Yaakov*, the G-d of Yaakov. He bases this on *Yeshayah* (29:23), which says והקדישו את קדוש יעקב—*They will sanctify the Holy One of Yaakov.*

The waters and mountains reacted to the *Adon*, the Master. As we mentioned, it was *through the Jewish people* that the world perceived the Master. The Maharal explains that both water and mountains responded to this because they represent the *chomer* of the world, which is incompatible with the *tzurah* of Hashem.[21] The revelation at the Yam Suf caused everything in the world that was incompatible to become destabilized. We can concretize this by imagining the reaction of a roomful of ordinary citizens when a king and his entourage walk through the door. The people would suddenly feel uncomfortable, out of place, and fearful of doing or saying the wrong thing. However, those in the room who already had a relationship with the king would feel more at ease. Likewise, when Hashem "walked through the door" by revealing Himself at the Yam Suf, the *kedushah* He brought to the entire world destabilized the mountains and waters. The true *tzurah* of Hashem impressed itself upon the world at the moment the Jewish people heeded Hashem's command and traveled forth across the sea. There was no person or entity on earth that did not, at this point, realize that creation existed to fulfill Hashem's purpose.

ההופכי, חולי

The Maharal points out that Dovid Hamelech once again inserts

---

21. The concept of *chomer* is a theme the Maharal mentions very often throughout his writings. *Chomer* is the substance and *tzurah* is the form. With a wooden board, the wood is the *chomer* and the form of the board is the *tzurah*, which is an incomplete state of reality. *Chomer* is used in various applications, for example water is *chomer*; it lacks any form of its own. A misguided person who acts on impulse is *chomer* without form, like water without a vessel that gives it purpose. *Tzurah* is the opposite; it has form, which might be a purpose or an idea to be realized. *Chomer* and *tzurah* represent two fundamentally conflicting concepts.

the letter *yud* twice in this *pasuk*, in addition to the five times it is used in the first *mizmor*. In the second *mizmor*, this duality follows the pattern we have noted. There is also a deeper understanding, which he derives from the *pasuk* in *Bereishis* that describes the creation of Adam: וייצר ה׳ אלקים את אדם עפר מן האדמה—*And Hashem formed man from the earth.* Rashi notes that the וייצר—*and He formed* is spelled with two *yuds* because man was created for two worlds, the physical world and *Olam Haba*. This is precisely the point of the second *mizmor's* duality.

For Your Sake

לא לנו ה׳ לא לנו כי לשמך תן כבוד על חסדך ועל אמתך. למה יאמרו הגוים איה נא אלקיהם. ואלקינו בשמים כל אשר חפץ עשה. עצביהם כסף וזהב מעשה ידי אדם. פה להם ולא ידברו עינים להם ולא יראו. אזנים להם ולא ישמעו אף להם ולא יריחון. ידיהם ולא ימישון רגליהם ולא יהלכו לא יהגו בגרונם. כמוהם יהיו עשיהם כל אשר בטח בהם. ישראל בטח בה׳ עזרם ומגנם הוא. בית אהרן בטחו בה׳ עזרם ומגנם הוא. יראי ה׳ בטחו בה׳ עזרם ומגנם הוא.

Not for our benefit, Hashem, not for our benefit but to give glory to Your Name, for the sake of Your kindness and Your truth. Why should the nations say, "Where is their G-d?" Our G-d is in heaven. Whatever He wants He does. Their idols are of silver and gold. They have a mouth but cannot speak, they have eyes but cannot see. They have ears but cannot hear, they have a nose but cannot smell. Their hands cannot feel, their feet cannot walk. They can emit no sound from their throat. Like them should be those who formed them, and all those who trust them.

Lo Lanu, an Overview

As we have discussed,[22] the first *mizmor* praises Hashem for creating and organizing the universe. The second *mizmor* glorifies Hashem for His miracles. The third *mizmor*, which begins *Not for our benefit, Hashem,* seems to interrupt this progression. The Maharal explains, however, that it is perfectly placed, for having recounted all Hashem has done for us, we wonder, "Why? What did we do to deserve the wonders of creation or a dramatic miracle like the splitting of the sea?"

In this *mizmor*, Dovid Hamelech provides us with four reasons. The first *pasuk* conveys three of them:

> *To give glory to Your Name, for the sake of Your kindness and Your truth.*
>
> Then we beseech Hashem: *Why should the nations say, "Where is their G-d?"*

In total, Dovid Hamelech offers four justifications for our request that Hashem intervene on our behalf. (This will be explained in detail later in this section.) In simple terms, this last verse tells Hashem, "If You do not involve Yourself in our well-being and the world will say to us, 'Jews, where is your G-d?' then You, Hashem, will *chas v'shalom* be perceived as unable to help Your people." This will cause a *chillul Hashem*, a desecration of G-d's Name. Indeed, this helplessness is the reality of their gods, for they are all useless and man-made. We conclude the *mizmor* by appealing to Hashem for His intervention and extolling the virtues of trusting in Him.

On a deeper level, the concern that the world will perceive Hashem as uninvolved or incapable of helping us flows from the principle we explored in the previous chapter: that the world knows us as "Yisrael, His dominions."

---

22. In the section of בצאת ישראל ממצרים.

This concept is known as *middas hamalchus. Malchus* means Kingship. Since the time of the exodus—when Hashem declared that we are His children, His firstborn—Hashem's kingship has been intertwined with the Jewish people. We are therefore inseparable from Hashem. If we are in a state of distress and no solution is forthcoming, it appears as if the King cannot even help His own subjects. They wonder, "Where is your G-d? Why isn't He helping you?" Therefore, this *mizmor* opens with the statement that it's *not for our benefit* that Hashem helps us. It's not because of our merit or the justness of our cause. We are merely the fortunate servants of His kingship.

Let's now look more closely at the reasons Hashem does indeed involve Himself in our world:

This first request for His involvement has three parts.

לא לנו ה׳—*Not for our benefit* (rather, for You)

כי לשמך תן כבוד—*But to give glory to Your Name*

על חסדך ועל אמתך—*For the sake of Your kindness and Your truth*

Before we discuss these three reasons, let us focus on the repetition of *lo lanu* at the beginning of this *mizmor*. The Maharal explains that the repetition emphasizes the fact that Hashem performs miracles for us even though we are unworthy. If the verse said *lo lanu* only once, it could imply, "Hashem, although you *could* do these miracles for us because we are worthy of Your intervention, please do them for the honor of Your Name." However, when we say *lo lanu* twice, we dispel any notion that we deserve Hashem's intervention and recognize that Hashem performs miracles because doing so expresses Who He is.

לא לנו ה׳ לא לנו, כי לשמך תן כבוד, על חסדך ועל אמתך—*Not for our benefit, Hashem, not for our benefit, but to give glory to Your Name for the sake of Your kindness and Your truth.*

Returning to the three reasons Hashem involves Himself in our world, the Maharal reveals that each reason addresses a different *middah* of Hashem.[23]

These are *din*, *chessed*, and *rachamim*.

Hashem interacts with the world according to these *middos*, based on the level of spiritual merit that exists. When the world is populated with righteous people, there is sufficient merit for those who are worthy enough to withstand the attribute of *din*. Therefore, Hashem acts with that *middah*.

Sometimes, however, the righteous cannot generate enough merit to deserve sustenance through *din*, and yet we are still deserving of Hashem's kindness because we ourselves are kind. In that case, we can depend upon Hashem's *chessed*. This is a secondary form of *din* because Hashem is still responding to our deeds, albeit in a less precise way than is required by *din*.

When we are not worthy of the first two attributes, Hashem calls upon His trait of *rachamim* (mercy).

In addition to these three attributes, we speak of another trait, *chein*, which we find in the context of *Birkas Hamazon*. We say that Hashem feeds the world *b'chein, b'chessed u'vrachamim*. *Chein*, which means "favor," stands in the place of *din* as the first *middah*. This implies that there is a connection between *din* and *chein*.

בחן בחסד וברחמים

The Maharal, in *Nesivos*, explains that these three *middos* listed in *Birkas Hamazon* represent three different ways in which Hashem sustains the world: judgment, kindness, and mercy. But why does the *tefillah* say *chein* instead of *din*? Furthermore, why does it matter which attributes Hashem uses to feed us?

---

23. *Middos* are the mechanisms through which Hashem impacts the world.

חן

The Maharal cites the story of Noach to explain the connection between *chein* and *din.* In Noach's generation, the world had lost its right to exist. The Heavenly Court decreed that it would be destroyed, but the Torah states that even in the face of this judgment, Noach was a righteous person, and therefore, *Noach found favor*–chein–*in Hashem's "eyes."* First the Torah identifies Noach as a righteous person, and then states that he found Hashem's favor. In contrast, the rest of the generation was subject to the attribute of *din*, which called for their annihilation. The Maharal concludes that *chein* is a trait that operates in a situation of *din*, protecting the righteous from the decree.

חסד

Chessed is a form of sustenance that requires no merit from the recipient. Rather, it emanates from the pure good of the giver. This is the sustenance that Hashem gives to animals since they cannot amass the merit that would enable them to "deserve" their sustenance on the scale of *din.* Hashem feeds them solely out of His kindness.

רחמים

A third segment of the world is sustained through *rachamim*—mercy. The Maharal identifies this group as small children.[24]

---

24. The difference between *chessed* and *rachamim* can be explained through two famous quotes regarding the creation of the world. The verse regarding *chessed* says, עולם חסד יבנה—*The world was created with the attribute of* chessed. The second, about *rachamim*, says מתחילה עלה במחשבה לברוא את העולם במידת הדין, ראה שאין העולם מתקיים שיתף עמו מידת הרחמים—*At first, Hashem created the world with the attribute of*

The Maharal then connects *Birkas Hamazon's* list of attributes, "*b'chein, b'chessed u'v'rachamim,*" to the three statements of *lo lanu*.

The first statement, which declares that we have no claim on Hashem's miraculous intervention, reflects the *middah* of *din*. We know that there's nothing a flawed human being can do to deserve, according to strict justice, the bounty that Hashem provides.

The next statement is our request for Hashem's Name to be glorified. This reflects the attribute of *rachamim* because, says the Maharal, "Mercy" is Hashem's great Name.[25] The third statement asks Hashem to act for the sake of His *chessed*.

To summarize, this chapter provides four reasons for Hashem's beneficial involvement with the Jewish people. These are *chessed*, *din*, and *rachamim*, corresponding to our three *Avos*, Avraham, Yitzchak, and Yaakov. The fourth reason, kingship, corresponds to Dovid Hamelech. In total, these four reasons represent what is known as the *merkava*, or chariot, through which Hashem involves Himself in this world.

---

justice. However, seeing that the world would not survive, He balanced justice with mercy.

Chessed is a goodness that is initiated not for the purpose of filling a void, but solely out of the kindness of the giver. For example, the world was built on *chessed* even though there was no creation before its existence, and therefore, there was nothing that could need or deserve the kindness. The *middah* of *chessed* was in itself the catalyst for the act of creation. This is the attribute of pure good that is initiated by the giver. *Rachamim*, however, is a goodness that fills a void; it is a response to a need. This is exemplified by the second quote: Hashem created the world based on the attribute of judgment, but the world couldn't survive because there was a tremendous deficiency. The attribute of *chessed* could not fill the void because it could not overcome a judgment that demanded adherence. The solution to this is the attribute of *rachamim*.

25. The great Name of Hashem is the Name of Mercy. The Maharal reveals the secret in the form of *gematria* and the usage of את בש. The holy Name of י-ק-ו-ק is מצפצ, which has a numerical value that is equal to ברחמים.

גוג ומגוג

The Maharal mentions a second opinion as to the reason for Hashem's intervention on behalf of the Jewish people. It is that *lo lanu* is a prophecy of the declaration Klal Yisrael will make upon the coming of Mashiach, when, as the prophets foretold, the war of Gog and Magog will occur. At that time, Hashem will intervene on behalf of His children without the impediment of judgment, but rather, with complete kindness. When we declare "not for our benefit, not for our benefit," we declare ourselves completely undeserving, and with that humble attitude, we will not be affected by the world's day of reckoning. Hashem will save us "not for our sake," but as an act of mercy.

עצביהם כסף וזהב מעשה ידי אדם—Their idols are [made out of] gold and silver, the work of human hands.

With these words, the *mizmor* begins a detailed description of the futile acts of idolators and the worthlessness of the idols they serve. What is the purpose of this lengthy elaboration? And how does it connect to the beginning of this *mizmor*?

First, let us delve into the specifics of the message. In describing the wasted efforts of idolaters, Dovid Hamelech cites seven different functions that are productive in humans but are worthless when applied to idols.

פה להם ולא ידברו—They have a mouth but cannot speak.
עינים להם ולא יראו—They have eyes but cannot see.
אזנים להם ולא ישמעו—They have ears but cannot hear.
אף להם ולא יריחון—They have a nose but cannot smell.
ידיהם ולא ימישון—Their hands cannot feel.
רגליהם ולא יהלכו—Their feet cannot walk.

לא יהגו בגרונם—*They can emit no sound from their throat.* What is the purpose of this lengthy description?

Physical Intermediaries of Heavenly Powers

The Maharal explains that ancient people understood the powers of stars and celestial bodies and made idols with human features to channel that power into the world. However, these human features are truly useless, for they are man-made and therefore, cannot perform their supposed function.

The Maharal notes that the *mizmor* lists a total of seven. These are divided into two groups, the first four and the last three. The first four mention the word *lahem*—"to them"—and the last three do not. The reason is that the first four, which are the mouth, eyes, ears and nose, are associated with the face and are located at a higher level than the body. The hands and the feet are with the body.

Dovid Hamelech begins with the most spiritual human organs and works his way down to the lowest level. Therefore, the *perek* starts with the mouth, the gateway to a human being's highest spiritual capacity. A person's capacity to speak is Hashem's unique endowment to humanity, shared by no other creation. Next are the eyes; they have the power to see into the distance, and we believe what we see. Ears can hear from afar. However, hearing is not as impactful a sense as vision. Below those organs is the nose, then the hands, and then the feet—the lowest part of the body. Given this order, the seventh and final feature, the throat, appears to be in the wrong place. Why is it last? Also, how is it functionally different from the mouth, which is mentioned first?

The Maharal addresses the placement of the throat in this listing by explaining that although the sound that emanates from the throat should be higher than all the six features that were mentioned above, for it is hidden and internal, this is only true when it is the throat of a real human being. In the idol-maker's futile duplication of what Hashem created, the inability to take a breath and emit a sound renders the idol's throat totally useless.[26]

כל אשר בוטח בהם כמוהם יהיו עשיהם—*Those who make them should become like them, all those who trust in them.*

ישראל בטח בה׳ עזרם ומגנם הוא—*The House of Yisrael trusts in Hashem, He is their help and their shield.*

בית אהרן בטחו בה׳ עזרם ומגנם הוא—*The House of Aharon trusts in Hashem, He is their help and their shield.*

יראי ה׳ בטחו בה׳ עזרם ומגנם הוא—*Those who fear Hashem trust in Hashem, He is their help and their shield.*

In the lines above, three groups are mentioned, the House of Yisrael, the House of Aharon, and those who fear Hashem. Each puts its trust in Hashem in a way that is based on its own unique connection to Him. What is the special character of each?

Three *Middos*

The House of Yisrael refers to the children of Hashem. They are connected to Him like a son to his father. Their trust is based on the unalterable nature of a connection between "blood relatives," which can never be severed.

The House of Aharon refers to those who serve Hashem out of love. These are the *kohanim* of the Jewish people who serve the Almighty out of their love for Him and His people. Confident in the power of that love, the *kohanim* trust in Him.

The third group refers to those who stand in awe of the Almighty and connect to Him through their trepidation. Because they are imbued with a strong sense of His power and might, they are confident that He can and will help them. They too trust completely in Hashem.

---

26. The idol's throat is lower even than hands and feet that have more external value than a throat that cannot make a sound, which is completely useless.

The unwavering trust and devotion of these three groups is the source of their blessing, as described in the next *mizmor*.

Trust Brings the Blessing

ה׳ זכרנו יברך יברך את בית ישראל יברך את בית אהרן. יברך יראי ה׳ הקטנים עם הגדלים. יסף ה׳ עליכם עליכם ועל בניכם. ברוכים אתם לה׳ עשה שמים וארץ. השמים שמים לה׳ והארץ נתן לבני אדם. לא המתים יהללו קה ולא כל ירדי דומה. ואנחנו נברך קה מעתה ועד עולם הללוקה.

Hashem Who has remembered us will bless, He will bless the House of Yisrael, He will bless the House of Aharon, He will bless those who fear Him, the small and the great. May Hashem increase blessings upon you, upon you and all your children. Blessed are you unto Hashem, the Creator of heaven and earth. The heavens are the heavens of G-d and the earth He gave to the sons of man. The dead do not praise Hashem, and neither those who have descended into silence. But we will bless Hashem from now until eternity, Hallelukah!

Blessings for Those Who Trust

This *mizmor* is a continuation from the previous *perek*. The three groups mentioned here [the House of Yisrael, the House of Aharon, and the House of those who fear Hashem] are the same ones named in the preceding paragraph. The repetition is to reassure us that Hashem is not only our protector but that He will shower His blessings upon those who trust Him. Everyone who can identify himself as a member of one of these groups—the House of Yisrael, the House of Aharon (*kohanim*), or *Yirei Hashem*,

G-d-fearing people—is "remembered" by Hashem. Their trust never goes unrewarded.[27]

Hashem's Unconditional Love

אהבתי כי ישמע ה׳ את קולי תחנוני. כי הטה אזנו לי ובימי אקרא. אפפוני חבלי מות ומצרי שאול מצאוני צרה ויגון אמצא. ובשם ה׳ אקרא אנא השם מלטה נפשי. חנון ה׳ וצדיק ואלקינו מרחם. שומר פתאים ה׳ דלותי ולי יהושיע. שובי נפשי למנוחיכי כי ה׳ גמל עליכי. כי חלצת נפשי ממות את עיני מן דמעה את רגלי מדחי. אתהלך לפני ה׳ בארצות החיים. האמנתי כי אדבר אני עניתי מאד. אני אמרתי בחפזי כל האדם כזב.

I love Hashem because He hears my voice, my prayers. For He turned His ear to me, all my days I will call upon Him. The pangs of death encompassed me, and the agonies of the grave came upon me. Trouble and sorrow I encounter, and I call upon the Name of Hashem. Please, Hashem, deliver my soul! Hashem is gracious and just, our G-d is compassionate. Hashem safeguards the simpletons; I was impoverished, and He saved me. Return, my soul, to your rest, for Hashem has dealt kindly with me. For You have delivered my soul from death, my eyes from tears, my foot from stumbling. I will walk before Hashem in the lands of the living. I had faith

27. These three groups are mentioned once more in Hallel after this. In the *perek* that begins with *Hodu*, each of the three groups gives their own unique כי לעולם חסדו—*praise of Hashem*. In total, these three groups appear three times in Hallel. First in לא לנו where it begins with their devotion and trust in the Almighty proclaiming that He is their shield. Then in this *perek*, their trust in turn becomes a source of His blessings upon them. And lastly, all three are mentioned in כי לעולם חסדו, where they give praise to Hashem for their unique relationship with Him.

though I say, I am greatly afflicted; [even when] I said in my haste, all men are deceitful.

Dovid Hamelech begins this *mizmor* by expressing the overpowering love he feels toward the One Who listens attentively and unfailingly to all the prayers of his heart. Beyond this simple interpretation, however, the Talmud and Midrash offer a different approach, which reveals Hashem's unconditional love for us.

The Gemara (*Pesachim* 118b) relates:

> *Rava taught: What is [the meaning of] the words, "I love Hashem because He hears [my voice and my supplications]?"* (Tehillim *116:1).* Knesses Yisrael *said: "Master of the Universe, when am I beloved by You? When You hear the voice of my supplications." I was brought low, and He saved me* (Tehillim *116:6).* Knesses Yisrael *said before the Holy One, blessed be He, Master of the Universe, "Although I am lowly in mitzvos, I am Yours; it is fitting that I should be saved."*

Rava explains that the Jewish nation feels Hashem's love when He listens to our supplications.

Hashem's Unconditional Love

The Maharal elaborates by first explaining why Rava alters the basic meaning of this verse. He explains that Rava accepts the simple meaning of the verse, which is that we love Hashem because He listens to our voice. However, that is not all Dovid meant to impart, for there is no need to state something so obvious. No one would praise his father, for instance, by saying, "I love you because you give me what I ask for." Everyone loves to be heard, and even more so when directing our prayers to Hashem, Who can fulfill any request.

Therefore, says Rava, the message is more than that we love having Hashem listen to our prayers; also, He loves to hear our voices as we make our requests. Meaning, the word אהבתי does not just mean "I love You when You listen," but also I am "beloved to You when I pray." He loves this to such a degree that even when we disobey His will, He continues to favor us and help us.

Why does He love for us to call to Him? It is simply because it shows that we have the humility to ask! This reveals the unconditional love between Hashem and His nation. With this first verse of the *mizmor*, we proclaim, "Just as we love when You pay attention to us, Hashem, may You too love to hear our voices, no matter how defiant or complacent we have become. You not only listen but You receive our requests with affection."

This is the nature of our loving relationship, and it sets the stage for the next few elements in this *mizmor*. But how did we merit such a relationship with Hashem? How did we become so close to Him?

The Source of Receiving

The Maharal cites the *Yalkut Shimoni* (p. 874), which explains this intimacy:

"The ears above are attuned to listen only to me," says Dovid Hamelech. This is based on his testimony in *Tehillim* (40:7) that states, *Neither the feast offering nor meal offering did You desire, yet You opened Your ears for me. Burnt offerings and sin offerings You did not request.* Hashem gave Dovid an exclusive audience without requiring that Dovid appease Him through offerings.

The Maharal explains that Hashem does not set preconditions to hear our prayers. He needs no offerings of appeasement to motivate Him to sustain the world; since He created the world, it is His will to maintain it. Therefore, it is logical that He would provide us with anything we are lacking. Nevertheless, this explanation applies to all creations, for Hashem created the entire world. Why do the Jewish people enjoy a greater level of access to Him than others do?

The Source of Creation

The answer is that the Jewish people are the reason for creation; therefore, they are the source of all that emanates from Hashem. This attachment is implied in the first word of the Torah as it describes the beginning of creation. Rashi quotes a midrash that states that the word "*Bereishis*" begins the Torah because it refers to "Yisrael, which is called the first (*reishis*)." Although the entire universe is His creation that He constantly maintains, He listens to the prayers of Klal Yisrael first and foremost because we are the purpose of everything He created.

כי הטה אזנו לי ובימי אקרא—*For He turned His ear to me, all my days I will call upon Him.*

The Maharal explains that "all my days" represents the blessings that Hashem bestows on a person. Dovid asks Hashem to continue to grant him His bounty day after day. Indeed, Hashem will never refuse to listen to His people.

This is the rationale for the statement (*Devarim* 4:7), *For which great nation has a god who is close to it as Hashem is whenever we call to Him?* In reality, if not for the Jewish people, Hashem would not listen to anyone. All the people of the world receive their sustenance through the Jewish people. As *Tehillim* (145:16) says, *He provides sustenance for all creations.*

Based on our unique bond with Hashem, Rava reasons we are indeed fortunate that Hashem listens to our prayers, but also, we are confident that He desires and treasures the sound of our prayers.

אפפוני חבלי מות ומצרי שאול מצאוני—*The pangs of death encompassed me, and the agonies of the grave came upon me.*

The simple meaning of these words is that Dovid is praising Hashem for saving him from his many brushes with death. The Maharal, citing a midrash, explains on a deeper level that this statement refers to two types of wicked people who plot against the righteous. "The pangs of death" are sinful Jewish people, whose guilt renders them deserving of death. The "agonies of the grave" are wicked gentiles whose destination in life is Gehinnom. Together, the wicked Jews and gentiles attempt to destroy virtuous people. Dovid therefore petitions Hashem to save him from these deplorable people. This *mizmor* continues with Dovid's requests for protection and salvation from evil.

ובשם ה׳ אקרא אנא ה׳ מלטה נפשי—*And I call upon the Name of Hashem. Please, Hashem, deliver my soul!*

The Maharal explains that Dovid Hamelech is beseeching Hashem to save his soul from those who seek to destroy him. This is an example of what the Maharal explained in the introduction to Hallel:[28] Since the praise is predicated on the righteous who are saved from Gehinnom, it also translates as being saved from the wicked Jews and gentiles who are destined for Gehinnom.

חנון ה׳ וצדיק—*Hashem is gracious and just.*

Hashem's Names reveal His different attributes. For example, *Yud-hei-vav-hei* represents a merciful G-d, while Elokim is a G-d of justice. Nevertheless, Hashem receives our prayers in all circumstances. By asking Hashem to continue sending us a flow of blessings when we call upon Him, we are appealing to His attributes of graciousness and justice.

ואלקינו מרחם—*Our G-d is compassionate.*

And when our enemies stand against us, encompassing us with the "pangs of death" of which Dovid Hamelech speaks, Hashem is a compassionate G-d Who defends us.[29]

---

28. Rabbi Nachman bar Yitzchak says that Hallel references the escape of the souls of the righteous from Gehinnom [מילוט נפשות של צדיקים מגיהנם] as it says, *Please, Hashem, save my soul.*

29. It is interesting to note that although generally the Name אלוקים represents

שומר פתאים ה׳—Hashem safeguards the simpletons.

Not only when we call out to Hashem, but even when we are foolish and we do not pray, Hashem still safeguards us, steering us away from harm.

דלותי ולי יהושיע—I was impoverished, and He saved me.

Not only when we are foolish and fail to pray, but even when we are "poor" in our performance of mitzvos, Hashem graciously finds reason to help us.

שובי נפשי למנוחיכי—Return, my soul, to your rest.

Not only when we are delinquent in performing Hashem's mitzvos, but even when we are just relaxing and not accomplishing anything, Hashem still acts kindly toward us.

כי ה׳ גמל עליכי—For Hashem has dealt kindly with me.

Here we perceive the full extent of Hashem's unconditional love for Klal Yisrael. He answers our prayers and looks out for us and will even be entirely benevolent—*gomel chessed*—to all, whether deserving or not.

כי חלצת נפשי ממות את עיני מן דמעה את רגלי מדחי—For You have delivered my soul from death, my eyes from tears, my feet from stumbling.

The Maharal notes that Hashem saved Dovid from three different types of misfortunes: death, tears, and stumbling. What do these three have in common?

Drained of Strength

The Maharal explains that there are three degrees of misfortunes that drain a person's strength. The worst is

---

His *middah* of דין, which means that Hashem is in the mode of judgment, here it is used in relation to His compassion.

death, a state in which a person literally has no life left in him. Stumbling is less draining, for that is a momentary loss of strength. Tears, however, are comparable to death, says the Maharal, because they stem from a feeling of helplessness. Both death and tears are a manifestation of a lack of energy, death in the physical sense and tears in the emotional sense. Dovid thanks Hashem for kindly protecting Him when he was threatened by death, and even when he faced the less dire situations that would have brought him to tears. He also recognizes that Hashem has protected "my feet from stumbling." Although he could quickly recover from stumbling, he appreciates that Hashem has ensured that his energy remains unimpeded by mishaps.

Neshamah, Nefesh, and *Guf*

The Maharal reveals another level of insight from this verse, explaining that the three misfortunes mentioned are each rooted in a different part of the human being: the soul, the eyes, and the feet. This parallels the three components of *neshamah*, *nefesh*, and *guf* that make up a person.

נפשי ממות—my soul from death
את עיני מן דמעה—my eyes from tears
רגלי מדחי—my feet from stumbling

As we have learned, a person is composed of three parts: the *neshamah*, which is completely above and detached from the influence of the body; the *nefesh*, the spiritual part of a person that is attached to his physical self; and the *guf*, the pure physical entity driven solely by desire and instinct. However, because the *guf* and the *nefesh* are connected to each other, they can exert influence on one another.

The Maharal links Dovid Hamelech's three statements of Hashem's protection to the totality of the human being, which encompasses the three parts listed above.

For a person to be completely sheltered, Hashem must protect all three parts from harm. The *neshamah*, which is everlasting, does not deteriorate. However, it could separate from the body, which is the mechanism of death. Tears express an experience of loss and despair, but this is a temporary state, while death is final and complete. Dovid is also grateful to Hashem for protecting him from faltering physically.

אתהלך לפני ה׳ בארצות החיים—*I will walk before Hashem in the lands of the living.*

The "lands of the living" refers to Eretz Yisrael. The Talmud Yerushalmi (*Kelayim* Chapter 9) explains that since the resurrection of the dead will occur in Eretz Yisrael, it is literally a land of life. The word "lands" is plural simply because we inherited the lands of the seven nations.

האמנתי כי אדבר אני עניתי מאוד אני אמרתי בחפזי כל האדם כזב—*I had faith though I say, I am greatly afflicted; [even when] I said in my haste, all men are deceitful.*

With these words, says the Maharal, Dovid Hamelech alludes to his encounter with Shaul Hamelech. Because Dovid maintained his faith in Hashem, he has been given the "podium" from which he can proclaim his thanks for Hashem's endless goodness.

Expressing Gratitude

מה אשיב לה׳ כל תגמולוהי עלי. כוס ישועות אשא ובשם ה׳ אקרא. נדרי לה׳ אשלם נגדה נא לכל עמו. יקר בעיני ה׳ המותה לחסידיו. אנא ה׳ כי אני עבדיך אני עבדך בן אמתך פתחת למוסרי. לך אזבח זבח תודה ובשם ה׳ אקרא. נדרי לה׳ אשלם נגדה נא לכל עמו. בחצרות בית ה׳ בתוככי ירושלים הללוקה.

With what can I repay Hashem for all His kindness to me? I will raise the cup of salvation and call upon the Name of Hashem. I will pay my vows to Hashem in the presence of all His people. Precious in the eyes of Hashem is the death of His pious ones. I thank You, Hashem, for I am Your servant. I am Your servant, the son of Your handmaid, You have unshackled my bonds. To You I will bring an offering of thanksgiving, and I will call upon the Name of Hashem. I will pay my vows to Hashem in the presence of all His people, in the courtyards of the House of Hashem in the midst of Yerushalayim. Hallelukah, praise Hashem.

מה אשיב לה׳ כל תגמולוהי עלי כוס ישועות אשא ובשם ה׳ אקרא—*With what can I repay Hashem for all His kindness to me? I will raise the cup of salvation and call upon the Name of Hashem.*

Dovid seems to be at a loss of words. The Malbim (*Tehillim ad loc.*) states that this chapter is a continuation of the previous chapter, which ended with Dovid's despairing statement, "I said in my haste, all men are deceitful." Yet after all the challenges, Hashem allows Dovid to survive. He is therefore overwhelmed with gratitude.

But Dovid's sentiment is not simply, "Thank You, Hashem, for keeping me alive." The Malbim explains that there is a unique nuance in this proclamation; Dovid is grateful that he survived because now he has a deeper appreciation of Hashem and can thank Him in a more profound way than was possible before the challenge that had beset him. *For better than Your kindness of life [is the opportunity that] my lips shall praise You* (*Tehillim* 63:4).

The Malbim's message is eye-opening. If Dovid had praised Hashem for saving him, that would have been self-centered. Rather, Dovid looks past the benefit he received and focuses on the fact that it taught him to recognize Hashem's goodness. *His experience showed him that Hashem's commitment to humanity has no limitations*, and he wrote this *mizmor* to share that awareness with the entire world.

The Maharal elucidates that when Dovid Hamelech asked, "With what can I repay Hashem?" he was so overwhelmed with gratitude that "thank you" was not enough to express his feelings. He sensed that Hashem had showered him with the maximum amount of good that a human could possibly absorb. The only reason that Hashem did not give more was because Dovid lacked the capacity to receive it. Were that not the case, Hashem's benevolence would have increased. This, says the Maharal, is the meaning of כל תגמולוהי עלי—*all the overwhelming kindness.*

כוס ישועות אשא—*I will raise the cup of salvation.*

Despite Dovid's inability to articulate his thanks, he desired to express it somehow. The mode he chose was to "raise the cup of salvation." The Maharal explains that by using a "cup," Dovid has captured the most appropriate metaphor for gratitude.

כוס—*Cup*

What is a cup of salvation? On a simple level, a cup symbolizes the concept of receiving because its main purpose is that of a receptacle. If there is a cup, that means that there is something to be poured into it. This idea is rooted in the concept of giving and receiving, which is a fundamental aspect of creation.[30]

---

30. For a deeper understanding, see Chapter 3, כוס = אלקים.

In general, for someone to receive, there must be something to be received, and some entity to accept it. For example, for someone to receive a dollar bill, there must be a bill to give and a hand to receive it. But first the recipient must be aware that the dollar is being given. Otherwise, he has no reason to stretch out his hand. Therefore, when we speak of a cup of salvation, we are referring not only to the receptacle but to the awareness that there is a "Giver" to fill the cup.

Conceptually, the same concept is true in terms of receiving ideas and emotional experiences. We cannot receive that which is being transmitted unless we have the intellectual or emotional capacity to do so. The giver and the receiver are both an essential part of the process.

For example, let us say that someone needs financial advice. If he has a knowledgeable friend but is unaware of that person's knowledge, he won't consult him and will miss out on the benefit of the advice the friend could have given. If he learns of that friend's knowledge, he will certainly seek his advice. When he becomes aware of the treasury of information his friend possesses, he can be a cup to receive.

The second part of the equation is the receiver's capacity. An example is a student sitting in an algebra class who hasn't yet studied basic arithmetic. Without that background, he cannot receive the lessons. He lacks a cup that can contain that which is being given.

To summarize, in the Torah, a "cup" signifies the recognition of the giver and of what is being dispensed. These two elements give the recipient the capacity to receive.

A Cup of Salvation

The same is true when a recipient shows gratitude. Conceptually, a person can "place" all his emotions and expressions of gratitude into a "cup." He does this by recognizing the source of the goodness he has received and showing appreciation in an appropriate way.

What is the appropriate way? It is not merely a "thank you." Rather, it involves sharing and publicizing the events for which he is grateful. To "raise our cup" is to express our thanks in a public forum. It is similar to the concept of a *seudas hoda'ah*, a meal to give thanks for a miracle.[31] This concept of sharing our personal salvation is deeply rooted in our prayers. We proclaim our thanks three times a day when we recite the *Modim* section of *Shemoneh Esrei*: נודה לך ונספר תהילתך—*We thank You and relate Your praise.*

ונספר תהילתך—*And Relate Your Praise*

When we publicize the events of salvation, we are "raising our cup," as if we're sharing a *l'chaim* in Hashem's honor. This is what a Jew is expected to do when Hashem bestows good on him. Someone who fails to do so, says the Maharal, identifies himself as a *kofui tovah*—"an ingrate." Not only does such a person fail to express thanks, but he fails to even recognize what has been done for him.

---

31. A *seudas hoda'ah* is a meal of gratitude that one is obligated to make when he/she has been saved from a potential tragedy or illness. It is based on the laws of the *korban todah*, a "thank you sacrifice." This is a sacrifice that is accompanied by forty loaves of bread/matzah that need to be eaten within one day. It is a very large amount of food that is impossible to be eaten by just a handful of people. Therefore, the host must invite many people and publicize his gratitude.

With this explanation, we can better understand Dovid Hamelech's statement, "With what can I repay Hashem for all His kindness to me? I will raise the cup of salvation and call upon the Name of Hashem." The positive feelings of receiving help, care, support, salvation, or validation all need to be "placed in a cup of appreciation" and raised in thanks. Dovid's gratitude is not about his own benefits, but rather about the many opportunities Hashem has given him to extoll His goodness. Dovid is overjoyed to announce his gratitude to the world by "raising a cup" and blessing Hashem for all that He has bequeathed to him.

Dovid is particularly focusing on his good fortune in having been a witness—through his own salvation and redemption—to Hashem's kindness. By raising this "cup of salvation," he fulfills his obligation to thank Hashem and demonstrates that he is not among those categorized as an ingrate.

ובשם ה׳ אקרא—*And the Name of Hashem I will invoke.*

As we mentioned at the end of the last chapter, Dovid was in despair, feeling that "all men are deceitful" and that life was an exercise in futility. Often, when people are in the midst of turmoil, they make vows to Hashem that they will fulfill if they merit to be saved.[32] Once Dovid Hamelech is redeemed, he wishes to repay Hashem for His kindness. Therefore, he says, "I will pay my vows to Hashem in the presence of all His people," acknowledging that since Hashem has redeemed him, it is his responsibility to fulfill his vows.

---

32. This is as Yaakov did in *Parshas Vayeitzei* when וידר יעקב נדר לאמר אם יהיה אלקים עמדי ושמרני בדרך הזה אשר אנכי הולך ונתן לי לחם לאכל ובגד ללבוש. Before Yaakov departs from the site of his monumental dream of the ladder, he vows to Hashem that if he is successful on his journey, he will keep his word and fulfill all that he has accepted upon himself.

יקר בעיני השם המותה לחסידיו—*Precious in the eyes of Hashem is the death of His pious ones.*

The literal definition of the word *yakar* is precious, meaning that which is of great value. However, the *Targum* uses the word *yakar* interchangeably with *kaved*, which means heavy or difficult. The Maharal expounds that a *tzaddik's* passing is *yakar*, both precious and difficult, for Hashem.[33]

This is a puzzling statement. If Hashem did not wish to remove the *tzaddikim* from the world, He would have all the power to keep them alive forever. What is this verse conveying?

The Maharal provides a fascinating explanation. Hashem makes miracles to save righteous people. He did this for Avraham when he was thrown into the fiery furnace, as well as for Chananyah, Mishael, and Azariah who were also saved from Nevuchadnezzar's fire. Logic indicates that if Hashem could save them once, He could have continued to alter the course of nature and allowed them to live forever. *Tzaddikim* who have subjugated their physical desires to the will of Hashem and risen above nature should not be bound by the laws of nature. However, the righteous are humble; they don't expect any special treatment. Rather, they request that Hashem treat them as He does everyone else, according to the laws of nature. Since it is natural to die, their will was to die and share the fate of all mankind.

The Maharal bases this explanation on the midrash *Bereishis Rabbah*,[34] which offers examples of Avraham, Yitzchak, and Yaakov acknowledging that they would die. The *kedushah* of the of the *Avos* and their connection to Hashem created a life that was infinite. Only because of their acceptance of death, was their

33. Nothing of course is actually difficult for Hashem. The idea presented is that *tzaddikim* are such an integral part of the world that it is difficult to have them depart from it.

34. לא היה ראוי מיתה לצדיקים אלא בשביל ששאלו המיתה בפיהם אברהם אמר אנכי הולך ערירי יצחק אמר ואברכך לפני מותי יעקב אמר אמותה הפעם.

death inevitable. Hashem actualizes their humble requests, leaving, however, the underlying feeling that life should be eternal.

The words of Dovid are clear: "Precious in the eyes of Hashem is the death of His pious ones."

אני עבדך בן אמתך—*I am Your servant, the son of Your handmaid.*

What is the significance of being a servant who is born to a handmaid? The Maharal explains that when Dovid states that he is the son of Hashem's handmaid, he claims that he isn't just an acquired slave who was born in freedom elsewhere. Rather, he says, "I was born in Your home to Your handmaid. I totally belong to You, Hashem. Therefore..."

פתחת למוסרי—*You have unshackled my bonds.*

Here Dovid acknowledges that he only has strength because Hashem set it free for him, allowing him to utilize his potential. It all belongs to Hashem and therefore, says Dovid, "I totally belong to You."

Hashem's Universal Praise

הללו את השם כל גוים שבחוהו כל האמים. כי גבר עלינו חסדו ואמת ה' לעולם הללוקה—*Praise Hashem, all nations! Extol Him all peoples! For His kindness was overwhelming to us and the truth of Hashem is everlasting, Hallelukah!*

Let us delve into this verse by examining three questions. First, why are the nations of the world praising Hashem? Second, why are they defined as two different groups—*goyim* (nations) and *amim* (peoples)? Finally, how does the last statement—that Hashem's truth is everlasting—tie into the exhortation for all nations to praise Hashem?

נסים גבורות וחסדים—*Miracles, might, and kindness*

The Maharal explains these terms based on a Gemara (*Pesachim* 118b) that asks why the nations of the world praise Hashem for His might and His miracles, which benefit the Jewish people. Shouldn't the obligation to offer these praises fall to the Jewish people who are the beneficiaries? The Gemara answers that sometimes when nations of the world know of Hashem's might and miracles, they are inspired to praise Him. For example, the entire world was inspired by the splitting of the Yam Suf. When the other nations praise Hashem—posits the Gemara—this tells the Jewish people that we are all the more obligated to do so.

In addition, the Maharal finds in this Gemara a deeper meaning, which reveals the special and exclusive relationship that the Jewish people are privileged to have with Hashem. Although Hashem, through His miracles, demonstrates His might to the nations of the world, those acts emanate from attributes other than His attribute of *chessed,*[35] for Hashem's kindness is exclusively focused on the Jewish people. This explains the juxtaposition of the "all peoples" with "for His kindness was overwhelming *to us.*"

ואמת ה׳ לעולם—*And the truth of Hashem is everlasting.*

The Maharal further explains that miracles, might, and kindness—three modes[36] through which Hashem interacts with the world—

35. The Maharal says that miracles emanate from Hashem's "great Name" and *gevuros* from the attribute of *din*. These correspond to the two categories גויים [nations] and האומים [peoples].

36. These are the same three that are mentioned previously in the chapter לא לנו. These three attributes, כי לשמך תן כבוד, על חסדך ועל אמתך, are each the catalyst for miracles, greatness/might, and kindness.

are all based on Hashem's attribute of truth. This means that Hashem's kindness to His people is not merely a show of favoritism, but rather, it is woven into the fabric of creation. It is an integral truth. The same holds for miracles and might.

As an example, the Maharal cites the Gemara mentioned above.[37] When Nimrod threw Avraham into the fiery furnace, the Angel Gavriel said to Hashem, "G-d of the Universe, since I am the Angel of fire, may I descend and cool the fire and save Avraham from the flames?" Hashem responded, "I am an individual exclusive in My world. So too, Avraham is unique and individual in his world. It is appropriate for one individual to save another individual." Yet because Hakadosh Baruch Hu does not withhold the reward due to any creature, He told Gavriel that he would be privileged to save three of Avraham's descendants.

Paying with Gratitude

הודו לה׳ כי טוב כי לעולם חסדו
יאמר נא ישראל כי לעולם חסדו
יאמרו נא בית אהרן כי לעולם חסדו
יאמרו נא יראי ה׳ כי לעולם חסדו

Give thanks to Hashem for He is good, His kindness endures forever.
Let Yisrael say now, His kindness endures forever.

---

37. בשעה שהפיל נמרוד הרשע את אברהם אבינו לתוך כבשן האש, אמר גבריאל לפני הקדוש ברוך הוא, רבש״ע ארד ואצנן ואציל את הצדיק מכבשן האש, אמר לו הקב״ה אני יחיד בעולמי והוא יחיד בעולמו נאה ליחיד להציל את היחיד. ולפי שהקב״ה אינו מקפח שכר כל בריה אמר תזכה ותציל שלשה מבני בניו. דרש ר״ש השלוני בשעה שהפיל נבוכדנצר הרשע חנניה מישאל ועזריה לתוך כבשן האש עמד יורקמו שר הברד לפני הקב״ה אמר לפניו רבש״ע ארד ואצנן את הכבשן ואציל לצדיקים הללו מכבשן האש, אמר לו גבריאל אין גבורתו של הקב״ה בכך, שאתה שר ברד והכל יודעין שהמים מכבין את האש, אלא אני שר של אש ארד ואקרר מבפנים ואקדיח מבחוץ ואעשה נס בתוך נס, אמר לו הקב״ה רד, באותה שעה פתח גבריאל ואמר ואמת ה׳ לעולם.

Let the House of Aharon say now, His kindness endures forever.
Let those who fear G-d say now, His kindness endures forever.

הודו לה׳ כי טוב כי לעולם חסדו—*Give thanks to Hashem for He is good, His kindness endures forever.*

The final chapter of Hallel begins and ends with the statement *Hodu LaHashem*—"Give thanks to Hashem." (As mentioned earlier, the opening verse of Hallel also begins and ends with *Hallelukah*.) When a paragraph begins and ends with the same statement, it means that statement encapsulates its entire message. Since this chapter begins and ends with *Hodu LaHashem*, it demonstrates that the entire psalm is one of complete gratitude. Simply stated, it is as though a person is saying, "I'm just reaching out to You to say thank You."

Other than being grateful, is there anything that is accomplished with our declaration of thankfulness?

Deserving Goodness

The Maharal quotes the midrash[38] that states, "Saying thank you is a form of payment." This means that when a person is grateful and gives thanks for the goodness he received, he has, in a sense, "paid" for the goodness and is now the rightful owner of that goodness. By showing gratitude, one becomes rightfully deserving of the goodness that has been bestowed, and the "thank you" is a form of payment.

What is accomplished by obtaining His goodness through gratitude?

---

38. מדרש תהלים [שוח״ט קי״ח] כי אין לישראל שיאמרו להקב״ה אלא הודייה בלבד על כל הטובה שהוא עושה עמהם שנאמר ה׳ אלקי אתה ארוממך.

This act of *acquiring* the goodness creates a *transactional relationship with Hashem.* This is a deep concept, for not only are we giving thanks, we are also allowing ourselves to become attached to Hashem. Where else do we find that saying thank you allows us to connect with Hashem?

Modim with a Bow

When we give thanks in our daily *Shemoneh Esrei*, we bend and bow—a form of *hisbatlus*—total subjugation and attachment. Bending and bowing exhibit a person's dependence on the one to whom he bows,[39] and **the ultimate attachment that we have to Hashem is measured by our capacity for gratitude**. The degree to which a person is capable of attaching himself to Hashem depends on the level of gratitude he is able to express. This is the logic behind the *minhag* to bow during prayer. In our *perek*, Dovid Hamelech—according to the Maharal's insight—is presenting us with various forms of connection to Hashem.

Different Forms of Attachment

Each of the opening four sentences of the *perek* repeats the words כי לעולם חסדו—*His kindness endures forever*. The reason for this repetition is that each of these categories represents a different level of connection to Hashem; the closer the connection, the greater the appreciation.

The first *Hodu LaHashem*, explains the Maharal, is a general statement that encompasses all of mankind. Dovid Hamelech is calling out to all people, regardless

39. In the Megillah, Mordechai would not bow to Haman under any circumstances. He would absolutely not show any form of *hisbatlus* toward Haman.

of their differences, to show gratitude toward Hashem. As creations of Hashem, we are all endowed with the capacity to give gratitude.

Following this, there are three subcategories, each with its own unique form of connection to Hashem.

- The Jewish people
- *Kohanim*
- Those who fear Hashem

יאמר נא ישראל כי לעולם חסדו—*Let Yisrael say now, His kindness endures forever.*

Why is this phrase written in the singular form (*yomar*) rather than plural (*yomru*)? The Maharal explains that Yisrael here refers not to the Jewish people as a whole, but rather to our forefather Yaakov who was given the name Yisrael. Yaakov's name change to Yisrael was a testimony to his profound connection to Hashem. In that battle with the angel—whom our sages identify as the Satan—the angel was unable to reveal any separation between Yaakov and Hashem.[40] Having survived this battle, Yaakov achieved heavenly greatness and merited a name that contained angelic powers. Just as angelic names often have the name of Hashem—*Kel*—as a suffix (e.g., *Gavriel, Michael*), so too does *Yisrael.* Indeed, in our prayers on Rosh Hashanah and Yom Kippur, we proclaim: "Our name is included in Your Name."[41] This unique connection to Hashem as children of Yisrael/Yaakov merits a singular expression of gratitude, *Yomar na Yisrael.*

יאמרו נא בית אהרן כי לעולם חסדו—*Let the House of Aharon say now, His kindness endures forever.*

The next group is the House of Aharon, who are defined by their love for the Jewish people. Aharon is known as a pursuer of

---

40. See Day Three: Welcoming Yaakov (Nighttime).

41. שמנו קראת בשמך.

peace, אוהב שלום ורודף שלום.[42] This attribute of love is the next level of closeness and allows those who belong to the House of Aharon to perceive Hashem's kindness in a unique way, meriting their own כי לעולם חסדו.

יאמרו נא יראי ה׳ כי לעולם חסדו—*Let those who fear Hashem say now, His kindness endures forever.*

The fourth and final category consists of those who fear Hashem. The Maharal explains that this *yirah* is borne from a profound clarity of Hashem's greatness. When Yaakov realized that he had stumbled upon the place that would eventually become the site of the Beis Hamikdash, he exclaimed, מה נורא המקום הזה—"*How awesome and intimidating is this place!*" The deeper one's understanding of Hashem, the more he is moved to glorify Him. Those who experience this level of awareness express the highest form of gratitude.

Turning Pain into Praise

מן המצר קראתי קה ענני במרחב קה. ה׳ לי לא אירא מה יעשה לי אדם. ה׳ לי בעזרי ואני אראה בשנאי. טוב לחסות בה׳ מבטח באדם. טוב לחסות בה׳ מבטוח בנדיבים. כל גוים סבבוני בשם ה׳ כי אמילם. סבוני גם סבבוני בשם ה׳ כי אמילם. סבוני כדבורים דעכו כאש קוצים בשם ה׳ כי אמילם. דחה דחיתני לנפל וה׳ עזרני. עזי וזמרת קה ויהי לי לישועה. קול רנה וישועה באהלי צדיקים ימין ה׳ עשה חיל. ימין ה׳ רוממה ימין ה׳ עשה חיל. לא אמות כי אחיה ואספר מעשה קה. יסר יסרני קה ולמות לא נתנני. פתחו לי שערי צדק אבא בם אודה קה. זה השער לה׳ צדיקים יבואו בו. אודך כי עניתני ותהי לי לישועה. אבן מאסו הבונים היתה לראש פינה. מאת ה׳ היתה זאת היא נפלאת בעינינו. זה היום עשה ה׳ נגילה ונשמחה בו.

42. See Day Five: Welcoming Aharon (Nighttime).

Out of narrow confines I called to Hashem. Hashem answered me with expansiveness. Hashem is with me, I will not fear, for in what way can man disturb me? Hashem is with me through those who help me, therefore, I can face my enemies. It is better to take refuge in Hashem than to rely on man. It is better to take refuge in Hashem rather than to rely on nobles.

All the nations surround me, in the Name of Hashem, I cut them down! They encircle me, they also surround me, in the Name of Hashem, I cut them down! They encircle me like bees, but they are extinguished like a fire of thorns, in the name of Hashem, I cut them down! You pushed me hard that I might fall but Hashem assisted me. Hashem is my might and my praise, and He was a salvation for me. The sound of rejoicing and salvation is in the tents of the righteous. The right hand of Hashem performs deeds of valor. The right hand of Hashem is exalted; the right hand of Hashem performs deeds of valor. I shall not die but I shall live and relate the deeds of Hashem. Hashem has chastened me intensely, but He did not give me over to death.

Open for me the gates of justice. I will enter them and give thanks to Hashem. This is the gate of Hashem; the honorable will enter it. I thank You for You have answered me and You have been my deliverance. The stone that was scorned by the builders has become the cornerstone. This was indeed from Hashem; it is wondrous in our eyes. This is the day Hashem has made; we will be glad and rejoice in it.

מן המצר קראתי קה—*Out of narrow confines I called to Hashem.* ענני במרחב קה—*Hashem answered me with expansiveness.*

As this *mizmor* begins, we see a shift from the theme of praising Hashem to one of calling out to Him from dire straits. How are we to understand this change?

The Maharal quotes the *Midrash Tehillim* (see below)[43] that elaborates on the different Names of Hashem that Dovid Hamelech could have uttered when making his request. He employs the Name י-ה.

In general, we find that we can address our prayers to any of Hashem's many Names and we will be answered from that Name. For example, explains the midrash, if someone cries out to Hashem with the Name of Shakkai, as in *And may Kel Shakkai bless you*, they are answered and blessed with the name Shakkai, as in the verse, *I am Kel Shakkai. Be fruitful and multiply*.

The same is true with the name Elokim, as in *Hashem my G-d (Elokim), what can You give me [seeing that I am childless]?* The prayer is answered in the name of Elokim, as the verse says, *And their cries went up to Elokim.*

This midrash reveals how accessible and responsive Hashem is to the righteous who seek His assistance. With whatever name a *tzaddik* turns to Hashem, He responds. The message is that Hashem is completely devoted to His people, regardless of the circumstances and the Name by which the *tzaddik* calls upon Him. However, there is a message in Dovid Hamelech's choice of this particular Name.

The Name י-ה; the Name of Creation

Dovid is calling out to Hashem from pain—from the narrow straits that press upon him from all sides. The Maharal explains that the reason Dovid chose the

---

43. מן המצר קראתי קה, מה הוא מן המצה, בכל לשון שישראל קורין להקדוש ברוך הוא הוא עונה אותם. בשדי שנאמר ואל שדי יברך אותך, וענה אותם בשדי שנאמר אני אל שדי פרה רבה. קראוהו באלקים שנאמר ה׳ אלקים מה תתן לי, וענה אותם באלקים שנאמר ותעל שועתם אל האלקים. קראוהו בה׳ שנאמר ונצעק אל ה׳, וענה אותם בה׳ שנאמר וישמע ה׳ את קולנו. קראוהו בקה שנאמר מן המיצר קראתי קה ענני במרחב קה. וכן הוא אומר כי מי גוי גדול אשר לו אלקים קרובים אליו כה׳ אלקינו בכל קראנו אליו.

Name י-ה is because it is the Name that eliminates pain and constraints.

This is because י-ה is the Name Hashem used to create *Olam Hazeh* and *Olam Haba.* As it is written, "For with the Name י-ה Hashem formed the [two] worlds. The letter *hei* is the source of this world and the letter *yud* is [the source of] the next world." It is the source through which this world can expand to a future boundless world.

Hashem's Goodness: The Source of Creation

The premise of the two worlds is that Hashem created the first world as a place where a person earns his reward, which he then receives when he "graduates" to the next world. Because the next world's sole purpose is to serve as the venue in which people can acquire their reward for the lives they have lived, the next world provides the ultimate purpose of this world. By creating a place dedicated to bestowing good upon His children, Hashem's goodness and His desire to bestow goodness on His creation is revealed.

Since the Name י-ה is the source of both this world and the next world, the Name energizes pure goodness. When Dovid calls out to Hashem to release his constraints, he does so using the Name that is the source of the good in this world. Although a person has encountered pain, tapping into creation and accessing this Name counteracts his pain. Since the world was created to bestow good on its inhabitants, the Name that created the world is the appropriate Name to mention, for it activates the "powers of good in creation." Therefore, through this Name, a person can ask Hashem to free him of his restraints.

ה׳ לי לא אירא מה יעשה לי אדם—Hashem is with me; I will not fear, for in what way can man disturb me?

ה׳ לי בעזרי ואני אראה בשנאי—Hashem is with me through those who help me, and therefore I can face my enemies.

The Maharal notes that the *mizmor* recognizes Hashem's assistance in two different ways. First, Dovid says simply, "Hashem is with me; I will not fear." Second, he says, "Hashem is with me through those who help me." These two expressions would seem to relate two different scenarios that require different types of involvement from Hashem. What distinguishes these two expressions? Further, why does Dovid say Hashem is "with me"—"*li*"—twice?

The Maharal explains that the dangers facing Dovid are many and varied. Sometimes, he faces an enemy he does not wish to destroy, such as his father-in-law, King Shaul. Although Shaul wanted to kill Dovid, Dovid chose not to fight. At other times, however, he faces an enemy he needs to eliminate and must therefore fight a war.

In the first situation, where the enemy remains alive, Dovid would be fearless, trusting that because "Hashem is with me, I will not fear"; he is untouchable. He has no reason to fear, because no one can harm him with Hashem as his protection. In the second situation, when the enemy needs to be eliminated, Dovid knows he can rely on Hashem to provide him with all the resources he needs to win the war.

טוב לחסות בה׳ מבטח באדם—It is better to take refuge in Hashem than to rely on man.

טוב לחסות בה׳ מבטוח בנדיבים—It is better to take refuge in Hashem rather than to rely on nobles.

These two statements about relying on Hashem over "man" and over "nobles" parallel the two earlier statements of "Hashem is with me." In both cases, the meaning is that man cannot save

Dovid from an enemy he doesn't wish to kill, nor can nobles give him resources that will defeat the enemies he does need to eliminate. In either scenario, Hashem is the only reliable ally.

We are surrounded!

כל גוים סבבוני בשם ה' כי אמילם—*All the nations surround me. In the name of Hashem, I cut them down!*

Having described two forms of personal conflict, Dovid Hamelech describes three different forms of opposition that the Jewish people face from the nations that surround them. By repeating the phrase *ki amilam* three times, he indicates that there are three forms of opposition. Each form of conflict is more dramatic than the one before it. The Maharal provides many explanations of these conflicts.

The first level of opposition, *kol goyim*, is generic; it is the natural competition of one nation against another. Such a war against the Jewish nation does not arise out of special enmity toward the Jews, but rather because it is the nature of nations to wage war and vie for power. Since nations each have their own unique, distinct perspective, explains the Maharal, their goals are bound to conflict. This is the type of war expressed by the verse: *All the nations surround me.*

סבוני גם סבבוני בשם ה' כי אמילם—*They encircle me, they also surround me, in the Name of Hashem, I cut them down!*

The second degree of conflict is based on the Jewish people's identity in contrast to the entire world. While all nations are indeed different from each other, they also bear a certain commonality that is not shared by the Jewish people. We are considered "outsiders" in the context of the global family of nations. Therefore, we experience a unique form of opposition, which Dovid Hamelech describes with the second verse: *They encircle me, they also surround me.* The seeming redundancy of "encircle" and "surround" expresses this additional layer of separation from the other nations, and the additional layer of conflict it engenders.

סבוני כדבורים דעכו כאש קוצים בשם ה׳ כי אמילם—*They encircle me like bees, but they are extinguished like a fire of thorns. In the Name of Hashem, I cut them down.*

The third level of opposition, according to the Maharal, arises when the Jewish people's only road to success is through the demise of the other nations. As it is written regarding Yaakov and Eisav, *When one falls, the other one rises, and then when the one who has fallen rises, the one who has risen falls*. When Dovid says, "They encircle me like bees," he is saying that just as there can be no peace treaty between a stinging bee and its victim, this winner-takes-all conflict between the Jewish people and their opponents is an irreconcilable rift. With this form of opposition and the other two as well, Dovid proclaims, "In the Name of Hashem, I cut them down!" In short, relying on Hashem provides a Jew with power against all opposition.

Battling the Jewish People

The Maharal provides a second fascinating insight into the meaning of these three types of opposition. In the first explanation, he focused on why the nations oppose us. Now, he examines how they oppose us. *All the nations surround me* highlights the fact that the "nations" are many and the Jewish people are but one.[44] With all their power, they are unsuccessful, for, *In the Name of Hashem, I cut them down!* Undaunted, they try again. *They encircle me, they also surround me*, redoubling their efforts, but once again, *In the Name of Hashem, I cut them down!* Finally, on the third attempt, they try to

---

44. As we say in the *Al Hanissim* of Chanukah, רבים ביד מעטים—*Many in the hands of the few.*

overwhelm us with an army of tens of thousands. Dovid Hamelech describes this with the analogy of swarms of bees attacking one individual. As the Maharal explains, there is no end to the number of bees in an attacking swarm, but once again, *In the Name of Hashem, I cut them down!*

The Battle of Gog and Magog

The Maharal then cites a midrash that offers a third explanation of *all the nations surround me*, which reveals that the three forms of opposition refer to a prophetic vision of the ultimate redemption ushered in by the war of Gog and Magog.

On Shabbos of Chol Hamoed Sukkos, we read in the *haftorah* about the war of Gog and Magog (*Yechezkel* 38). This war is not waged as a war of nations, but rather as a direct assault on Hashem. Dovid Hamelech, in *Tehillim* (2:2), calls it an attack *on Hashem and His Mashiach.* The *Navi* identifies this as the final war in the history of the world. Only those who accept Hashem as the sovereign King will remain alive; all others will perish. According to the midrash, this apocalyptic war will have three stages, represented by the three ways of being surrounded that are mentioned in this portion of Hallel.

At this time of reckoning, each of the three battles will be waged by the nation of Gog through an attack on Yerushalayim. The three attacks—which are Gog's attempt to stop the coming of Mashiach—will fail. Instead, each defeat will make Hashem's glory increasingly evident, until it is undeniable to anyone whose eyes are open. The ultimate victory brings forth Mashiach and the Final Redemption.

These three battles parallel the three attributes of the great, mighty, and awesome G-d (*Hagadol, Hagibor, v'Hanora*), which we mention in our daily prayer. As we have discussed, those traits also relate to the three *Avos*, Avraham, Yitzchak, and Yaakov. Thus, each time the Jewish people are victorious, a different form of glory is attributed to Hashem's Name. The Maharal explains the three battles.

The Great Battle

In its first assault, Gog will lead *many* nations against Israel, as the *pasuk* says, *All the nations surround me.* Gog's strategy is to wage a battle with a great army, but Dovid Hamelech does not fear being outnumbered, for, *In the Name of Hashem, I cut them down!* When the enemy attacks with a show of greatness, Hashem's victory depicts His "greater greatness." This gives glory to the Name of Hashem by revealing His identity as *Hagadol.*

The Mighty Battle

In the second battle, Gog will redouble his efforts, mounting a greater attack with a greater show of strength. This is the reason for the double language of *They encircle me, they also surround me.* The Maharal explains that Gog will fight "on the second occasion with might and force," but once again, says Dovid, *In the Name of Hashem, I cut them down!* The dynamic at work here is like that in *Tehillim* (2:1-2): *Why have the nations gathered and [why do] kingdoms think vain things? Kings of a land stand up and nobles take counsel together against Hashem and against His anointed.* Since the battle is against Hashem, the appropriate response is, *In the Name of Hashem, I cut them down!* By granting victory in this battle, Hashem reveals to the world that His might is the ultimate force; He is glorified through His *gevurah.*

The Awesome Battle

Gog sees his third battle as his last opportunity to triumph over Hashem. He therefore wages an all-out battle, deploying a totally disproportionate number of troops. This is a strategy of "shock and awe" against Hashem and His people. But there is no awe greater than that which is due to Hashem. Therefore, in victory, Hashem is glorified through His *middah* of *nora*, awesomeness.

קול רנה וישועה באהלי צדיקים—*The sound of rejoicing and salvation is in the tents of the righteous.*

The Maharal writes that when our world resounds with people rejoicing in the hope of salvation, Hashem is stirred to display His supremacy and fight on our behalf. As Dovid Hamelech continues, *The right hand of Hashem performs deeds of valor.* The Maharal clarifies that when we confidently sing and rejoice in Hashem's salvation even before we see His involvement, we elevate Hashem's right hand.

The Three Right Hands

ימין ה׳ עשה חיל ימין ה׳ רוממה ימין ה׳ עשה חיל—*The right hand of Hashem performs deeds of valor. The right hand of Hashem is exalted; the right hand of Hashem performs deeds of valor.*

What is the right hand of Hashem and why is it mentioned three times?

In general, *the right hand of Hashem* relates to Hashem's forceful involvement in earthly matters. The paradigm for this is the splitting of the sea, when Hashem held back the waters to enable His nation to cross, and then drowned the Egyptians, thus saving the Jewish people. The *pasuk* in *Az Yashir*, the song of praise the Jews sang in gratitude for this redemption, says, *Your right hand, Hashem, is adorned with strength. Your right hand, Hashem, smashes enemies.*

The *Sefer Rokeach* identifies a third mention of the right hand in *Az Yashir*: *You stretch out Your right hand.* Thus, *Az Yashir* parallels the three mentions of Hashem's right hand that we see in this portion of Hallel. The *Rokeach* sees a connection as well to the three declarations of *In the Name of Hashem, I cut them down!* Hashem's right hand is responsible for each of our three victories over those who surround and attack us.

The right hand of Hashem performs deeds of valor. The right hand of Hashem is exalted; the right hand of Hashem performs deeds of valor.

The first declaration, *The right hand of Hashem performs deeds of valor*, refers to His deeds in this world. The second statement, *The right hand of Hashem is exalted*, means that His right hand is raised up to the place known as *Marom*, which is the heaven above. The third mention of Hashem's right hand describes His power of salvation that comes from a place above the heavens, known as *Olam Ha'elyon*—the Upper World.

In all, the phrase *yemin Hashem*—"the right hand of Hashem"—is mentioned three times. These refer to the three worlds we mentioned above, in the section of *Hallelu avdei Hashem*, that correspond to the three repetitions of *kadosh kadosh kadosh*. Therefore, says the Maharal, when the righteous sing the praises of Hashem three times, they raise the power of Hashem throughout all three worlds.

לא אמות כי אחיה ואספר מעשה קה—*I shall not die but I shall live and relate the deeds of Hashem.*

The Maharal explains that Dovid's desire to live is not motivated by a fear of death. Rather, he wants to live so that he can continue to reveal Hashem's greatness. As we mentioned earlier in the chapter of *Mah ashiv la'Hashem*, Dovid's gratitude to Hashem is not for his personal redemption but rather for the opportunity to give Hashem his thanks.

יסר יסרני קה ולמות לא נתנני—*Hashem has chastened me intensely, but He did not give me over to death.*

Dovid recognizes that Hashem has treated him justly, with afflictions he deserved. Nevertheless, he thanks Hashem for preserving his life and not allowing him to fall prey to his enemies. This expression is extremely powerful, for it shows Dovid Hamelech's inner strength, which enabled him to accept suffering and always appreciate that, as dire the situation might be, *He did not give me over to death.* He is grateful to be alive.

אודך כי עניתני ותהי לי לישועה—*I thank You for You have answered me and You have been my deliverance.*

Dovid began this chapter with the words, *Out of narrow confines I called to Hashem.* Why is he thanking Hashem again for rescuing him from a difficult situation? Did he not already express this form of thanks in the chapter beginning with the word אהבתי, *I love Hashem because He hears my voice, my prayers*? There, the *pasuk* also speaks of Hashem rescuing Dovid from danger: *The pangs of death encompassed me, and the agonies of the grave came upon me. Trouble and sorrow I encounter, and I call upon the Name of Hashem. Please, Hashem, deliver my soul!* What is the difference between this expression of thanks, *You have been my deliverance* and *Hodu la'Hashem ki tov*—"Give thanks to Hashem for He is good," which is said in a previous *perek*?

The Maharal explains that previously, Dovid was thanking Hashem for protecting him by preventing a painful situation that appeared imminent. In that context, he thanks Hashem with *Hodu la'Hashem ki tov.* Here, however, his gratitude emerges *min hameitzar*—from a place of constraints. He calls to Hashem **from the midst of his** troubles, and thanks Him, *because You have answered me and You have been my deliverance.*

אבן מאסו הבונים היתה לראש פינה—*The stone scorned by the builders has become the cornerstone.*

Dovid Hamelech states that he has not only been saved, but that this redemption has become the cornerstone. It is interesting to note that although a "cornerstone" is placed at the foundation of a building, it is known as *rosh*, which means "head." How could the cornerstone that is at the bottom also be considered "the head"? There is a powerful message here. Every time a person goes through a difficult time, he can draw strength from previous situations in which he was saved. The past becomes the present and leads a person with confidence through his difficulty.

מאת ה׳ היתה זאת היא נפלאת בעינינו—This was indeed from Hashem; it is wondrous in our eyes.

Dovid recognizes that his deliverance was completely miraculous. The Maharal explains the deeper meaning of this statement, which is connected to the previous statement about our redemption being our "cornerstone." The wonders and miracles that Hashem performs are rooted in *Bereishis*, "the beginning." We should never think that when we are redeemed and released from dire straits, it is because Hashem has "changed His mind" about our situation. On the contrary, Hashem is all-knowing and everything that happens to us, the good and the bad, is part of His Master plan, which is totally wondrous to us when we behold it.

Therefore, we continue:

זה היום עשה ה׳ נגילה ונשמחה בו—This day Hashem has made, let us be glad and rejoice on it!

When a person comes to the realization that everything that has happened is meant to be, and nothing has deviated one iota from Hashem's plan, he can rise above his stress and anxiety and embrace and **rejoice** in all that He has given us.

אנא ה׳ הושיעה נא אנא ה׳ הצליחה נא—Please, Hashem, help us now! Please, Hashem, bring us success now!

Since this chapter begins with *Out of narrow confines I called to Hashem*, we continue with a plea to Hashem to help us and give us success now. Although we call to Him from a difficult situation, we express confidence that we will be delivered!

הודו לה׳ כי טוב כי לעולם חסדו—*Give thanks to Hashem for He is good. His kindness endures forever.*

The Maharal concludes: We began Chapter 118 with the words *Give thanks to Hashem*, and conclude with the exact same words, for we are declaring that all we can do is to thank Hashem for all the good that He has done!

APPENDIX

The Origin of the Name Yom Tov

The Jewish people use the Hebrew words "Yom Tov"—meaning "good day"—to identify the Jewish holidays. These include Pesach, Shavuos, and Sukkos, as well as Rosh Hashanah and Yom Kippur. Purim and Chanukah are certainly days of celebration; however, since work is not prohibited on those days as it is on the other holidays, they are not called Yom Tov.

Where does this name come from? What is its origin and when was it first used? It isn't biblical, for in the Torah, holidays are called either *regalim*, *chagim*, or *mo'adim*. What caused us to adopt the name Yom Tov?

Megillas Esther

The first use of Yom Tov in this context seems to be in *Megillas Esther*. After the Jewish people defeated their enemies, Mordechai desired to establish Purim as a holiday that would resemble the holidays of the Torah. He proposed that Purim too should be celebrated by refraining from work, except for that which is required to prepare food. The source of his request is in the Megillah:

> *Mordechai recorded these events and sent letters to all the Jews who were in all the provinces of King Achashverosh, charging them to observe the fourteenth and fifteenth day of the month of Adar each year. These were the days on which the Jews*

gained relief from their enemies and the month that had turned about for them from one of sorrow to gladness and ***from mourning to a festival****. They were to observe these days with feasting and gladness, sending delicacies to one another, and gifts to the poor.*

מאבל ליום טוב—*From Mourning to Festivity*

The portrayal of the Purim victory as a transition "from mourning to a festival" is fitting. The Jewish people in that era experienced a miracle that brought them from the brink of annihilation to triumph. The depth of their despair upon hearing Haman's decree is captured in the use of the word *aveilus*, the word usually used to identify the period of mourning following the death of a family member.

Indeed, the Purim story was one of redemption. The Jewish people "came back to life" from a near-death experience. Haman had succeeded in launching his genocidal plan; the decree was passed as a law, and the day of doom was less than a year away. Only with Hashem's intervention were the Jews saved. The threat of the decree and the deliverance from its seemingly irreversible consequences formed the backdrop against which Mordechai declared the holiday of Purim as a "Yom Tov."

- What was his rationale for creating this concept of Yom Tov?
- Why did Mordechai request the observance of Purim to be accepted as a day of cessation from work?
- Why did he not use the traditional terms, *mo'ed* or *chag*,[1] that the Torah uses?

These questions can be explained on multiple levels.

---

1. The mention of *aveilus* is understandable as the Jews were on the brink of total annihilation, yet the name Yom Tov requires an explanation.

Mo'adim

The source for holidays in the Torah is found in *Parshas Emor*, which states, *These are the holidays of Hashem, days of holy festivity that you shall observe in their times.* The Torah then elaborates on this subject, starting with Shabbos and then detailing the unique themes, observances, and character of each of the *mo'adim*. Despite their distinctiveness, they are bound by one common thread, which is the commandment, *and you shall bring a sacrifice to Hashem*, meaning to the Beis Hamikdash. These offerings were the essential common element of all the Torah's *chagim*.

Additionally, as we mentioned, one of the names of Jewish holidays is *regel*, which means foot. This is because the Torah commands all Jewish men to travel to the Beis Hamikdash three times a year in order "to see and be seen by" Hashem. The mitzvah, called *aliyah l'regel*, requires men to travel from their homes to bring their sacrifices and celebrate at least one day of the *chag* with Hashem in the Beis Hamikdash.[2] As the Torah states, *Three times a year all your males shall appear before Hashem.* Even the name *chag* is connected to the concept and requirement of a *chagigah* sacrifice. Clearly, the most complete observance of the *mo'adim* requires a Beis Hamikdash.

Yom Tov Without a Beis Hamikdash

Without the Beis Hamikdash, how could Purim fit into this paradigm of what a *chag* should be? The Megillah declares, *The Jews had light, happiness* (simchah), *rejoicing, and honor.* The word *simchah* is generally associated with holidays because the Torah commands, *And you shall be joyous in the presence of Hashem.*[3] The salvation of Purim created a *simchah* that needed to be

---

2. This was the requirement for Pesach, Shavuos, and Sukkos, but not for Rosh Hashanah and Yom Kippur. The concept of the three holidays known as *Shalosh Regalim* are discussed in a different chapter.

3. The concepts of *simchah* and the Beis Hamikdash are intertwined. The

memorialized so that the Jewish people could thank and praise Hashem for His intervention. It also needed to be harnessed so that we would forever have a point of access to the energy that was revealed on the days of the miracle.

However, since the events of Purim occurred between the first and second Beis Hamikdash, the focal point of the Torah's holidays was missing. There was no possibility of fulfilling the mitzvah of *aliyah l'regel* or bringing a *korban* for the *mo'ed* or *chagigah* offering. Calling the holiday a *mo'ed* or a *chag* would therefore not be appropriate. Because the Jewish people would not be able to celebrate this *simchah* as biblical holidays were celebrated, Mordechai understood that he would have to create a holiday that was different from the existing *mo'adim*. He wanted it to resemble a day of rest, and yet it needed its own distinct mode of celebration.[4]

The Introduction of Yom Tov

Hence, Mordechai created more than a new name to describe the celebration; he created a ***new concept*** for this holy day: the concept of Yom Tov. The Gemara in *Maseches Megillah* refers to this idea in its discussion of the *pasuk, The Jews had light and happiness and rejoicing and honor.* It expounds that "light" means

---

Gemara states (as codified in the *Shulchan Aruch*) that since the destruction of the Beis Hamikdash, it is prohibited for one to be full of *simchah*.

4. At the time Purim was established, the Jewish people and the Sanhedrin accepted Mordechai's idea of a new holiday. However, they rejected his idea that it should be "a day of rest." Instead, the Yom Tov of Purim was created with alternative expressions of celebration: reading the Megillah, distributing assistance to the needy, giving presents to friends, and gathering together for a festive holiday meal. If people were to stop work, they would do so according to the halachah governing observance of a *minhag*—a custom. Fittingly, the third *perek* in *Maseches Megillah*, called *Makom Shenahagu*, discusses various rules associated with customs, which are not as restrictive as those pertaining to matters of halachah.

Torah, *simchah* means Yom Tov, joy means *bris milah,* and honor means the mitzvah of *tefillin.*

The Maharal has a penetrating explanation; an introduction is required:

With no possibility of a *mo'ed* that would resemble the existing *mo'adim,* why did Mordechai feel such a pressing urgency to make Purim a Yom Tov? The answer is found in Reb Tzadok Hakohen's discussion of Purim in his *sefer Resisi Leilah.*

Simchah Refers to Yom Tov

Holidays are known as days of *simchah,* and Purim was of course no different. With the victory over their archenemy Amalek, the Jewish people recognized Hashem's divine intervention and were inspired with so much gratitude that the elders and leaders understood the need for a holiday. Although the holiness of a Beis Hamikdash was missing, there was another option—the **holiness of the Jewish people**. The new holiday couldn't revolve around the Beis Hamikdash, but Klal Yisrael had a *kedushah* of its own, and that was an acceptable alternative. An explanation is forthcoming.

נורא אלקים ממקדשיך—*Hashem's Awesomeness Emanates from His Mikdash*

The Beis Hamikdash is the palace within which Hashem rests His presence. As Dovid Hamelech proclaims, "Your awesomeness (*nora*) is rooted and emanates from Your Temple." The Talmud (*Maseches Tamid*) describes the commandment to have twenty-four guards from the tribe of Levi stationed in specific locations around the Temple. The Gemara asks, *Does Hashem need people to watch and protect Him?* The answer is, of course, Hashem doesn't require protection, but because the Mikdash is where the King of kings resides, and earthly kings have guards, the Temple should have no less. This displays the Jewish people's awe—*nora*—and reverence for Hashem's palace. The Beis Hamikdash is the King's residence, the epicenter of *nora.*

Another source that connects *nora* with the Beis Hamikdash is Yaakov's dream of the ladder that extended from earth to heaven, with angels ascending and descending it. When he awoke, says the Torah, he was fearful, and he said, "How awesome (*nora*) is this place. This is none other than the House of Hashem, and here are the gates of Heaven."

The attribute of *nora* existed in the Beis Hamikdash only when the Jewish people respected Hashem and His mitzvos. Under those circumstances, miracles that defied nature happened there every day. The mishnah (*Avos* 5) states that ten daily miracles occurred in the Beis Hamikdash, making Hashem's presence undeniable. Thus, all who visited there would refer to Hashem as *Hagadol, Hagibor, v'Hanora*, acknowledging the awe they felt in His presence.

However, with the decline of the moral and spiritual stature of the Jewish people, the sanctity of the Beis Hamikdash was diminished. When the Babylonians conquered it, says the Gemara (*Yoma* 68b), the prophet Yirmiyahu cried out, "Hashem, where is Your awesomeness?" He thenceforth omitted the term *nora* from his praises of Hashem.[5]

---

5. The source for this is found in the Gemara (*Yoma* 69b), which relates that Rabbi Yehoshua, the son of Levi, asked (rhetorically) why the Men of the Great Assembly were given this name. The Gemara answers that they returned the glory of old: Moshe Rabbeinu praised Hashem with the declaration, "For Hashem is your G-d, He is the G-d of the powers and the Lord of the Lords, the great, mighty, and awesome (*Hagadol, Hagibor, v'Hanora*) G-d, Who does not show favor and Who does not accept a bribe" (*Devarim* 10:17). Yet when Yirmiyahu saw Gentiles defiling the Temple, he lamented, "Hashem, where is Your awesomeness (*nora*)!" The Gemara continues, stating that when Daniel saw the Jewish people subjugated by their enemies, he cried, "Hashem, where is Your strength (*gevurah*)!" Therefore, when Daniel prayed to Hashem, he omitted the word *Hagibor*—"the Mighty." (Both Yirmiyahu and Daniel were referencing the statement made generations earlier by Moshe Rabbeinu.)

Anshei Knesses Hagedolah

The *Anshei Knesses Hagedolah*—"Men of the Great Assembly," the ruling body of the Jewish people after the first Beis Hamikdash was destroyed, restored the term *nora* to its rightful place. In fact, the Gemara explains that this assembly was called "great" because *They returned the glory of Hashem [the title* nora*] to its origin*. But with the Beis Hamikdash lying in ruins, on what basis did they do so?

The Jews: A Testimony to Hashem

The *Anshei Knesses Hagedolah* found the answer in the survival of the Jewish people. They declared, "How can one sheep survive among seventy wolves?" The seventy wolves are a reference to the nations, who would eat us alive if they could. But what is stopping them? A sheep can't protect itself from even one wolf. How does it survive? The only possible answer is Divine intervention; Hashem does not permit our destruction. The fact that the Jewish people survived the destruction of the Temple and the exile, that we continue to survive and even revive, is an expression of the eternal protection of the Almighty G-d. Our existence proves His might and awesomeness. The fact that we, His children, defy all natural rules of nations and continue to flourish is a testimony that Hashem, the great, mighty, awesome G-d, is still involved. The survival of the Jewish nation reawakened the great Name of Hashem—*Hanora*—the Awesome One.

However, the Men of the Great Assembly perceived the world from a different perspective. They saw the destruction and exile as just the opposite of what it seemed. They reasoned that with all the success of the enemy, the Jewish people should not have been able to survive. Their survival is testimony to Hashem's greatness and awesomeness! Without His constant protection and intervention, the Jewish people would have been long gone. Therefore, the Men of the Great Assembly countered the laments of Yirmiyahu and Daniel and proclaimed Hashem's greatness, might, and awesomeness through the survival of the Jewish people.

Two Types of *Nora*

With the *Anshei Knesses Hagedolah's* new insight, it became apparent that although the Beis Hamikdash was destroyed and its honor, glory, and awesomeness were decimated, Hashem's glory would continue to emanate through His children. The attribute of *nora* that had once been found in one place on earth—the Beis Hamikdash—was now found in mankind, through one nation among all of humanity.

My *rebbi*, Rav Moshe Shapiro *zt"l*, explained a verse in our morning prayers that is a source for the parallel between these two versions of *nora*. He quoted the *pasuk* in the *tefillah* of *Hodu* that says, *Hashem's attribute of awesomeness emanates from the Mikdash. He gives strength and power to the nation, Blessed is Hashem!*[6] The first part of the verse proclaims that Hashem's awesome presence is in the Beis Hamikdash; the second part refers to when there is no Beis Hamikdash, in which case His awesomeness is evidenced by the fact that *He gives strength and power to His nation*, which refers to the Jewish people's survival.

On a deeper level, the declaration of *nora* is not based on our surviving the destruction of the Beis Hamikdash, but rather on *the destruction itself.* The Jewish people should have been destroyed along with the Beis Hamikdash, but instead, Hashem sent His nation out of the land where they could survive and thrive. He "evacuated us" from the war zone so that the full wrath of the destruction would not destroy us. That too is a testimony to Hashem's awesomeness.[7]

---

6. נורא אלקים ממקדשיך קל ישראל הוא נותן עז ותעצמות לעם ברוך אלקים.

7. On a deeper level, the attribute of *nora* had shifted; it was once found in a defined place, the Beis Hamikdash, and it was now replaced with the revelation of the source of *kedushah* of the Beis Hamikdash which emanates from His people. Meaning, although the *middah* of *nora* no longer existed in the House of Hashem, it was revealed through those who possess the image of Hashem.

Thus, when the *Anshei Knesses Hagedolah* composed the *Shemoneh Esrei*, they reinstated the name *Nora*. As the Gemara states, they successfully returned glory to the Name of Hashem. There was no Beis Hamikdash to invoke the fear of Hashem, but there was a nation—the Jewish people! And Hashem's awesome presence among His nation was never more evident than in the miracle of Purim.

Purim: The Revelation of Awesomeness

Re-examining the story of Purim, we can gain a new appreciation of this holiday's identity as a Yom Tov. Before the miraculous redemption, Haman had succeeded in procuring a royal decree allowing the seventy "wolves," the vast conglomeration of nations that comprised the Persian Empire, to "eat the sheep." The law had been passed and the countdown to doomsday—13 Adar—had begun, and Haman looked forward with confidence to a Jew-free world. Instead, the Jews not only survived, but also, *Many from the nations became Jews* because they feared the Jewish people. As the Megillah continues, *fear fell upon them [the nations]* and they realized that there was only one way to deal with the Jews: to join them, because with Hashem's protection, they were invincible. Hashem had shown His awesomeness to the world through the Jewish people. Thus, Purim can be described simply as the Yom Tov that celebrates the Jewish people's awesomeness.

The Maharal (*Sefer Ohr Chadash*) writes that the victory over Haman was not simply a local individual triumph; it affected the entire universe. This is because Haman was Amalek's descendant, and a victory over Amalek constituted the removal of an impediment that hobbled the world's ability to perceive Hashem. This is an important key to understanding the source of *simchah* on Purim, and on Yom Tov in general.

Amalek: The Archenemy of Good

Since the Jews left Egypt and became a nation, Amalek has been our enemy and impediment to our connection to Hashem. This, says the Maharal, is because Amalek obstructs the unity of the world under Hashem. Even our connection to Torah is negatively affected by Amalek.[8] This first emerged when the Jewish people were traveling from Egypt to Har Sinai to receive the Torah; Amalek attacked, causing the appearance of vulnerability in Hashem's sovereignty. Hashem then "raised His hand" in an oath that neither His Name nor His throne would be complete until the children of Amalek were eradicated from the world.

This established a force and counterforce: The greater Amalek grows, the less connection the world has to Hashem; the weaker Amalek becomes, the greater the connection. Therefore, when Haman, his children, and his supporters were killed, the Jewish people were able to renew their connection to Hashem. The Maharal explains that this is why the victory over Amalek enabled the Jewish people to complete their acceptance of the Torah in an unprecedented way. As the Megillah recounts, *Kimu v'kiblu*—"They rose up and they accepted" the Torah anew.

ליהודים היתה אורה—*The Jews Had Light, Honor, and Happiness*

With this victory against Amalek—the obstructor of Hashem's light—the Megillah's words, *The Jews had light, happiness, joy, and honor*, come alive. The Jews who lived through this episode forged so vibrant a connection to Hashem that they merited a light that supersedes creation itself. That light, our Sages explain, is the Torah.

However, the Jews had received the Torah at Har Sinai many

---

8. The name Amalek has a numerical value of 240, the same value as ספק/doubt. Amalek's presence and values create doubt in the world that Hashem is meant to govern.

centuries earlier. How could they receive it again? The Maharal explains that indeed we possessed the Torah, but as long as Amalek was exerting its full power in the world, our connection to Hashem was far below its potential. Only when Amalek was slain could this connection blossom and flourish as never before. The people accepted the Torah again, this time out of love! Naturally, Purim, the time of this passionate reunion of the Torah with the Jewish people, is saturated with unparalleled happiness. The Maharal named his *sefer* on Purim *Ohr Chadash*—"A New Light," based on the Megillah's celebratory words, *The Jews had light*, for we saw the Torah as a purer, brighter light than we had ever known.

This is the source of all the Jewish people's achievements—light, happiness, joy, and honor. The Maharal connects each one to all of the others. The Jews' renewed connection to the Torah was itself a reason for a holiday. Furthermore, they experienced such happiness that it had to be embodied in a Yom Tov. Continuing this concept, the Maharal explains that the mitzvos of *tefillin* and *bris milah* each represent the body's ability to reach an exalted level of holiness. The holiness of *bris milah* completes us, allowing us to resemble Adam before the sin,[9] and donning *tefillin* connects our body to the Name of Hashem.[10]

To summarize, the victory over Haman and his nation brought the Jewish people light (Torah), which in turn brought them happiness (Yom Tov), which in turn gave them joy (*bris milah*), and brought them renewed honor (*tefillin*). From a broader perspective, we see that what the Jewish people achieved on Purim through their victory over Amalek was in fact one overall achievement; it

---

9. The Midrash explains that the foreskin appeared on Adam only after he sinned. Adam was originally created without the foreskin.

10. The Gemara says that when the nations of the world see the *tefillin* on the heads of the Jewish people, they are in fear and awe of the Jewish people.

was a total unification of body and soul, comprised of four components (light, happiness, joy, and honor).

There are multiple associations between "light" and "good." The first is that the Torah, which we have just defined as "light," is also the essence of good. As the *pasuk* (*Mishlei* 4:2) declares regarding the Torah, *For it is a good acquisition I have given them*. It is also associated with light, as in the *pasuk*, *For a mitzvah is a candle and Torah is light* (*Mishlei* 6:23). Therefore, the renewed acceptance of Torah created "good light," which ultimately expressed itself in a new holiday.

Yom Tov: A Good Day

The first time the word *tov* is found in the Torah in reference to light is on Day One of creation (*Bereishis* 1:4), "And He saw the light and it was good." On the first day of creation, light was all that existed, and it was good. The light of Purim, a day that was only good, is associated to this day with its pure light. Thus, the "good" in Yom Tov represents Hashem's presence as it connected to the Jewish people and gave them access to a "good/light day."

On a slightly deeper level, light is associated with life, and darkness with death. Rav Moshe Shapiro *zt"l* explained that when a person is surrounded by complete darkness, everything that exists around him is "dead" to him since he has no access to anything. Conversely, light reveals everything, bringing meaning and life. This is the goodness Hashem expressed on Day One of creation, and it is the "*tov*" in Yom Tov.

The Maharal (*Chiddushei Hagados*) says that when the Jews experienced the victory over Amalek and rose from a state of mourning to Yom Tov, they previewed the good that will enter the world with the eradication of Amalek: *On that day, Hashem will be One and His Name will be One.*

The good and the light that the Jewish people experienced

through the miracle of Purim were pure and uncontaminated by Amalek's poison. This was a new beginning for the Jewish people, and it created the concept of Yom Tov for all the holidays. For although the Jewish people no longer had a Beis Hamikdash in which to celebrate the *mo'adim*, they did, however, find within themselves Yom Tov.

A Cessation of Pesach

There is an additional reason for all of the holidays identified as Yamim Tovim. On the year that the Jewish people celebrated Purim, they had no Pesach. The decree to kill all the Jews had been passed on the thirteenth of Nissan, a mere two days before Pesach, and they needed to take drastic action to beg Hashem to rescind the decree. Therefore, the Jews of Shushan fasted for three days and nights. No one ate matzah or *maror*. No one held a Seder, nor did the Jews fulfill their obligation to view themselves as though they had personally left Egypt.

Since every holiday including Shabbos is *zecher l'Yetzias Mitzrayim*—"a memorial to the exodus"—the Purim decree had cut off the Jewish people's connection not only to Pesach but to every other Yom Tov and commandment.[11] With the salvation of Purim, the transformation of darkness to light, the time had come to reconnect to all the Yamim Tovim.

Ohr Chodosh—a New Light

Furthermore, the Maharal cites a parallel in the Gemara (*Bava Metzia* 83) that compares this world to evening, and the future world of *Olam Haba* to daylight. In the evening, there is an absence

---

11. Since the Yom Tov of Pesach is the cornerstone of our relationship with Hashem—as stated in the first of the *Aseres Hadibros*, *I am Hashem, your G-d, Who took you out of Egypt*—its observance serves as an annual foundation for our connection to Hashem. That year, however, Bnei Yisrael did not celebrate Pesach, breaking that continuous chain. Purim re-established that link.

of light that prevents us from accurately perceiving the reality around us. In the clear light of daytime, however, everything is perceived as it is.

In a world where Hashem's presence is recognized, everything that exists is based on its relationship with Him. It is illuminated by His light, and therefore we see what truly exists.

Conversely, things that exist only because Hashem has hidden His presence from us are not real—they are like the monsters children "see" in a dark room. This is the message the Maharal expresses when he compares this world to darkness. When the annihilation of the Jewish people was decreed, the world plummeted into complete darkness; the presence of Hashem was nowhere to be found. With the total reversal of the decree, the Jewish people emerged from mourning into a state of existing in the truest sense of the word. This opens our eyes to the meaning of the "good day" that Purim celebrates: Purim offered a glimpse of pure, true light that the world had never seen before, and it redefined all the *mo'adim* into Yamim Tovim.